1090833

364.133
Dabn   Dabney, Joseph Earl
               Mountain spirits
8.95

DATE DUE		
MAR 10 '75	APR 1 1985	
APR 28 75	FEB 1 1986	
MAY 24 75	JAN 23 1980	
JUL 1 3 1976	MAR 26 1990	
JUN 4 1977	FEB. 1 1977	
JUN 1 7 1977		
AUG 1 6 1977		
APR 2 0 19		
MAY 1 2		
SEP 81		
APR 2 3 1984		

MOUNTAIN
SPIRITS

MOUNTAIN SPIRITS

A CHRONICLE OF *Corn Whiskey* FROM *King James' Ulster Plantation* TO *America's Appalachians* AND THE *Moonshine Life*

Joseph Earl Dabney

CHARLES SCRIBNER'S SONS   NEW YORK

Library of Congress Cataloging in Publication Data

Dabney, Joseph.
   Mountain spirits.
   Bibliography: p.
   1. Liquor traffic—Southern States—History.
2. Whiskey.   3. Liquor traffic—Southern States—
Taxation—History.   I. Title.
HD9357.A2D32   364.1'33   73-1121
ISBN 0-684-13705-4

3 5 7 9 11 13 15 17 19 H/C 20 18 16 14 12 10 8 6 4

To my wife Susanne

The author acknowledges with appreciation permission to quote from the following books: on p. xvi, Horace Kephart, *Our Southern Highlanders* (by permission of The Macmillan Company); on p. 17, Hamper McBee, *Cumberland Moonshiner* (by permission of Guy Carawan); on p. 19, Jonathan Daniels, *Tar Heels: A Portrait of North Carolina* (by permission of Mr. Daniels); on pp. 20 and 130, Margaret Warner Morley, *The Carolina Mountains* (by permission of Houghton-Mifflin Company); on p. 42, Bernard DeVoto, *The Hour* (by permission of Houghton-Mifflin Company); on pp. 69, 70, and 73, Hariette Simpson Arnow, *Flowering of the Cumberland* (by permission of The Macmillan Company); on p. 72, Frances Dugan and Jacqueline Bull, eds., *Bluegrass Craftsman* (by permission of Dr. Bull); on p. 75, E. Merton Coulter, *Georgia: A Short History* (by permission of Dr. Coulter); on p. 104, W. J. Cash, *The Mind of the South* (by permission of Random House, Inc.); on pp. 134 and 135, Ernie Pyle, *The Home Country* (by permission of William Morrow and Company); on p. 201, Judge Felix E. Alley, *Random Thoughts and the Musings of a Mountaineer*; on pp. 208 and 209, Eliot Wigginton, *Foxfire I* (by permission of Mr. Wigginton).

Acknowledgments

It would have been impossible for me to have attempted writing *Mountain Spirits* without the conviction that I eventually could call on scores of experts on the subject as well as many, many others who would have peripheral information, suggestions, and guidance.

To the United States Treasury Department, I owe a special debt of gratitude. At the start of my preliminary research, I was aided immeasurably by Joseph Rosapepe, former director of information for the Internal Revenue Service. In the course of the research, the people in the Treasury Department's Bureau of Alcohol, Tobacco, and Firearms gave me valuable assistance, and my thanks go to William N. Griffin, Atlanta regional director of ATF, and to these ATF officials: William R. Thompson, Miles Keathley, Edward Hughes, Clarence E. Paul, Miss Pearl Wilder, Byron Reed, Robert Lane, Bob Scott, John T. Guy, Charles Talbert, George Corley, and Gene E. Childers. I am grateful to Warren McConnell and Scott Waffle of the Washington ATF headquarters for reviewing the manuscript. A number of retired ATF agents gave valuable help: Charles S. Nicholson, John Nelson Petre, James Stratigos, Duff Floyd, Wallace Wheeler, Homer Powell, Hobart Henson, and L. B. Britton. Retired Georgia state revenue agents Ed Barnes, Joe Jeff Moore, Marshall Bryan and David Ayers were extremely helpful, as were J. Carroll Cate, former prohibition officer in east Tennessee, Obe Pruitt, retired deputy U.S. marshal in north Georgia, and Jesse James Bailey, former sheriff of Buncombe and Madison Counties, North Carolina.

I would also like to acknowledge and express appreciation to Fred Goswick, owner of the authentic Moonshine Museum of Dawsonville, Georgia. Fred not only gave me the idea for *Mountain Spirits* but also provided valuable advice and assistance over the three-year period of research.

Librarians were a great help, and I want particularly to thank the people at the Atlanta Public Library and especially Miss Alberta Carruth, now retired, of the Library's General Reference Department. My appreciation also goes to these other libraries and librarians: Pack Memorial Library, Asheville, North Carolina, James Meehan, curator of the North Carolina Room; Lawson McGee Library, Knoxville, Mrs. Virginia Edgel of the McClung Room; Louisville Free Public Library, Martin F. Schmidt, head, Kentucky Division; Appalachian State University Library, Boone, North Carolina, Mrs. Audrey Hartley; Chattanooga Public Library, Marion Smith, Historical Room; The Hurty-Peck Library of Beverage Literature, Santa Ana, California, A. W. Noling; University of Kentucky Library, Dr. Jacqueline Bull, head, Special Collections; West Virginia University Library, Mrs. Louise Topliffe, bibliographer; TVA Library, Knoxville, Jesse Mills, librarian; U.S. Regional Archives, East Point, Georgia, Ed Weldon and Arthur Ryden; Duke University Library, Miss Florence Blakely; Library of Congress Archives of Folk Songs, Joseph C. Hickerson; Library of Charlotte and Mecklenberg County, Miss Mary L. Phillips, local history librarian; University of North Carolina Library, North Carolina Collection, William S. Powell, curator; John Edwards Memorial Foundation, University of California at Los Angeles, Norman Cohen; the Licensed Beverage Industries, New York; Maryland Historical Society, Baltimore, P. William Filby, librarian; Tennessee State Library and Archives, Nashville, Mrs. Ellen D. Ross; the Public Library of Cincinnati and Hamilton County, John Mullane; Virginia State Library, Richmond, Milton Russell; Historical Society of Pennsylvania; Scotch Irish Society of the United States of America; West Virginia Department of Archives and History; New York Public Library; Emory University Library; Richmond Public Library, Mrs. Lucille Gaines, reference librarian; Free Library of Philadelphia, Robert Scutter; Kanawha County Public Library, Charleston, West Virginia; Carnegie Library of Pittsburgh, Mrs. Julia Cunningham; The *Asheville Citizen* Library, Mrs. Fred Hearn; the *Atlanta Journal-Constitution* Library, Mrs. Louette Hardigree, librarian.

Next, my thanks to newspapers and columnists who publicized my appeal for information. In particular, I am indebted to Celestine Sibley and Bob Harrell of *The Atlanta Constitution*, whose help was crucial; and to John Parris of the *Asheville Citizen*, North Carolina. Similar appreciation goes to the following: Hugh Park, *Atlanta Journal*; Lydel Sims, *Memphis Commercial Appeal*; Howard Jacobs, *New Orleans Times-Picayune*; Bob Herguth, *Chicago Daily News*; Bob Ward, *Huntsville Times*, Alabama; Sylvan Meyer and John Keasler, *Miami Daily News*; Bob Talbert, *Detroit Free Press*; Sam Griffin, *Post-Searchlight*, Bainbridge, Georgia; Ed Holman, *Northside Neighbor*, Atlanta; Tony Maddox, *Forsyth News*, Cumming, Georgia; Hassie Hancock, *Gateway*, Bremen, Georgia; Troy Houser,

Acknowledgments

Courier, Forest City, North Carolina; and Ralph Owen, *North Georgia Tribune,* Canton, Georgia.

Thanks also go to the following newspapers: *Charlotte News, Kingsport News, Huntsville Times, Chattanooga Times, Bristol Herald, The Daily Times* (Gainesville, Georgia), *Jackson Daily News* (Jackson, Mississippi), and the *New York Times Book Review.*

Local historians who answered my appeals were very helpful, and I'd like to thank Mrs. Jo Walker, Country Music Assn., Nashville, Tennessee; Mrs. N. Charlene Turner, North Carolina Folklore Society; Charles Guthrie, Kentucky Folklore Record; Dr. Ralph Hyde, Tennessee Folklore Society, and professor at Middle Tennessee State University; Dr. Cratis Williams, Appalachian State University, Boone, North Carolina; Eliot Wigginton, Rabun Gap-Nacoochee School, Georgia; Joe Boyer, Blue Ridge, Georgia; Kenyon Withrow, Polkville, North Carolina; M. D. Beal, Gatlinburg, Tennessee; John Burrison, folklore professor, Georgia State University, Atlanta; Dr. Dave Thomas and Dr. Bill Egerton, Oglethorpe College, Atlanta; Prof. Charles Wellborn, University of Florida; Dr. Floyd Watkins, Emory University, Atlanta; Edwin A. Davis, managing editor, *Louisiana History;* Gilbert E. Govan, Chattanooga; and John Gordon, Jr., Hartwell, Georgia. Jack Plampin and "Pic" Pequignot of the Tax Paid Liquor Council, Inc., better known as the Anti-Moonshine League, gave valuable assistance.

Also my thanks to Dave Wright, WFMY–TV, Greensboro, North Carolina; and Fred Griffith, WEWS, Cleveland, Ohio.

I wish to thank the following historians for their help and, in some cases, for their kind permissions to quote from their books: Mrs. Harriette Simpson Arnow, Ann Arbor, Michigan; Jonathan Daniels, Hilton Head Island, South Carolina; Parke Rouse, Williamsburg, Virginia; Mrs. Wilma Dykeman Stokely, Newport, Tennessee; Dr. E. Merton Coulter, Athens, Georgia; H. G. Crowgey, Wilmington, North Carolina; James G. Leyburn, Lexington, Virginia; Leland D. Baldwin, Santa Barbara, California; and Eliot Wigginton, Rabun Gap, Georgia.

The following provided valuable suggestions:

TENNESSEE: Creed Bates, John A. Chambliss, Carlos C. Campbell, E. S. Gaither, Mr. and Mrs. J. D. Marlowe, John O. Morrell, John Lopez, Mrs. Hubert Reese, Al Payne, Wilbur Piper, Mrs. Bob Sherrill, Paul Sutton, Ted Tindell, Lant Wood.

GEORGIA: Bonnelle Akins, Mrs. J. D. Anthony, Eddie Barker,

Virgil Chumley, Leon Colwell, George Cornett, C. A. Dabney, Harris Dalton, Frederick Delves, Henry Dillard, Carl Dodd, Ed Dodd, Leon English, Eston Gallant, Paul Gibson, Don Kosin, R. W. Langston, Curtis Luke, C. H. McKennon, Dent Myers, Clayton Penhalgon, Don Pfitzer, Bud Reed, Ed Reich, Dave Rife, Darb Rusk, Roy A. Shore, Phoebe Smith, Cecil Stockard, Frank Rickman, Luke Teasley, C. H. Todd, Mrs. Alan Wansley, Mrs. Vinnie Williams, Herbert Willcox, Sidney Witlen, and Mrs. June Smith Woodruff.

ALABAMA: A. Lynne Brannen, Mrs. Cora Carter Gamblin, Mrs. Robert R. Head, and Mrs. Patsy Norton.

Also: Wayne Pryor, California; Frank Dornheim, Kentucky; Dr. Moray C. Coop and Mrs. Joan Hunter Dittmer, Texas; Col. Leland S. Devore Jr., Maryland; T. T. Holm, Massachusetts; Harold Everett and William B. Tanner, Mississippi; Karal Ann Marling, New York; Leon B. Winer, New Jersey; John J. Lamb, Pennsylvania; and Mrs. L. B. Ellis, Earl G. Jackson, and Malcolm Jamieson, Virginia.

Invaluable help was given to me by six individuals to whom I wish to express deep appreciation: Turner M. Hiers, for photographic help; Ralph Bugg, for his expert editorial suggestions; and Mrs. Arthur Reynolds, Mrs. Rubye Rackley, and Mrs. Betty Tucker for typing assistance. To my wife Susanne I owe the deepest gratitude. Her unfailing encouragement sustained me from the conception of the idea through the long period of spare time researching and writing.

To Tom Hill of Atlanta, the skilled artist who produces the Sunday *Mark Trail* strip, my thanks for his excellent illustrative sketches.

Last but certainly not least is an important group of individuals many of whom must go unnamed but who contributed crucial material. These were a score of ex-moonshiners who willingly consented to being interviewed. I have named only eight in the book—John Henry Chumley of Dawsonville, Georgia; Semmie Free, Tiger, Georgia; Peg Fields, Jasper, Georgia; Hubert Howell, Cartersville, Georgia; Arthur Young, Tate City, Georgia; Hamper McBee, Monteagle, Tennessee; Robert Lee Blue, Bennettsville, South Carolina; and the late John Henry Hardin of Georgia. (I have also mentioned by name ex-trippers Fred Goswick, the late Lloyd Seay, Roy Hall, and Legs Law.) To them, and to the many others who remain anonymous or whose quotes were attributed to fictitious names, I wish to express my thanks.

Joseph Earl Dabney
Atlanta, Georgia

Contents

Foreword: A Case of Malum Prohibitum

The making, the drinking, and the marketing of corn whiskey are deeply enmeshed in the rural and pioneer Southern mystique, much more deeply than perhaps many Southern social historians have been aware. The fiery beverage has been rooted in the lives of the people in the Appalachian South for over two and a quarter centuries—and long before that in the lives of their ancestors in England, Scotland, and Ireland.

Over its broad sweep, the history of corn whiskey is really a story of pioneer America, beginning in the mid-1700s with the settlement of the eastern seaboard interior by thousands of hardy immigrants from Europe and Great Britain—particularly the Ulstermen, the "Scotch-Irish." The immigrants brought grain whiskey with them and used it to sustain themselves as they carved a new nation "beyond the Blue Ridge," down the great valley from Pennsylvania through Virginia, into the Carolinas, Georgia, and Tennessee, and through the Cumberland Gap and Wilderness Trail, into Kentucky. These were a people who helped save the new nation with their valiant Revolutionary War victory at Kings Mountain, a battle we will look at in a later chapter.

The history of corn whiskey is also the saga of a poor but proud and striving people, fighting not only against the seemingly insurmountable odds of the frontier, but also against what they considered to be unjust government interference. This latter fight, one of whose early climaxes was the Whiskey Rebellion in 1794, has continued against the fabled "revenooers" to the present day, just as whiskey-making has continued.

For decades now, around ninety per cent of the county's illicit distilling has been done in the Southeastern region—which, incidentally, contains most of the nation's dry counties, 446 to be exact. Georgia, with 116 dry counties as compared to only 43 wet ones, reigns supreme as the moonshine-producing champion of the country (and probably the consuming champion as well), annually nosing out Alabama for the honor. According to the federal government, in volume of production, these states are followed by North Carolina,

South Carolina, Tennessee, Mississippi, Florida, and Kentucky, in that order.

During fiscal year 1972, the U. S. Treasury Department's Bureau of Alcohol, Tobacco, and Firearms, the agency concerned with illegal whiskey-making, destroyed 2,090 illicit distilleries, and poured out almost one and a quarter million gallons of fermented mash and 67,000 gallons of untaxed white (distilled but unaged) whiskey. In carrying out these raids, the "feds" arrested 3,191 people. But this is only the tip of the iceberg. During the year 1972, according to estimates prepared by the Licensed Beverage Industries, Inc., America's illicit distilleries turned out more than nine million gallons of white whiskey. This illegal whiskey, the LBI says, defrauded the federal treasury of 97 million dollars (at the federal tax rate of $10.50 per gallon) and cheated state and community coffers of an additional thirty-five million dollars.

But however startling these statistics, they have to be put into perspective. The truth is that compared to equivalent figures for five, ten, and twenty years ago, the "corn likker" craft is dying fast. There has been a downhill skid in moonshining since the days of National Prohibition. During the height of the Noble Experiment, in the year 1925 alone, prohibition agents seized 29,087 stills and arrested over seventy-six thousand people!

Mountain Spirits is in part the story of this decline. But more fascinating to me—lauching me into the research that led to this book by way of interviews with a score of ex-distillers in four states, an equal number of federal and state alcohol revenue men, plus communications with hundreds of other people knowledgeable about the fascinating folklore of this "ancient art of the hills"—is its story of a people. When I began delving into this subject as a hobby in the fall of 1970, I was almost totally ignorant of what moonshine-making was all about. After concluding my research (and bringing home about fifty cassettes of tape), it was clear that moonshining was and is a terribly personal enterprise, so personal you really can't talk about a "typical" moonshiner. In the book I have tried to recreate his individualistic, exciting, but disappearing world.

This is an appropriate place to explain a few terms basic to the story of corn whiskey. The term "moonshiner" derives from "moonlighter." It was used in England prior to the 1700s to describe the night-time smugglers of brandy from Holland and France onto the British coast. *A Classical Dictionary of the Vulgar Tongue*, published in 1785, declared: "The white brandy smuggled on the coasts of Kent and Sussex is called moonshine." When the term caught on in America is not clear, but it likely came with the imposition of the excise taxes (which became permanent in 1862), when many whiskey-makers went underground, figuratively and in some cases, literally, carrying out their illicit "stilling" at night. J. C. Campbell noted in *The Southern Highlander and His Homeland*: "He is called moonshiner because it is supposed that he engages in his illicit traffic on moonlight nights when there is enough light to make work easy and enough darkness to make him secure."

In some areas of the Appalachians, notably in North Carolina, southwest Virginia and Georgia, pioneer moonshiners were called "blockaders" and their product "blockade whiskey." In all likelihood, the term derived from the blockade-running prior to and during the Revolutionary War, the War of 1812, and the Civil War, when contraband was rammed through coastal blockades.

A term often used synonymously with moonshiner is "bootlegger." But the bootlegger, in most cases, is a different individual entirely. The moonshiner is the maker of illicit whiskey, while the bootlegger strictly speaking is the seller. (He could also be the seller, under illegal conditions, of legal liquor.)

The original bootlegger was the person who, in the early days of the American colonies, and in the face of laws prohibiting it, smuggled intoxicating spirits to the Indians in flasks concealed in the top of his boots. Over a century later in 1871, when the first federal revenue stamps for whiskey came out, bootleggers would use their boots to hold a few stamps which they would stick on a bottle if challenged by a revenuer. Of course, it is possible that a moonshiner could also be a bootlegger, and there have been many instances of this occurring, particularly among small operators with a neighborhood "fruit jar trade" clientele. But in general, most traditional moonshiners have restricted their illicit activity to making, leaving the transportation and marketing to others albeit, in many cases, their kin.

Today there are still a number of active "pure corn" distillers left in the hills—mostly old men in their eighty's and ninety's—who occasionally make "runs" on their copper pot stills, just as their fathers and grandfathers before them; these purists are admittedly rare. But the current moonshine scene is populated mostly by big-time bootleg syndicate operators with huge "groundhog" stills and "steamers" and —more and more in recent years—giant "pan" stills. These syndicate operators are really entrepreneurs in the modern sense, and their distillers are usually hired hands, some of whom are quite skilled in the art of distillation.

Now, readers who know of the present-day moonshining record— one of greed, gangsterism, and bribery, with poison pouring out of filthy stills—will perhaps consider this volume to be overromanticized. But I have been interested in the moonshine genus, the traditionalist who was handed the craft from his father and grandfather and who considered it a God-given right not subject to federal intervention. Indeed, in legal terms, moonshining has been defined by federal law as *malum prohibitum*, which means that it is bad because there is a law against it, not bad in itself. Into this legal category, for example, fall offenses against our tax and parking laws. What the moonshiner does when he makes "likker in the woods" is to avoid payment of taxes. Hence he is a tax violator rather than a criminal, whose crime is defined as *malum per se*, or *malum in se*, bad in itself.

So perhaps readers will have to take into consideration my admitted prejudice in favor of the corn whiskey traditionalists—the "copper pot craftsmen," the mountain people who were "borned into" and "raised" in liquor lore. As the late Horace Kephart, the great chronicler of the Great Smoky Mountains, observed in his classic book, *Our Southern Highlanders*:

> The little moonshiner . . . fights fair, according to his code, and singlehandedly against tremendous odds. He is innocent of graft. There is nothing between him and the whole power of the Federal Government, except his own wits and a well-worn Winchester or muzzle-loader. . . . This man is usually a good enough citizen in other ways, of decent standing in his own community, and a right good fellow toward all of the world, save revenue officers. Although a criminal in the eyes of the law, he is soundly convinced that the law is unjust and that he is only exercising his natural rights. Such a man . . . suffers none of the moral degradation that comes from violating his conscience; his self-respect is whole.

Kephart's observations were made prior to the days of National Prohibition, which saw the beginning of the decline and degeneration of the really pure corn practitioner. But today there still remain these old-timers who were "borned into likker," who are "soundly convinced" they are exercising their "natural rights," whose "self-respect is whole." It is their story we shall be observing in this saga of pure corn.

Drawing by Tom Hill

A Corn Whiskey Glossary

Some terms you ought to know about—a few of which already have been explained—as you read the rest of this book.

Backins: The weak whiskey (usually below 90 proof) at the end of a double run, or at the end of a run through a thumper (doubler). "Backins" is the whiskey that "breaks at the worm" —drops in proof.

Bale: Metal strip across top of still cap, tied to "ears" on cap to keep top from popping off during cooking. (Some operators put rocks on the top.)

Bead: The bubbles that form when you shake liquor. An experienced distiller can evaluate the proof of the liquor by the size and position of the bubbles on the surface and whether it is pure corn whiskey or a combination of corn and sugar.

Beading Oil: A cooking oil used by modern moonshiners to create a false bead on low grade whiskey and give the impression that it has a high proof.

Beer: The product of the first stage of whiskey-making; fermented mash. It is sometimes called "distiller's beer" or "fermented wort," when it has fermented sufficiently for distilling. Many distillers prefer to drink it rather than whiskey, which comes from the next stage. They often drink it with the help of hollow quills that they pull from creek banks.

Blockader: An expression in the Appalachian meaning moonshiner. It is a carryover from Revolutionary War days. Many Appalachian whiskey-makers were known as "blockaders" and their white whiskey was known as "blockade likker," due to the fact that untaxed whiskey had to "run the blockade" of revenuers.

Bootleg Bonnet: This is the old-time moonshine hat, made of black felt. These caps are turned upside down and tacked on top of a barrel and used to strain fresh whiskey.

Bootleg Turn: Sliding a whiskey-carrying car into the opposite direction at a high rate of speed in order to escape from pursuing officers. This is done by putting on the brakes and making a turn at a coordinated moment.

Branch: A small tributary. Usual site of a still.

Cap: The removable top third of a still, which fits snugly into the top, or collar, of the pot. Alcohol vapors collect in the cap on the way to the condenser.

Cap Arm: Built into the cap, this is a pipe that conveys the alcoholic vapors to the thumper keg or to the condenser.

Cape: The area of greatest circumference on a still pot, usually just below the collar.

Case: Six gallons of moonshine liquor. Packed as twelve half-gallon jars in a corrugated case, or six one-gallon plastic jugs.

Condenser: The metal device (usually copper) in which the alcoholic vapors are converted into liquid.

Copper Pot: Sometimes called a "copper," or kettle, this still, with roots going back to Scotland and Ireland, was a favorite along the Appalachians and can still be found in isolated spots in the hills. It has three forms—the "turnip," round and fat; the "half turnip"; and the upright copper pot, shaped like a metal drum and placed vertically in the furnace. Also called the buccaneer, the blockade still, and mountain teapot.

Doubled and Twisted: See *doubling liquor.*

Doubler: See *thump barrel.*

Doubling Liquor: Whiskey run through a copper pot still twice, which produces a proof of well over 100. Sometimes known as high wines or "doubled and twisted whiskey."

Feints: The leftover liquid in a thumper keg after a run. Sometimes referred to as "thumper tails." These are withdrawn after a run and replaced with fresh beer or backings, to provide alcohol for the thumper's doubling effect.

Fermenter: Container for mash. Can be barrels, boxes, or vats.

Fire in the Hole: A term some moonshine families in southern Kentucky used to signal their men that the "law" was near.

Flake Stand: A box or barrel in which the condenser is placed. Water flows constantly into and out of the stand, cooling the condenser, and causing the whiskey vapors to liquefy. See *condenser.*

Foreshot: First whiskey to come out of the condenser at the beginning of a run. Sometimes referred to as "high shots," "high wines," or "alkihol."

Fusel oil: Bitter oily liquid, mostly amyl alcohol, found in whiskey which has not been distilled thoroughly or to a high enough proof.

Gauger: An exciseman in the British Isles, the equivalent of America's latter-day revenuer. His job was to gauge the amount and proof of whiskey and to collect the excise taxes.

Groundhog: This still, sometimes called a "hog," is usually found dug into the side of a hill or bank and is usually a huge metal cylinder with a wooden top and bottom. The bottom is placed about a foot or two underneath the ground. The furnace is the air space around and outside the cylinder. The flames wrap around it on either side and exit at the top on the back side. The mash is fermented in the groundhog pot.

Headache Stick: The long vapor line pipe that goes down into the thumper keg. The hot vapors flow into the beer at the bottom of the keg, and the doubled vapors exit from the shorter, second pipe at top. See *thumper barrel.*

High Shots: See *foreshot.*

In: A moonshine term meaning the containers used for fermenting have been filled with mash. "Mashed in," in other words.

Jacket: A one-gallon tin can moonshine haulers used during and after Prohibition to carry whiskey. Five cans usually were tied in a one-bushel onion sack, with slits cut for the mouth of each can.

Jars: A moonshiner term for whiskey containers, be they made of glass, tin, plastic, or ceramic.

Lay-Worm or Branch Type: A number of equal lengths of copper tubing joined by angle pipes and laid flat in a rectangular cooler box or in a stream of water. Some of these condensers measure eight to twelve feet long.

Malt: Sprouted grain, dried and ground up. Usually barley or corn. Malt contains diastase, which helps break down carbohydrates in grain meal and convert them into sugar.

Mash: The mixture of raw and cooked meal, water, malt, and sometimes yeast, which ferments into "beer" prior to distillation.

Mash Stick: A hardwood stick about eight feet long used periodically to stir the mash. Pegs are put into the end of the stick so that the distiller can "comb" the mash and break up solid matter.

Mess: A distilling rig on the Southeastern coastal plain.

Metal Pot: The ATF defines this still as one constructed of any metal other than copper, no matter what shape or size. Many moonshiners in recent years have resorted to tin, galvanized metal and in some cases, aluminum. A localized version of the metal pot still is the "silver cloud," common in East Tennessee, particularly around Cosby. They are cylindrical pots made of galvanized steel, with heat being applied by burners through single or twin flues through the lower third of the pot. Another type of metal pot is a "steel drum still," made of drums welded together end to end, and laid horizontally over the furnace, with a hole cut in the top for the cap.

Money Piece: Where the whiskey "pays off"—emerges—out of the condenser. See *condenser*.

Pan: Most pan stills are solid metal, usually quarter-inch welded steel or iron. And most are huge rectangular, box-like containers, with a two-foot hole in the top for the cap. The mash is both fermented and distilled in the same container (although in some push-button operations, mash is mixed nearby and pumped into the pan for fermentation and distillation). Most pan-type stills in north Georgia have a capacity of from 800 to 2,250 gallons. In south Georgia, they are somewhat larger, with up to 3,000 gallons capacity. Many pan distilleries have a number of pans and are distilled in sequence. An outfit with three 1800-gallon pans would rotate every three days, since it takes three days for fermentation. A variation of the pan still is the "coffin" with a dome cap like a coffin.

Pile: A pan-type still in the mountains.

Plug Stick: A hardwood stick with rags tied to one end. It is placed in the slop arm, sealing the inside of the still pot when pulled tight.

Pot-Tail: The mash left after a distillation. In copper pot stills, this leftover is dipped out and "slopped back" into the mash barrels and mixed with subsequent batches to be fermented. The result is sour mash whiskey. In groundhog and pan stills, the pot-tail is left in the bottom, and sugar and meal are added for fermentation for subsequent distillations.

Pre-Heater: Sometimes called the "heater box." Just about the most

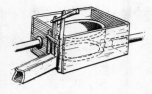

efficient add-on to a still. This is a square wooden box built adjacent to and somewhat higher than the still. It is used to heat mash to the point of distillation. Hot vapors from the still are piped through the heater box into the condenser.

Proof: The proportion of alcohol in whiskey. One-hundred-proof whiskey has 50 per cent alcohol. British proof is 57.1 per cent alcohol by volume.

Proof Vial: A small glass tube used to test the whiskey bead. The operator would shake the vial of whiskey and hold it horizontally to check the bead. Some distillers added drops of water to determine the proof and the volume of water needed for the "blending tub." Most of the vials held exactly one ounce, such as a Bateman Drop bottle.

Quill: A straw used to sample still beer, which many moonshiners considered a tasty drink. "Oh boy," said one. "I liked that beer better than a pig loves slop."

Relay Barrel: A dry barrel used to catch "puke" overflow during a hot distillation.

Rig: A distillery setup.

Run: One whiskey distilling cycle. "We're going to have a run today."

Runners: Whiskey transporters, also known as trippers or haulers.

Shack: A crude shed built over a moonshine still. Term sometimes used to describe distillery itself. "He has a 'shack' behind his house."

Sign: The physical evidence leading to a distillery: tracks, broken undergrowth, spilled sugar, a trail. A favorite moonshiner expression was "put out the sign," i.e., sweep away the tracks. Revenue agents sought to "find the sign" or "cut off the sign."

Singlings: Whiskey run through a single pot still once, without being run through a doubler.

Slop: Same as pot-tail.

Slopping Back: Using hot pot-tails from a run to "start" a new batch of mash, yielding sour mash whiskey.

Steamer: This still utilizes steam which is piped to an adjoining wooden or metal distilling pot containing the beer (mash). The steam-producing unit may be a homemade steel drum boiler—called a "stack steamer" or "double drum steamer"— or a commercial boiler. Some homemade steamers have metal drums laid or suspended horizontally over a furnace. The still pot itself is usually built of wood. The "Wilkesboro type" in the North Carolina Piedmont consists of a stave-type barrel, into which the steam from the boiler is piped.

Still: Colloquial for distillery. A still is one cooker, pot, or kettle in a distillery complex, which may have several stills.

Strainer: The filtering unit at the bottom of con- denser. Old-timers used charcoals and cloth in a one-gallon funnel.

Swab Stick: A hickory stick with the end beat up like an old toothbrush. Used by operators to scrub out the still and to keep the mash from sticking to the still wall before reaching a boil. Sometimes called a stir stick.

Tempering Tub: Tub used to blend various proofs of whiskey and cut it with water or backings, giving the whiskey from a particular run a uniform proof.

Thump Barrel: Also known as the doubler, thum- per, or thump keg. This container is charged with fresh beer or backings. Vapors from the pot bubble through, giving a second distilla- tion called "thump likker."

Thumper tails: See *feints*.

Trippers: Same as moonshine haulers or runners.

Twist: Comes from the term "double and twisted" and refers to the fact that doubled whiskey makes a final twist when it leaves the end of the condenser. In the 1920s, Georgia distillers cut willow saplings, charred them over a fire, washed them off, and put them at the end of the condenser worm. One account said that after trickling and twisting down a sixteen-foot pole, whiskey was doubled and twisted the equivalent of eight years of aging.

Up: Term used to indicate the distillery is filled with beer and is ready for distillation.

Workway: Main path leading to a distillery. Sometimes known as the "still path" or walkway.

Worm: Copper condensing coil placed in the flake stand. See *lay-worm*.

I

THE CRAFT

Mother Corn—giver of life.
Old Indian Saying

The ABC's of Pure Corn

Here's to Old Corn Likker,
Whitens the teeth,
Perfumes the breath,
And makes childbirth a pleasure.
—North Carolina folksaying

There's gold in them there mountains,
There's gold in them there hills;
The natives there are getting it,
By operating stills.
—John Judge, Jr.
Noble Experiments, 1930

I T is a federal offense in America to distill alcohol without a federal permit or even to possess a workable, unregistered still.

But it wasn't always that way.

For 241 years of America's colonial and pioneer history, whiskey-making was an inalienable right of all citizens, an occupation free of federal restriction.* Which in part explains why it took on such major proportions as a "cottage industry" on thousands of farms across the Appalachians and why, when whiskey-making without a license permanently became a federal offense in 1862, the result was widespread illicit moonshine activity, which has carried down to today.

Indeed, for the proud Scotch-Irish people who predominated on the frontier, whiskey-making inevitably was linked to freedom, and

* Whiskey was untaxed in the U.S. up to 1791, and then from 1802 to 1862 (with the exception of three years following the War of 1812).

the various taxes imposed against it time and again in Great Britain and America were looked on as expressions of government tyranny. "Whiskey and freedom gang thegither," wrote the Scot poet Bobbie Burns.

To appreciate the full story of corn whiskey's history in America, one needs to know something about the nature of the enterprise, and the fundamentals of how alcohol is made. Since these fundamentals constitute a kind of practical guide to the making of corn whiskey, the consequences of violating the federal statutes in this regard cannot be emphasized too strongly. Violation of any one count of the federal liquor laws can result in a fine of up to $10,000 or a sentence of up to ten years in prison, or both.

Now, the manufacture of alcohol is a natural process, and man's intervention is required only to arrange the raw materials in the proper proportion and sequence and to apply the necessary heat and cooling along the way.

There are two basic steps involved: fermentation and distillation. Practically all foodstuffs, vegetables, fruit, and grain are fermentable —a natural phenomenon—and practically all of them at one time or another have been utilized to produce wine, beer, or alcohol. Beer, made from grain, and wine, made from berries and fruit, are the result of fermentation, and they end up with an alcoholic content— usually of sixteen per cent or less.

During the fermentation process, the starches in the grain (or the fruit) are broken down through saccharification into sugars and then the sugars into alcohol. This process is speeded up greatly by the infusion of sugar, yeast, and/or malt. Yeast speeds up fermentation by twelve hours. Sugar hurries it along additionally and increases the alcoholic yield considerably.

In whiskey-making, the basic fermenting mixture of grain, water, and other ingredients is called "mash." Mash containing a heavy proportion of sugar and yeast usually ferments in three to four days. However, pure corn meal alone, without sugar (though with the sprouted grain which is called "malt" and which is explained below), can take five to ten days to ferment and, if the temperature is not high enough, up to fourteen days or more.

Old-time distillers say the key to making a good run—a batch of whiskey—and drawing out the biggest quantity of alcohol, lies in the fermenting stage of the art, "mashing in" the grain, sugar (when used), and water, keeping it stirred, and applying adequate malt and/or yeast.

"It's like a woman making biscuits," allowed "Short" Stanton, a veteran Greene County, Tennessee, ex-distiller. "If she don't know how to mix that dough in the bread bowl over thar, when she puts 'em in the pan, they ain't no count. You don't make likker in a outfit. You make it over thar in the mash barrels."

Soon after the meal, water, sugar, and malt are mixed in the mash box or barrel, carbonic gas bubbles begin rising to the surface, forming, along with some of the grain, a thick, foamy "cap." Some distillers add rye meal or wheat bran as an additional cap to contain the mash and speed fermentation. Later—the interval depending on whether sugar was used—the mash bubbles so much that it starts rolling, literally, and keeps on for a day and a half or two days. When the bubbles stop rising, and the cap disappears, the mash, now called "corn beer" or distiller's beer, becomes a soupy yellow and is ready to be distilled.

At this "high point," the beer contains ten or more per cent of alcohol essence, and has a slightly sweet taste with a sharp sour tang. If it is not distilled promptly, it begins to lose its alcoholic content and turns more and more sour. Federal agents who come onto fermenting mash can tell immediately what stage of the cycle it is in, first by taste, and next by the "smack," the feel, of the mixture when the fingers are dipped into it. A clear liquid with little smack (little stickiness or tackiness) means it's about ready for the cooking pot and distillation. If the mash is a long way from the distilling stage, agents usually elect to "save" the still and come back and raid it on the morning of the distillation, in order to capture the operators on the scene.

In earlier times, when sugar and yeast were not readily available, the distiller had to ferment his mash a lot longer than is common today. Some used honey or sorghum, known as "long sweetin'," which speeded things up a bit and helped the yield. In place of yeast, he made his own malt, sprouted grain which is dried and ground up. (Incidentally, it is a federal crime to grind sprouted corn or barley.) Malt, which was called "drake's tail" by pioneers, contains the enzyme diastase which converts the raw corn meal starches into sugar, through a saccharification process. Wild yeast spores that are present in the air multiply on contact with the meal in the mash and speed up the fermentation. In effect, the malt (and/or yeast) produce the souring catalyst for the mash in much the way that a pinch or two of sourdough will carry on the fermentation cycle for succeeding batches of dough.

To go from the fermented mash to alcohol itself requires the additional step of distillation. In this process the essence, or spirits, of the fermented liquid is separated from the water by being heated to the appropriate temperature. Wine heated to 173 degrees Fahrenheit gives off an alcoholic vapor which, when cooled and condensed back into liquid form, becomes brandy. Similarly, the distiller's beer produced by fermented grain-based mash produces grain alcohol—whiskey—when heated and vaporized at the same temperature. The higher the heat during the distillation, the greater the amount of water and impurities in the proportion of the final product.

The use of leftover soured slop from a still pot following a run—distributed back into the mash and sometimes referred to as "slopping back" or "dipping back"—continues the yeasting cycle for eight or ten subsequent runs, until the operator decides to "slop out" and begin anew. The first run of whiskey results in a sweet mash liquor. The subsequent slopping back distillations—usually with the addition of a lot of sugar and lesser amounts of grain—result in sour mash whiskey. "When whiskey gets good," says veteran distiller Hamper McBee of Tennessee, "is when it runs four times [on the same basic mash]. Then you get some good whiskey—the kind you can drink without a carbide for a chaser."

Distilling being an essentially individual affair, there are many variations in the whiskey-making process. Here, in the words of different old-timers, are personal tips and suggestions on how they did it "in the old days."*

PUTTING IN A STILL

A retired whiskey-maker from Stillhouse Branch, North Carolina, explains the special attention that some corn liquor men paid to the water they used.

* The first comment comes from an interview by columnist John Parris of the *Asheville Citizen*. The remainder are taken from interviews I conducted.

6

"The beer won't pay off as good if the water comes from a branch that's got touch-me-nots along its banks. . . . They denote hard water and hard water won't make corn whiskey. For making moonshine, find yourself a branch where red horsemint grows. You can't go wrong. Another way to test the water . . . is to see if it will 'bead.'† All you do is take a jar of water from the branch and shake it up. If the bubbles rise when it's tilted, then you know you've got the kind of water it takes to make good whiskey."

SPROUTING MALT

A seventy-three-year-old retired distiller from Laughingal, Georgia, tells of the value of using malt and how it is made. "We put our shelled corn in a tow sack and poured hot water over it and put it in a sawdust pile. Just covered it up. In about three days, it'd have stringers about two, three inches long. All tangled up. You just spread it out and let it dry in the sun for two, three days. Carry it to the mill and have it ground."

"In the wintertime," another maker from Rabun County, Georgia, said, "you have to dig a hole in the ground. Put your grain in it in a sack and pour warm water over it. Then cover it over with straw and let it sprout. Sometimes takes four days. Then you put it out to dry and took it to an old water-powered mill somewhere and had it ground. Back when I was a boy, that was the only kind of mill they wuz."

KEEPING MASH WARM AND USING IT

Keeping mash warm in winter was a problem. "We had a still one time on the quarry hill," a northeast Georgian told me, "and we buried twenty barrels. We got rye straw and hay and packed it around them. It was pretty severe winter, but the mash 'kicked over' in five or six days." (Many distillers found burying mash barrels also

† See the glossary for terms that need further clarification.

7

insured against excessive heating in summer. Too much heat will cause wild yeast "vinegar mother" to form, in effect killing the mash.) Another way to keep mash warm in winter is to bury the barrels or boxes in a sawdust pile. "The heat from that sawdust makes it work right along," an old-timer remembered. A third popular method was to bury vats in hot manure piles, "mother nature's heating system."

"When the mash starts workin', it rises up," declared an old-timer from Track Rock Gap, Georgia. "You gotta leave it eight inches from the top [of the barrel]. That malt'll come up there thick. If it's still workin', it's 'wild in the still.' That kind 'pukes' [meaning the beer belches through the vapor line prematurely before it is distilled]. Got to let it settle down. It's all right when it begins to spot [clear] just a little. You can see the clear spots. Then when it settles down . . . down . . . down . . . the cap's about dropped on it. It's ready to run likker! Ready to run likker! You've got eight hours to cook it. Otherwise it'll go bad on you."

FIRING THE STILL "JUST RIGHT"

Firing a still furnace is an art in itself, because the idea is to keep the heat close to the alcohol vaporizing level—173 degrees (F)—but not much higher. An old-timer from near Blairsville, Georgia, recalled this stage:

"I've seen faar at night just lap its tongue out in front of the still. The blaze crosses itself when you're faarin' one hard. You get that furnace throat just exactly right, it'll cross its tongue.

"After a while—it don't take too long—your furnace is good and hot, you'll see a little steam look like comin' out of the worm. Next thing you'll see directly a drop, maybe two or three drops. Then it'll piss just a little. After a while, when you begin to see drops comin' fast, you say, 'She's gonna get riiiiiiiiiggghhhhhhhhhttt now.' Directly she'll start pourin' out of the worm. *Then you're makin' likker.* You don't want to faar it too hard. You can puke a doublin' if you do. You want to run it slow and steady. That whiskey'll get out there [out of the worm] and hold its tail, like a saddle horse kinda. It'll get out there just as steady. . . ."

A "half turnip" copper pot still at the 1973 Georgia Mountain Fair. A former moonshiner, seventy-year-old Arthur Young, who used this type of still as a young man in the Smoky Mountains of North Carolina, adds a piece of wood to the furnace. The furnace is well doubed with clay, to keep the heat in. The flames come up inside it, wrap around the pot, and exit at the flue on the front, roughly at a point to the side of Mr. Young's hat brim—so the furnace's nickname, an "eyebrow singer." The still's cap arm at left leads to the thump keg, where the whiskey receives a second distillation on the same run.

Copper pot rig on display in the Moonshine Museum, Dawsonville, Georgia. The vapor flows from the cap arm into the thump keg, then into the heater box in the rear, and from there into a lay worm copper condenser which is in a simulated stream to the rear. The big mash barrels are old style hand-made 220-gallon barrels with special hickory straps, latched together with notches.

Two groundhog stills at the Moonshine Museum. The still pot is the round metal container under the barrel cap. When the mash has fermented, the operator "caps down" his still and fires the furnace, in this case a 55-gallon drum cut in half. The flames wrap around the pot and exit at a flue on the back. The vapors collect in the barrel cap, then go to a thumper keg and to the condenser, off to the left (not seen). The advantage of the groundhog still over the copper pot is that it could be used for both fermenting and distilling and could be easily set into a creek bank or hillside. With its wooden top and bottom, it also conserved precious metal.

Mash bubbling
during fermentation.

Freshly run moonshine whiskey.

Typical old stone jug from
a registered corn whiskey
distillery in Atlanta.

A copper pot still in operation. Water is piped into the flake stand by a metal pipe at the left. A thump keg on the rock in the center provides a second distillation. Note cover of mountain "laurels"—rhododendron—over the still site. (National Park Service photo).

A former moonshiner, Hamper McBee, looks over a destroyed distillery set beside a cave in the Cumberland Plateau around Chattanooga, Tennessee. A stream of limestone water ran from inside the cave to a sinkhole near the front. Many an illicit whiskey distillery such as this one was seized and destroyed after an angry housewife reported the activity to the law. "They get mad 'cause their old man is drunk and turn somebody in for making whiskey. I reckon they think that'll break 'em from drinking. They was a lot of stills turned up by these mad wives." (Photo by Duval Cravens, Jr.).

Black moonshiner pictured at work at his still at Southern Pines, located in the sandhills section of North Carolina. The still is a metal pot with a thump keg and condenser. Mash barrels are at the left. In addition to whiskey made of grain, meal and sugar, some moonshine through the sandhills region was made of molasses. It was called "monkey rum." (Photo from the Wittemann Collection, Library of Congress).

A 520-gallon "silver cloud" pot still captured in Cocke County, Tennessee. Note the two flues going through the galvanized steel pot. This still was fired by liquified petroleum gas. The photo suggests why so-called silver clouds, very popular in the Cosby (Cocke County) area of east Tennessee, are said to resemble a silver cloud on a hillside, particularly at night under the light of a bright moon.

MOVING FROM A SINGLING RUN
TO A DOUBLING

After the distiller has run eight barrels of mash through the still to make singlings, he is ready to start on his doubling run. The same distiller from Blairsville, Georgia, quoted above, describes this phase:

"You run them singlin's 'til as long as they got any strength in 'em, then you put your hands under the worm, rub 'em and inhale. When they smell right sour, the alkihol's out. It's ready to change boils, and you refill the pot with those singlin's for a doublin' run.

"But first, you draw your fire and clean your still. Ever' little spot. Everything's got to be clean about likker. Wash your still . . . wash your vessels after a run. If you're thumpin', wash that thump keg every time you run a boil of likker. *Wash* that thing. *Clean* that thump barrel. *Wash* the heater box. *Wash* 'em connections. That don't leave no feinty taste. When that bead breaks when you run them low wines in there, it gets down to a funky scent, leaves a bad odor in the connections, and on your next run, that likker's gonna knock that bad odor out and that's in your likker there, you see."

TELLING WHEN WHISKEY IS ABOUT
TO BREAK AT THE WORM

The maker keeps a close watch on the distillate coming out of the worm to make sure he pulls away his tub when the whiskey breaks at the worm, when the proof drops sharply. A one-time maker from Habersham County, Georgia, had a sharp eye for the break. "I could stand as fer as from here to that door yander and I could tell just when it would break. It quits runnin' nearly . . . the power and the strength stops—drops to a stream a little bigger than a match stem. I could take my finger and wet it that way and put it to my mouth and I could tell just the second I tasted it . . . it didn't have the power."

Another maker from Union County, Georgia, remarked:

"When thump likker shows its low bead, it ain't long before it's

9

through. Lots of times I could tell when the bead broke because it changed that twist. I'd say, 'It's broke boys,' and go over and test it and it'd be dead."

PROOFING WHISKEY BY ITS BEAD

Next comes proofing the whiskey by its bead, as explained by a former moonshine hauler—a tripper.

"If it's high proof—say 115 to 120—a big bead will jump up there on top [of the whiskey] when you shake it. If the proof is lower, the bead goes away faster and is smaller. Hand a mountain man a pint of whiskey and the first thing he'll do is shake it. The longer those beads stay on there the higher the proof.

"There's a way of putting a false bead by using beading oil or lye. You put the oil in when the likker first comes out of the still. The way you tell . . . when the bead hops all the way out and sits on top of the surface, it's false. A true bead will stop half in the likker and half out on top."

The proof of whiskey today is estimated this way: Its advertised proof figure is twice the amount of the alcohol content. If it is labeled 100 proof, this means it is 50 per cent alcohol. The British centuries ago established proof at 57.1 per cent alcohol. It had been found that whiskey with that proportion of alcohol, mixed with gunpowder, gave off a steady blue flame. An ancient British dictionary described this as "gunpowder proof,"* which the British government adopted in 1816 as being 100 proof. The U.S. copied the principle but, to make it easier to calculate, ruled 100 proof whiskey to be 50 per cent alcohol. The British still have proof of 57.1 per cent alcohol by volume, which translates to 114.2 proof American!

Some distillers who are not confident of their estimates of the bead toward the end of a run have been known to throw a cup full of whiskey into the furnace. If it blazes up well, they are assured the proof is still strong. Early revenue officers of the American frontier

* Early American Whiskey historian Harrison Hall of Philadelphia described "gunpowder proof" this way: "Pour a small quantity of spirit on a small heap of gunpowder and kindle it. The spirit burns quietly on the surface of the powder until it is all consumed, and the last portion fires the powder if the spirit was pure; but if watery, the powder becomes too damp and will not explode."

used something called a Dicus hydrometer. In the case of most distillers in the Appalachians up through the early 1900s, proof was
checked with a proof vial—a small bottle-like device, to which they
would add drops of water to the whiskey. "You'd get it two-thirds
full of likker," a retired maker remembered, "and put twenty drops
of water in it. If the twenty drops killed it, knocked the head off of
it, that meant it was 100 proof likker." In general, though, most
distillers merely shook a vial and judged the proof by the bead.

STRAINING FRESH WHISKEY

Filtering whiskey—purging it of its impurities—also has a tech-
nology of its own. Although most modern-day moonshiners shun
filters, many makers of earlier days used "bootleg bonnets," to strain
the fresh whiskey. They would tack the hats across the top of the keg
under the worm. But the most popular method of the old-timers was
to use homemade charcoals. Here's how Peg Fields, a retired distiller
from Pickens County, Georgia, did it:

"We had a big funnel set in a two-gallon bucket, and we placed it
right under the worm. We faared with hickory wood most of the
time. We'd burn them faar coals and wash 'em off in the branch.
We'd put a flanigan cloth or two in the funnel bottom and fill it with
them coals, the whiskey coming from the condenser down through
the coals into the bucket. If you used barley malt [to make the
liquor], the whiskey left grease on the coals. Wasn't much left when
we used corn malt. But those coals cleaned the whiskey up and left it
just as clear as could be."

Distillers on the Cumberland Plateau in Tennessee, who special-
ized in improving raw whiskey by "rectifying" it (another term for
purging), set up elaborate filter systems. They would take an empty
keg and place in it a layer of felt, a layer of maple charcoal, a layer
of sand and a layer of gravel. Then they primed it with ten gallons of
high proof whiskey, sending the whiskey through the several layers.
But most illicit distillers never went to such elaborate extents. (Some
distillers even purged impurities by placing a charred peach seed or a
few spoons of ground charcoal into a jar of whiskey.)

AGING CORN WHISKEY

Most corn whiskey over the years has been sold fresh and unaged
—seldom over a week old—which meant that it was clear, "white
lightning," as it was called. But many of the registered, family-
operated "government distilleries" that proliferated following the
Civil War, charred their barrels in the bourbon tradition to age their
whiskey, giving it color and a smoother taste. A retired tripper from
Cobb County, Georgia, remembered how his grandfather did it in the
late 1800s in Dawson County:

"He burned the barrels out with still alcohol. He'd take high shots
and slush 'em around in the barrel. Set it on fire and let that blue
flame shoot out. Then wash it out with boiling water and clean out
the ashes. It would char it down about a half inch deep. You always
charter [sic] old barrels that way to burn out the old fusel oil."

But makers virtually always aged their "drinking likker." Different
people had different ways. From a retired maker in Jasper, Georgia:

"You take a white oak or a hickory tree and split off little pieces
about half as big as your finger. Take six or eight pieces and fry 'em
good and brown in an old pan outside. Drop five or six in a gallon
jug of whiskey. Ever time you go by it, just shake it a little. First
thing you know, it's as pretty and red as any bonded whiskey you
ever saw."

From a distiller near Greeneville, Tennessee:

"You put your whiskey in a charred keg. Go to the keg about
twice a day and shake her real good. In three weeks, it'll be cherry
red. That's some of the *best* likker that you've ever stuck in your
mouth. She'll char more that way in three weeks than hit will settin'
right there perfectly still in six months. That kerreck."

AVOIDING DETECTION BY THE REVENUE

While making whiskey was his primary objective, the illicit distiller's second priority was keeping out of the sight of the law. "Trails

are what lead the law to your still," said an ex-moonshiner of Gwinnett County, Georgia. "If you make a path, it's just like pouring paint up through the woods. What we'd do, we'd take our sugar and barley malt and meal and yeast in a truck. But that truck never left the road. We'd pull out big two-by-ten timbers and lay them from the truck to the high bank up into the woods. Then we left no tracks on the bank at all. Then nobody could tell where the path was. We always walked to the still by a different direction. We'd go this way today, ten feet over the next day."

GETTING AWAY FROM THE REVENUERS

"I learned never to run by a tree that you couldn't see the back side of," a Tiger, Georgia, distilling veteran told me. "First and only time I got caught was when I was fourteen year old. I outrun two of the officers. First I ever seed in my life. Then I went and run about a hundred and fifty yards from there and went past a big mountain oak. Dennis Hughes [a revenue officer] was a standin' right behind it and grabbed me. Then I was caught. If I'd a seed him, he wouldn't have caught me. If you can get a revenuer in a thickety place, it's no trouble to get away."

Most old-time moonshiners cut a number of paths from their still in different directions through the mountain laurel. Then when they had to run during a raid, they could confuse the officers by taking one of their many paths. Frank Rickman, son of the late beloved sheriff of Rabun County, Georgia, remembered one of the last of the double and twisted old-timers. He had located his still out on the point of a ridge and spaded a little trench about six inches deep and a half inch wide to run the water around the hill to his still. He brushed leaves over the trench. Lawmen would walk over it and never realize that water was running down the ditch. Out from his still, the old man trimmed out little trails through the laurels, "just a forkin' ever which a way," Rickman remembered. "When he'd start to escape, he'd get out of sight quick, then before you could get onto his plan, he was gone. You couldn't tell which one of the trails he went on. Like gettin' lost in town, you know."

THE FINE ART: MAKING A RUN OF
PURE CORN WHISKEY

Toward the end of my research into corn whiskey lore, I was fortunate to meet and interview Arthur Young, a seventy-year-old native of the Smoky Mountains. During his youth, Mr. Young learned all about the pure corn art which was done, of course, without the use of any manufactured ingredients—that is, yeast, sugar or store-bought malt. The only ingredients used in the old days were corn or rye meal and home-sprouted and ground malt, and, of course, good soft water from a clear mountain stream. Mr. Young is also a musician, and before he turned twenty quit making liquor and devoted his energies to, among other things, fiddling on a Stradivarius violin (made in 1700) that he inherited from his father and his "greater grandfather" who brought it over from England. In previous visits to the Appalachian foothills of far northeast Georgia, I had heard about Mr. Young's intimate knowledge of the distilling art (as well as his musicianship), but it took some doing to find him. He resides in a little mountain farming community called Tate City, deep into the Appalachian ridges along the headwaters of the Tallulah River. When I reached his home, situated beside a one-lane dirt road on a bluff overlooking the Tallulah River valley miles from a paved road, I found Mr. Young sitting out in his front yard.

"I was born in 1903 in the Smokies under Clingman's Dome, North Carolina," he told me. "I fooled with whiskey from the age of sixteen until I was nineteen. Quit fooling with it when I got another job. Drove horses for thirty-five years for these old logging companies. I quit whiskey. Wasn't nothing in it, you couldn't get nothin' fer it anyhow. Likker then sold for $1.50 a gallon. Likker that would sell today for $24.00 a gallon. Course most likker today is chemicals. It's never seen no still. That's the kind of inspectors the government's got on it now. Back in my day, they wan't any government likker. Whole United States was dry. It was all blockade likker."

Mr. Young explained how he and his associates made corn whiskey in the old way, singling and doubling with a copper pot still. First of all, he had his copper pots made by a skilled still-maker. Then he

selected a secluded spot beside a "bold" stream of water and built up
a furnace from rocks gathered from the water bed. He fashioned his
condenser on the spot, making it into a worm.

"First we got a copper tube three-quarters or an inch in diameter,
about sixteen, eighteen feet long—long enough so that when it is
curled, it would go from the bottom of a fifty-gallon barrel to the top.
We poured either sand or sawdust in the tube to keep it from crimp-
ing and twisted it around a stump. Placed this worm inside the barrel
and fitted the top of the tube to the cap arm from the still. We never
did use a thump keg. Went directly from the pot to the worm. We put
a trough into the barrel—the flake stand—and ran cool water
through it all the time."

Here follows Mr. Young's description of how he went about the
process of making singling and doubling (or double and twisted)
whiskey on a fifty-gallon pot still:

"If a man had a fifty-gallon still, he'd need about eight bushels of
meal—ground from choice white corn only.

"In addition to your still and worm [and flake stand barrel], you
need eight fifty-gallon barrels. To start off with, you put a half bushel
of meal in each barrel. Then you 'cook in' the other half of the
meal—four bushels—in your still pot. Just heat it up and make a
mush of it, like cornmeal batter. Then you divide that back into the
eight barrels. So what you'd have in each of those barrels would be a
half bushel of cooked meal and a half bushel of raw meal.

"You leave it a couple of days, then you have to go and break it
up, and thin it with water, and mix it up with a stir stick. At that
point, you add a couple of gallons of ground corn malt and a gallon
of rye meal. Some folks sprinkled rye meal on top to form a cap and
keep the mash warm. Others just stirred it up. It'd come to the top
soon anyway—all grain does. Six days later, when that cap falls and
the top gets clear, the mash had become 'beer' and it was ready to
run off."

One by one, Mr. Young said, he distilled all eight barrels. From
each of these singling runs, he said, you could expect to get six to
eight gallons of "singlings," or low wines. Then, "you take those fifty
gallons of singlings and cook them through the still again. That's
your doublin' run; that's when the alkihol comes. It'd be real *alkihol*.
Be high proof, too high to bead. That's grain alkihol. Those first
shots be 150, 160 proof. As it continues to distill, the whiskey proof

gets weaker and atter while it comes down to a bead [about 120 proof].

"Finally, it comes to a good bead, about 100 proof. Corn whiskey has a lot smaller bead than this sugar whiskey nowadays. Sugar puts a big coarse bead on it. Now pure corn whiskey comes down to a *fine* bead. About the size of a number six or number seven shot, not much bigger than a bb shot. Sometime later, the whiskey breaks at the worm, as they say. It starts smelling and tasting sour. That's below 90 proof. You're supposed to take all the whiskey that comes out from then on—the backin's—and put it in a barrel with the singlin's for the next doublin' run."

From fifty gallons of singlings, the distiller expected to get between sixteen and twenty gallons of "doubling likker." "I just always figured it'd make two gallons and a half to the bushel of meal," Mr. Young said. "Then you'd 'fourth' that with water, which in this case [eight bushels at two and a half gallons meant twenty gallons of whiskey] would amount to five gallons of water, bringing your yield to twenty-five gallons of doubling whiskey. Some people cut the proof down with backin's," Mr. Young said, "but we didn't. We took cold spring water and poured in that. Cuttin' with water makes the best likker . . . the sweetest-tasting likker. Lots of folks would boil the water first and let it cool off, then added it to the whiskey."

While whiskey-making, illicit style, essentially was a case of "helping nature along"—and seemingly a joy ride—it was also a tough, back-breaking occupation, requiring a lot of plain hard work and steel nerves. Many older mountain men with crooked backs can attest to their younger days of "rawhiding" sugar and meal into tough mountain terrain and then barrels of whiskey on the opposite trip out.

As Mr. Young observed: "I usta hear people complain that these whiskey men ought to get out and work for a living. The fact was, *they* were the ones were *really* working already."

I remember asking an old-timer from Mountain City, Georgia, if he enjoyed his former life as a moonshiner:

"Oh, it was excitin' at times, but it's not a life of sunshine, I'll clue ye. It's nothing but hard work and the very hardest. You stay out there and take all kinds of exposure. If you ain't got a shed over you and if it comes up a rain, you stand right there and take it. If it snows, you stand right there and take it. Lot of time, maybe you got no way to ride and you too fer back in the mountains to walk out and you just got to stay and take it."

Hamper McBee put in his share of hard labor making moonshine in the Cumberland Mountains northwest of Chattanooga. On a record he cut, called *The Cumberland Moonshiner*, Hamper commented about the image of the lazy whiskey-maker:

"Ain't no lazy man gonna make no whiskey . . . I hear a lot of women at our home say 'so-and-so too lazy to work, all they do is make whiskey.' They ought to try it sometime if they think it's a snap. Ride the sugar down the mountains and it wet, slippery, and you're falling and a stumbling and getting down there a chopping wood and it wet and trying to get a fire and run that stuff and don't know whether you're agonna run into the revenue or not and then have to pack that stuff back out of them mountains. It's a blooming job . . ."

Against these odds, extremely hard work, the ever present danger of being caught by the law and the relatively low compensation— why have men across the South continued to make whiskey illicitly over the years?

A distiller from Bartow County, Georgia, offered one rationale:

"Moonshining gets into your blood just like sawmilling and digging gold. Once a gold digger, always a gold digger. Once a blockader, always a blockader at heart."

Appalachian researcher John Gordon, writing in the *Georgia Review*, had another explanation:

"Mountain people are action seekers. They live episodically and they live for adventure. Moonshining is for some of them the ultimate adventure."

2

The Taste of Corn Whiskey

That pure corn, it was just as mild as it
could be. It was up there close to 100
proof, too. . . . You could just turn it up
and drink it like drinking water.
—Old-time Georgia corn
whiskey distiller, Peg Fields

When you absorb a deep swig of it, you
have all the sensations of having swal-
lowed a lighted kerosene lamp.
—Irvin S. Cobb

YOU can get hundreds of descriptions of corn whiskey, all the
way from the superlative to the obscene. Irvin Cobb, the Kentucky
humorist who tickled America's funny bones during the 1930s, was
wont to throw around disparaging remarks about corn whiskey,
which was understandable since he was a great promoter of bourbon,
a more sophisticated cousin of corn. (True corn whiskey has eighty
per cent corn; bourbon, fifty-one per cent, plus a dab of rye.) He
often called corn whiskey *moonshine* to make sure serious connoisseurs didn't confuse it with bourbon. Cobb, a Kentucky colonel,
advised his friends who just *had* to imbibe corn (and apparently
there were a lot of them), to always do so while sitting flat on the
floor, so they wouldn't have so far to fall. He even went so far as to
describe "this here fiery stuff called corn whiskey" as "An unlawful
offshoot from the bourbon tribe . . . an illegitimate orphan of the
Royal Line, born out of wedlock in the moon, left as a foundling on
the doorstep of some convenient bootlegger and abounding in fusel
oil."

Another report from the same period, the height of corn whiskey's romantic appeal, is provided by historian Jonathan Daniels, whose comments suggest that the widespread adulation of the drink was like unto the fox who lost his tail while pointing to taillessness as perfection:

> At its best, aged in home-sized kegs, which could be purchased at most chain stores, corn liquor was a potable drink full of the mule's heels. Gentlemen exchanged private systems for reducing the shock to the palate, which extended all the way from the introduction of dried fruits into the liquor to advanced chemical procedures. Sometimes they succeeded. But at their worst, corn liquor and monkey rum (which in North Carolina was the distilled syrup of sorghum cane) were concoctions taken stoically, with retching and running eyes, for the effect beyond the first fusel oil belch. There was certainly a democracy in drinking then. Rich and poor drank with the same gasping. Indeed, when a death by gunshot wound resulted in the revelation of the details of a party in one of the State's richest houses, it came out that, before the gun went off, they had been drinking corn whiskey and chasing it down with near beer.

Of course, a lot depends on the quality of corn your informants drink, particularly whether their supplier really turned out a pure corn product or whether, as in the unfortunate case of many modern-day sugarhead moonshiners, the beverage came from fast-fermenting, almost pure sugar mash. With pure corn, as we have noted, it takes upwards of a week or two, depending on the weather, to convert the grain from starch to sugar, and then to alcohol, prior to the final process of distillation. By starting off with mostly sugar, and adding a relatively small amount of grain, a distiller can cut his fermentation time considerably and subsequently reduce his total production time to just over three days. It figures that he can make quite a bit more money this way which explains why the ranks of the deliberate, conscientious corn whiskey craftsman went into a terrible tailspin during Prohibition, when the number of buyers for home-made spirits increased explosively.

Still, devotees of corn likker swear by it.

"I'm a tellin' you the truth," a tobacco-chewing maker told me in Greene County, Tennessee, between spits. "I wouldn't give *one* gallon of good moonshine likker—me t' make it—fer five gallon of *any* of the bonded likker they air. Most of that gov'mint likker will hurt you worser than any moonshine, even that Cawsbey Special [moonshine from Cosby, Tennessee]. I'd ruther go right down to Cawsbey and walk right up to the outfit and watch it run outa that silver cloud still and buy it and drink it as to buy this bonded stuff. The gov'mint says old silver cloud likker is poison. The gov'mint is just as much wrong about that as anything. Fer if silver cloud likker killed all the people that drunk it, why Vietnam over hyar ain't killed nobody in comparison." The grizzled veteran stood his ground proudly in front of his weather-beaten frame shack beneath the towering Smoky Mountain range.

Government whiskey, he declared, was just too weak for his palate. He was used to homemade corn of 120 proof and higher—and what he liked particularly were the "high shots" that even he admitted would "take your breath away." The sensation produced by high shot was characterized this way by Appalachian historian Margaret Warner Morley in *The Carolina Mountains:*

> Pure corn whiskey for the first second after it is taken in the mouth seems as inoffensive as the water it looks like, with a delicate flavor of wild flowers. But wait another second and you will think you have performed the juggler's feat of eating fire. In time it might ripen, but it never has time. It is the only thing in the South that cannot wait for consumption . . .

Many old-time mountain men drink high proof corn whiskey "neat" without a quiver. It is said in the hills, "A mountain man likes his coffee strong enough to float an iron wedge, and likker strong enough to make a rabbit spit in a bulldog's face."

Another vote on the affirmative side comes from Fred Goswick of Dawsonville, Georgia. Goswick, an ex-tripper who operates the world's most elaborate "moonshine museum" in the heart of what once was north Georgia's corn whiskey belt north of Atlanta, swears that if you get the real article, properly double distilled by a corn whiskey craftsman, you will have a liquor second to none of the whiskies produced in a legal distillery. Indeed, Goswick insists that with the old-time homemade whiskey, a person didn't have to worry about a hangover.

"Old-timers took a drink of corn whiskey ever mornin', and again at night and a few snorts in the day and it didn't hurt them. Reason was it had hardly no fusel oils. They fired it real slow, both on the first and second runs. After the first run, they cleaned out the pot real good and on the second time round, they took special pains to fire it *just right*. You know alcohol boils at 173 degrees. When you get much over 176 degrees, you stand the chance of boiling some of the water and that gets that fusel oil mixed in it."

But to the uninitiated, of course, high proof corn whiskey can be quite devastating. A former state revenuer in Atlanta recalled a trip he made in the late 1930s:

"I had a '34 Ford. It was a cold night. I put a few pints of corn whiskey in the radiator and put some in my own radiator. A Yankee was riding with us, and said he was freezing to death. We gave him a drink. It was over 100 proof. His tongue lit up like fire bugs. He tried to holler. We stopped the car and he broke off ice in the ditch and ate it."

Another story was told to me by a secretary at Lockheed's aircraft plant near Atlanta who vividly remembered taking her first drink of corn whiskey twenty-odd years ago. Having heard of the potent elixir made by the illicit distillers in east Tennessee, she prevailed on friends from Knoxville to bring some of the good stuff. So on a Saturday night, in hushed reverence, a foursome gathered around their quart of corn shimmering on the kitchen table. Like all freshly run, unaged corn whiskey, it was clear and innocent looking, containing a goodly proportion of bubbles when you shook it. The hostess got out tall tea glasses and poured everyone a glassful. Following appropriate toasts to the copper pot artisans of east Tennessee, they downed their drinks straight. Within minutes, one by one, the three guests toppled over and had to be put to bed. The hostess, shocked by the crisis, amazingly remained untouched by the effects of the alcohol, and calmly administered aid and comfort to the others. The next morning, however, as she was cooking breakfast, the effect of the whiskey caught up with her and she ended up in bed for three days. Her lasting remembrance: "It was like swallowing sugar that was on fire."

Despite all the tales, wild and otherwise, about corn whiskey's throat-searing potency, many communities in the South have taken pride over the years in the quality of their homemade spirits, a pride resulting from the craftsmanship handed down from father to son over many generations. This has been particularly true in the Appalachian mountain and foothill country, from West Virginia to north Alabama. But grain whiskey craftsmanship has extended to a number of areas in Dixie's lowlands as well. During the 1930s, the Coffee County Chamber of Commerce in deep south Georgia traditionally gave visiting VIPs a quart of their famous "Coffee Country rye."

"The whole county took pride in it," recalled an *Atlanta Constitution* photographer of that era. "We never made a visit there but that we were treated to at least one Mason jar full of their pride and joy. And it was 'good stuff,' too." Good stuff is a term used often to describe high quality liquid corn.

During the pre-Prohibition era, and even up to the early days of World War II, good corn whiskey was found in some of the finest hotels of the legally dry South, particularly those hotels frequented by the politicians. Such a one was the old state-owned Henry Grady Hotel of Atlanta, demolished in 1972 to make way for a new seventy-story hotel. Stories were told of how Georgia politicians had loads of Rabun and Habersham Counties corn whiskey delivered to them in the Henry Grady in the 1930s, courtesy of state couriers.

It was in a famed resort hotel in Asheville, North Carolina, that Henry Ford was presented a jar of Appalachian pure corn. The late Thomas E. Dewey reportedly sampled corn whiskey during a governor's conference in Tennessee. Former Vice President "Cactus Jack" Garner also liked the corn whiskey that came from the makers in Tennessee. A famed soprano of the New York Metropolitan Opera, arriving on her annual visit to Atlanta for a two-week engagement of the Met, would always call for a half-gallon of "good north Georgia corn likker," which she toasted as being "without peer."

One of my informants from Asheville, North Carolina—a former hotel employee—recalls that the pure corn from nearby mountain stills was drunk with great appreciation by convention delegates at that city's leading downtown hotels. One noteworthy national convention, starting off with the opening night get-acquainted cocktail party, offered delegates "24-hour punch," a local delicacy made with corn whiskey, fruit juices, sugar and fruit peelings, all marinated for twenty-four hours. (High proof whiskey efficiently extracts the flavor from any fruit, being about the only solvent that can dissolve and extract the flavoring oil essence of fruits and herbs.) The delegates, who consumed the punch in vast quantities, couldn't climb out of bed the next morning, and the convention had to be postponed a day. The Asheville practice of serving punch with a corn whiskey base came to an embarrassing halt in the 1940s, when Federal agents swooped onto an opening night whing-ding and seized all of the untaxed booze.

As Asheville indicates, corn whiskey was not the only popular drink. In some sections of the South fruit brandies have been just as popular. The brandies, which bring a premium twenty-five dollars a gallon and more, are made of apples, peaches, prunes, grapes, and berries of all types. "Crazy apple," for example, is a mixture of corn whiskey and brandy combined during or after distilling. There are also various blends, such as the aforementioned 24-hour punch and "nose dive." A drink famous in Rabun County, Georgia, is called "mountain orange juice," whose recipe was concocted by a one-time top state politician. "Applejack," a drink famous since frontier days —primarily a high proof apple brandy, sometimes made even stronger by freezing it and pouring off the excess water—is still popular.

Appalachian brandy can be quite powerful. A resident of Sugar Valley, in northwest Georgia, who grew up on corn whiskey, remembers taking his first swig of apple brandy. "My uncle's pickup truck smelled a little like rotten apples and I asked him what he had in there. He had some apple brandy and offered me a drink. I guzzled it down like moonshine, and DAMN, *I must have farted fire*."

Well, we are still a long way from finding out what corn whiskey, or moonshine if you will, *really* tastes like. Perhaps the best way to approach the subject is to ferret out the nicknames the booze has inspired over the years. Of all the sobriquets, white lightning is the most graphic and perhaps the most popular.

Nobody knows exactly why this term caught on and lasted so long as a nickname. But pioneers were said to have considered that a bolt of white lightning would set fires that could not be extinguished, in contrast to the weaker red or reddish blue lightning. The fact that raw, clear corn distillate would set an almost unquenchable fire in one's innards, perhaps explains why many of the old folks gave it the white lightning label!

There are many, many southern nicknames which attest to the drink's searing potency. Here are three:

Block and tackle: This moonshine drink originated in the Okefenokee Swamp in deep south Georgia, a onetime hotbed of illicit whiskey-making. Swampers who took a drink of "block and tackle" were reputed to be able "to walk a block and to tackle anything in the swamp."

Squirrel likker: This is a hill country expression. After three or four drinks of "squirrel likker," imbibers would throw down their guns and climb the trees to get their squirrels.

Creepin' whiskey: The saying is that this liquor "creeps up behind you and knocks you to your knees."

Some fans call the drink "corn," while others qualify it a bit by the designations "pure corn," "corn juice," and "corn squeezin's." It is called "white mule" in areas of Kentucky and Tennessee, apparently due to its kick. In the Virginias and Kentucky and possibly in other areas, it is called "paleface" or "white likker." The Indians called it "firewater," while frontiersmen of the 1700s and 1800s referred to corn whiskey as "tiger spit," "black betsy," and "forty rod." The last was a favorite term for the homemade whiskey that was readily available on riverboats on the Ohio, Mississippi, and Missouri Rivers—after imbibing, the drinker was said to feel he was forty rods removed from reality! "Hooch" was a frontier term that came from the Indians who called it "hoochino." Hooch later signified white whiskey in Alaska, and also Prohibition-era moonshine. "Buckeye bark whiskey" got its name from the fact that moonshiners put buckeyes (inedible nuts that grow in the hills) into the newly-run liquor to give it a bourbon red color.

Like hooch, not all the terms refer to taste. "Blockade whiskey" was the name of the drink for many years in Appalachian areas—particularly in North Carolina and north Georgia. It is a term associated with the blockade runner of history.

Then there is *pure corn*. While most modern-day corn whiskey is really mostly a sugar product called "sugartop," the mountain whiskey of frontier days was water clear, made wholly from corn and corn malt (sprouted and ground) which was often converted into meal and malt in hand mills in the home or in nearby tub mills or, in later years, in grist mills. It was raw and fiery. Its makers had no sugar or yeast to mess it up and hence it was really pure corn. Francis Lynde, writing in the *Century Magazine* in 1929, quoted an old-time North Carolinian as saying:

Hit's a blamed ugly drink. I reckon there ain't no fightin'er liquor ever to come out'n a jug. Now there was the time when Jim Layne got hisself killed in that there *argymint* with Jud Byars. They'd both of 'em been fillin' up on *pine top* . . .

Now that's a name for corn whiskey you don't hear about these days—"pine top."

There are many corn whiskey connoisseurs today who swear that sugar really gives corn whiskey a bracing bounce. A recently retired maker in east Tennessee, for instance, swears that twenty-five pounds of sugar mixed with a bushel of cornmeal and water will produce a whiskey second to none. He said, "It's as good agin' as *pure corn* . . . no, three times as good."

There's a drink called "teedum barrel whiskey," which is usually the personal drinking liquor of a maker. This is usually kept in a keg or barrel in a cool stream or nearby bank for his personal consumption. Many connoisseurs willingly pay a higher price for a jar of teedum barrel.

Just about the wildest name for corn whiskey is the expression coined by an old-timer in Rabun County, Georgia: "sweet spirits of cats a fightin'." The story about "sweet spirits" was recounted to me by a resident of Dillard, Georgia, who remembered its originator as being "old man Brown" who lived in the "frazzled edge" of northeast Georgia next to North Carolina. "I was going with old man Brown's daughter. It was in 1931. One day about dinner time, he rode his donkey up to my gate and hollered. He cocked his eye and said, 'That thar gal of mine that you've been tryin' to spark has got that old hen-fluenzy. I just rid my donkey out here to see if I could get a little vial of sweet spirits of cats a fightin' to make her a little tea with.' That's the only time I've ever heard it called *that*!"

The names go on: "scorpion juice," "widow makers," "stump puller," "who shot John," "panther piss," "panther sweat," "wolf whiskey," "barbed wire brandy," "rim cuttin' my nose."

The people who in all likelihood currently know more about the taste of modern-day moonshine than any others are the ghetto blacks of southern cities, moonshine's greatest consumers. They have coined such nicknames as "alley bourbon," "city gin," "splo" (because of the "'splosion" it causes in your innards), and "cool water." This last term got its start because many shot houses cut their white whiskey so many times with water. Another ghetto nickname, again suggesting the power of the drink, is "ruckus juice" (pronounced *rookus*). "When you drink it, you will want to start a ruckus," says Atlanta black preacher, Rev. William Holmes Borders, who, being a teetotaler, has condemned many such rotgut ruckuses.

It is doubtful that one could ever arrive at a consensus on the taste of corn whiskey, due to the variations in the ingredients and methods of its manufacture.

About the best way to conclude this chapter is with an opinion from one who has been practicing the pure-corn making art for a lifetime, and who has equally high experience as a connoisseur. Into this category falls Semmie Free, an eighty-one-year-old man who lives in Rabun County in Georgia, near the country made famous by poet Sidney Lanier in his "Song of the Chattahoochee."

As I drove up to the farmhouse, on a knoll overlooking a lush valley surrounded by a semi-circle of peaks, Mr. Free came out in oversized blue denim overalls and greeted me warmly, giving me a big pumping handshake. He explained that he had had several snorts of liquid corn during the day and was happy and willing to talk about his favorite beverage. Within minutes, he was pulling his flat bottle from his pocket to offer me a swig as we sat on the front porch rocking in the double-size rocking chair. Then I popped the question:

Really, now, I inquired, what is it that is so great about corn whiskey?

"I can't tell you," he began, "but I'm damned sure I know how it tastes and how to make it. I got the record of makin' the best they is in the state of Georgie, anywhar."

Mr. Free, now slowed down with arthritis, said that he was literally raised from the cradle on homemade spirits.

"My daddy said they went to givin' corn whiskey to me when I was sure enough young, just a toddler, when they couldn't give me but one drop of sweetened likker. Said it wuddn't long until I got to where I could take two drops, then half a teaspoonful. Later on, I could take a bottle and take a drink. I knew how to handle it. Didn't never get drunk. Go so fer and quit. Carry it all day. Mother, she'd take a drink, but you couldn't call it drinkin', you know. All the old people, nearly, usta drink. When kin folks would come in, Daddy'd put a bottle or a jug on the table. Everybody kept a little flask of likker in his pocket.

"My daddy lived to one hundred and nine years and four months old. Gave him a long life, drinkin' likker did. It's what's keepin' me here now.

"Yeah, I've drunk a lot of corn likker in my time. Now you can't hardly get it. The people don't make it right any more."

Up the road apiece, in Dillard, Georgia, another ex-maker remembered the long-gone days of double distilled home-made spirits.

"Now pure corn, I've made some that was out of this world, nearly. Me and old Bill J. was talkin' the other day about what kind of liquor this younger generation is a making and a drinking. Bill asked me, 'What would these young boys say if we wuz to get us a rig and get back in the woods and make whiskey like we started out on, double distilled whiskey, and give one of them a drink of it. What would they say?' I replied that it would be so mild and meller that if they'd think it was wheat-bran backins and the first thing you knowed, their moccasins would be a sunnin'. That's right. That stuff'll fall on you like a ton of bricks, that pure corn will. It's so mild and meller. But there's no hangover. Only thing wrong with that pure corn whiskey, if you get too high on it, like tonight, you couldn't get to the branch fast enough the next day, wantin' water so bad."

II

THE HISTORY

Whiskey and freedom gang thegither

Robert Burns

3

To Usquebaugh with Love (Or, Moving the Cradle of Corn Whiskey to America)

> . . . Being moderatlie taken . . . it sloweth age, it strengtheneth youth, it helpeth digestion, it cutteth flegme, it abandoneth melancholie, it relisheth the heart, it lighteneth the mind, it quickeneth the spirits. . . . And trulie it is a soveraigne liquor, if it be orderlie taken.
> —Richard Staynhurst, Irish historian, on Irish whiskey, 1577

> Inspiring bold John Barleycorn!
> What dangers thou can'st mak' us scorn!
> Wi' tipenny we fear nae evil:
> Wi' usquebae, we'll face the devil.
> —Bobbie Burns, Scot poet and reluctant exciseman, in *Tam o'Shanter*

To get a handle on the roots of America's whiskey-distilling saga, which rolled down the Appalachian frontier in the 1700s and 1800s along with the winding trains of pack horses and the red, white, and blue Conestoga wagons, you must retrace the steps of our Scotch, Irish, French, German and English ancestors who brought the distilling art to our shores just over two centuries ago.

As we have seen, it's a relatively simple matter to distill alcohol. You merely heat the wine or beer to the magic temperature of 173 degrees (F). The resulting vapor lifts the alcohol essence out of the water, and the vapor is then reconverted to liquid by cooling. While this principle appears to be rather rudimentary today, it was an earthshaking development at the time of its discovery and was later

31

considered by the Europeans to have been a revelation from God. Indeed, for many years, the distilling secret—particularly when it reached Italy, Spain, and the heart of Europe—was hoarded and spirited among a selected and limited clientele, primarily the monks in the monastaries.

As might be imagined, the actual dawning of the distillation age is clouded in the mists of antiquity. Distilling, mostly from rice, had been under way in China, Japan, and India hundreds of years prior to the birth of Christ. Aristotle, born in 384 B.C., wrote in his *Metrology* about distilling seawater as well as wine.

But the first really authentic distillers—at least the people who imparted the revelation to the West—were probably the famous old Arabian and Egyptian alchemists who for some time had been trying to find or manufacture the elixir of life which was supposed to impart long (or eternal) life and health. The first alembics (distilling pots) were built in Egypt, and the term alcohol derives from the Arabian term *al-kohl*, which is described as a material produced by refinement. One of the popular heroes of the subsequent distillation saga was an Arabian alchemist, Abou-Moussah-Djafar-Al-Sofi (nicknamed Geber), who lived around A.D. 700 and who put the distillation principles to paper. Ironically, the Arabs were prohibited by their religion from drinking distilled spirits and fermented drinks. As the saying of the time went:

To drink is a Christian diversion
Unknown to the Turk or the Persian

Indeed it *was* a Christian diversion, but it began with fermented beverages. In A.D. 569, the Church in Britain (the Synod held by St. David) forebade intemperance among monks and priests. In 670, St. Gildas the Wise decreed, "If any monk through drinking too freely gets thick of speech so that he cannot join in the psalmody, he is to be deprived of his supper." From the time of its discovery, wine was a practical substitute for water (which at times was unfit to drink); it swept across the Mediterranean, through Europe and into the British Isles. (Actually, wine and beer had been around some five thousand years or so before man happened onto distillation. One of the first things Noah did when he got off the ark was to plant a vineyard.)

But just as night follows day, so distilled spirits were destined to follow fermentation, and when distillation came, the result was dubbed *aqua-vitae* (water of life), and became a highly prized wonder drug dispensed by the monks, the alchemists, and the apothecarists. About 1527, famed German surgeon Heironimus Brunswick published a paper describing *aqua-vitae* as "the mistress of all medicines." He wrote: "It eases the coming of the cold. It comforts the heart. It heals all old and new sores on the head. It causes a good color in a person . . ." Brunswick even claimed it would restore hair and would prevent deafness provided one placed a few drops in the ears on retiring every night. (Somewhat earlier in Italy, Leonardo da Vinci had discovered that *aqua-vitae* had another miraculous quality: by soaking his wooden mural panels in the distillate, the panels would become impervious to worms!)

Then from *aqua-vitae* we go to whiskey. The popular beliefs are that the distilling secret went from the Arabians to the Spaniards (possibly via the invading Moors) to Ireland where "whiskey" was invented. But there's another theory, perhaps a facetious one, that the Irish monks—some of whom were to have received their revelation from Saint Patrick around A.D. 400—were the progenitors who spread the word to Europe! One of the wilder stories in this connection is that Saint Patrick probably brought the secret back to Ireland from Egypt, where he picked it up from the famed alchemists!

But then, Saint Pat wasn't Irish. He was a Scot Lowlander born at Dumbarton near the Firth of Clyde, where he lived until he was kidnapped by Irish Celts at age sixteen and spirited away to Northern Ireland—which in a way would give the credit for whiskey to the Scots.

No need to dwell on just who discovered what and when. The matter remains, to this day, very much in the air and probably will never be settled. There is no doubt, however, that Ireland and Scotland were in the vanguard of the distilling saga and that it was in those countries that the name *whiskey* came into being. The Gaels of the old Ireland called it *usquebaugh*, Gaelic for *aqua-vitae*. From this it became *uisge-betha*, *uisge* and simply *whiskie* and/or *whiskey*.* The

* One unlikely version of the origin of the word *whiskey* is that in some out-of-the-way places in England where liquor was first distilled, smugglers used a horse-drawn vehicle, known as a whisk, to haul five- to ten-gallon kegs of spirits hidden under the seat, thereby enabling the distiller or free-trader to avoid paying the excise. The law at the time was that all spirits had to be hauled in sixty-gallon barrels, or larger, requiring heavy wagons. However, this theory carries little weight—no pun intended—because the excise was first enacted in the 1640s, and the term *usquebaugh* had been in use at least two centuries by that time.

ancient Irish called their early whiskey, distilled from barleycorn, *poteen* (pronounced put-cheen), which means, small pot. This term has carried down through the centuries. In 1170 the English invaders of Ireland found to their amazement that distilling spirits "was commonly known among the people and was carried out as a domestic art free from any restriction."

In nearby Scotland, whiskey was highly admired and extensively manufactured as early as the late 1400s. (The Scots traditionally have spelled *whisky* without an *e*, right to this day. So do the Canadians. The Irish and Americans spell it with an *e*. Just why this is so, nobody seems to know. One theory is that the thrifty Scot printers eliminated the *e* because it was a wasteful extravagance.) While grains spirits were known in Scotland's Highlands and its Lowlands to the west as *usquebaugh*, the early Scot distillers, just as the Irish, had a more familiar colloquialism—*poit du*—meaning "black pot." The Scots administered whiskey in "colds, fevers, and faintings," and it was a frequent prayer of theirs that "God may keep them from that disorder that whiskey [*sic*] will not cure."

The Scots' early and enduring love for whiskey was described vividly by Tobias Smollett in *Humphrey Clinker* when he noted that the Scots "regale themselves with whiskey, a malt spirit, as strong as Geneva, which they swallow in great quantities without any sign of inebriation: they are used to it from the cradle, and find it an excellent preservative against the winter cold. . . . I am told it is given with great success to infants, as a cordial, in the confluent smallpox, when the eruption seems to flag . . ." An exciseman added his admiration for the early Scots: "The ruddy complexions, nimbleness and strength of these people is not owing to water-drinking, but to the aqua-vitae, a malt spirit which is commonly used in that country, which serves for both victual and drink."

Meanwhile, the Irish were not lagging. According to an old Irish song:

> *A sup of good whiskey will make you glad.*
> *Too much of the creatur will make you mad.*
> *If you take it in reason, 'twill make you wise,*
> *If you drink to excess, it'll close your eyes.*

This leads us into considering that hardy race of people, the

"Scotch-Irish," those rollicking, whiskey-making, hard-drinking, hard-fighting folks of legend and folklore, who also were real. The Scotch-Irish brought corn whiskey-making to America. More than anyone else, they popularized it—despite the mighty inroads of "rumbullion" (rum).

Strictly speaking, the Scotch-Irish were neither Scotch nor Irish. It is most accurate to describe them as Ulstermen, or Ulster Presbyterians, which is what most of them preferred to be called when they landed in America.

Here's how the Scotch-Irish came to be:

King James I, the first joint king of the two countries to come from Scotland, "planted" Protestants in the province of Ulster, the ten counties of Catholic Northern Ireland, beginning in 1610, with the aim in part of trying to make "wild Irish" more peaceful. Just before James' predecessor, Queen Elizabeth, had died, her British troops had finally brought the rebellious Irish in Ulster to heel after having literally burned and starved them into submission. At that point, Ulster's two clan chieftans, the Earl of Tyrone (Hugh O'Neill) and the Earl of Tyrconnel (Red Hugh O'Donnell), who had led the bloody rebellion with the backing of the Pope and with the help of troops from Spain, fled to France. With their departure, almost three million acres of land reverted to the British crown.

With the flight of the earls, King James gave his support to the expanded plantation idea, hoping "that the sea-coasts [of Ulster] might be possessed by Scottish men, who would be traders as proper for his Majestie's future advantage." Doubtless, he also envisioned the opportunity to spread the Protestant faith into Ulster. The Scottish lairds who received big land grants from James drew thousands of willing settlers from the ranks of the poor across the Lowlands, who leapt at the opportunity presented by the Ulster land. The Lowlanders could get on a thirty-one-year "feu"—virtually a lifetime lease —under general circumstances that were far better than those available under the caste system in Scotland. Further, social order did not operate so rigidly in Ulster, and the immigrant, however lowly in station, considered himself a "royal colonist." He could live where he pleased, could own a gun, could distill and drink his corn whiskey without interference (that is, before it was subjected to an excise), and, perhaps most important of all, he could worship as and where he pleased, which meant, of course, in the Presbyterian "kirk."

By 1640, there were forty thousand Scots in Ulster, drawn mainly by economic opportunities. Additional thousands came in succeeding years because of religious freedom.

Now, it was during the Ulster colonization that the English Parliament adopted excise laws against spirits—mainly to raise money to finance the suppression of the Civil War which broke out in 1642. Even though the people of London had rioted and burned down the excise house a few years before, King Charles needed money to suppress the Civil War, and forced Parliament to pass the excise imposition, which read:

Strong waters.

For all strong waters and aqua-vitae, imported or to be imported, to be paid by the first buyer thereof from the merchant or importer . . . after the rate of eight pence the gallon.

And for all strong waters and aqua-vitae made or distilled within the Realm, Dominion of Wales or Towne of Berwicke, the like rate to be paid by the maker or distiller thereof.

Scotland followed England's lead and, in 1644, passed an "Act of Excyse."

In Scotland and Ireland, rebellion broke out against the gaugers and excisemen. Scot poet Bobbie Burns, though himself to become an exciseman, declared angrily in verse:

> *Thae curst horse-leeches o' the Excise*
> *Wha mak the whisky stills their prize!*
> *Haud up thy han', De'il! ance, twice, thrice!*
> *There seize the blinkers! [wretches]*
> *And bake them up in brunstane pies*
> *For poor damn'd drinkers.*

The consequence of the excise duty in England was enormous. According to a historian, "almost every little creek or inlet on the long line of sea-coast, from Land's End to the fartherest point in Scotland, in both seas, the Irish and the North Sea, was a landing place for some kind of smuggled goods. Liquors were by far the most available commodities for the smuggler to handle. Although heavy and bulky, ardent spirits had an almost universal demand."

A Scot historian, Henry Grey Graham, noted, "From Holland and France and Spain, luggers brought their contraband cargoes. . . . No crime was so respectable as 'fair trading,' none was so widely spread. Along the quiet bays of the Solway, into caves under the rocky cliffs of Forfarshire . . . and even to the open shores of Fife, boats came with fine impunity and perfect confidence . . ."

The smuggler of Scotland—the term "smuggler" included both the person who sold the whiskey and the person who made it—became a highly respected citizen and not only had the sympathy of the people but their total cooperation. It was said that Scotland's illicit whiskey enterprise was "the secret half a country keeps." A special "smugglers' loft" was reserved in the Dundonald parish church where the free-traders sat on Sunday "with their wives gay in silks, highly respected by all the worshippers."

Everything else aside, the smuggler distilled a superior whiskey to that made by the Parliament whiskey distiller, who was saddled with high excise taxes, and therefore had to sell in large volume as quickly as he could. The smuggler, without such economic restraint, was able to double and triple distill his whiskey in leisurely fashion and turn out a high quality drink. It was said that at least half of the whiskey consumed in Scotland and England, even up to the early 1800s, was illicit. (Today's *Gaelic Old Smuggler Brand* scotch whiskey is said to be an heir of that era.)

In Ireland, where whiskey-making had been conducted in the homes, glens, and mountains for years without restriction, the excise came as a shock. Hatred of the duty "aroused the worst passions." It was felt by many Irishmen that to kill a gauger was anything but a crime. "Wherever it could be done with comparative safety, he was hunted to the death," noted a history of Ireland.

The most famous exciseman of them all, poet Bobbie Burns, was well aware of the odious image of the exciseman.

> *I'm turn'd a gauger—Peace be here!*
> *Parnassian queans, I fear, I fear,*
> *Ye'll now disdain me!*
> *And then my fifty pounds a year*
> *Will little gain me.*

The first verse of *The De'il's awa wi th' Exciseman*, went this way:

The De'il cam fiddlin' thro the town
And danced awa wi' th' Exciseman,
And ilka wife cried—'Auld Mahoun,
I wish you luck o' the prize, man!

The gauger, or exciseman, was Britain's equivalent to America's later-day revenuer. The name derived from the fact that he gauged or measured the contents and proof of whiskey and also collected the excise tax. Sometimes, particularly in the larger cities, he sold out to and accepted the bribes of the moonshiners, who bought protection as often as possible. The gauger became the wealthiest man of many a community, usually accepting his payoff in fine whiskey. To show his appreciation, before he would mount to go on a tour of a community, he would send out an advance runner to warn of his approach, so the whiskey-makers could haul out and put in safekeeping their precious pots and worms!

Meanwhile, in Ulster, the inquisitive Scotch-Irish had learned everything possible of the distilling art (in addition to what they already knew) from the renowned Irish poteen makers. While the structure of Irish society in effect prohibited the Scots from intermarrying with the Irish, the separation did not extend to the area of whiskey production. The fact was that the Irish at that time (as today) were past masters at distilling spirits, and in many areas, Irish poteen had a greater popularity than liquor made in Scotland. (Sometime before 1700, so the story goes, some of the legendary whiskey smugglers of time immemorial, the Scot Highlanders, also settled in Northern Ireland to add their contribution to the corn whiskey saga of the Scotch-Irish.)

During their years in Ulster, the Scots learned to drain the marshy bogs, converting former wasteland into fertile farms. The city of Belfast became a monument to Scot enterprise. The deep-water port literally was carved out of the bog, becoming Northern Ireland's center of export and import. The Scots introduced the potato. With the help of newly arrived Huguenot Protestants from France, who were great industrial technologists, they developed booming woolen and linen manufacturing industries.

But all of these industries were soon in dire straits, because the English industrial and agricultural interests could not stand the competition. Parliament was persuaded to enact laws which in effect virtually eliminated the exporting of goods and livestock from Ulster.

Of all the harsh penalties to hit the Ulstermen, "rack-renting" was the worst. The Scottish proprietors, who had benefited from the great improvements made by their tenants, "screwed up" and "racked" the rents to double and triple their previous amounts. Professor James C. Leyburn, writing about the Scotch-Irish, pointed out that the Ulster farmers, ". . . feeling a sense of injury and stubbornly refusing to accept what they regarded as an outrageous departure . . . resisted the rack-rent. The highest bidder for the new lease was therefore a native Irishman. The intransigent and dispossessed farmer had an alternative of leaving the country, to go either to Scotland, or . . . to cross to America. . . ."

One would think, author James Watt Raine noted, that the English government would have favored these Scotch Presbyterians who were their instrument for repressing the uprisings of the Irish Catholics, ". . . but the Stuart kings . . . badgered and irritated their Presbyterian 'plantations' even more unbearably than they treated the Catholics. No Irish ships were allowed to engage in foreign trade. . . . The people were not allowed to worship except in the State churches. The government prohibited them from exporting horses, cattle, or dairy products to England."

As a result, America beckoned. After only five generations in Ulster, the Ulstermen were ready to move on. And move they did, bringing with them to this country an almost pathological thirst for their own land, a strong Protestant faith and, withal, a great tradition of whiskey-making and free-trading.

In Maryland, Lord Baltimore held out the carrot stick of a three-thousand acre spread for any "adventurer" or "planter" who would bring thirty persons to his colony, promising as well "free liberty of religion."

But it was Quaker William Penn's wide open colony of Pennsylvania, with its great tolerance for people of all religions and its deep democratic ideals, that quickly was seen as presenting the greatest opportunity for the land-hungry Ulsterman. Thus to Pennyslvania they flocked and, at the first at least, received a warm welcome. The colony's provincial secretary, James Logan, issued an invitation to the first Ulstermen to come to the colony. He declared: "We were apprehensive from the Northern Indians. . . . I therefore thought it might be prudent to plant a settlement of such men as those who formerly had so bravely defended Londonderry and Inniskillen as a frontier in case of any disturbance . . ." Later, however, the Ulstermen flocked into the colony in such numbers that Logan, himself a Scotch-Irishman who had been signed up as Provincial Secretary by William Penn, became apprehensive. He wrote in 1729:

It looks as if Ireland is to send all its inhabitants hither, for last week not less than six ships arrived, and every day, two or three arrive also. The common fear is that if they thus continue to come they will make themselves proprietors of the Province. It is strange that they thus crowd where they are not wanted. . . .

The first big wave of Scotch-Irish immigration began about 1717 when Lord Donegal led the way in rack-renting his Ulster tenants in County Antrim. In 1716, rot had decimated flocks of sheep. In 1718, smallpox spread over Ulster. Over and above all this, from 1714–19 six years of drought ruined crops of flax and exploded what was left of the linen industry.

So to America they came. It was almost a repeat of the Scots' experience in moving to Northern Ireland. Only this time, the individual Ulsterman was making an irrevocable break with Europe on behalf of America. But he was ready to take the risk. He was fed up with the persecution of the monarchs and the Parliament and the landed gentry and fed up with the excise. He was ambitious to "become his own man." And in some part, he really just wanted to move, a characteristic that would surface time and time again after he arrived in America.

It is estimated that a quarter million Ulstermen poured into America during the five heavy waves of the great migration of 1717–1776, and some estimates go as high as four hundred thousand. (They followed and joined waves of German peasants and French Huguenots.) While they landed at many ports from Boston to Charleston, most of them came into Philadelphia, New Castle, and Chester, flocking into Pennsylvania and its "three lower counties" which were to become Delaware.

Thousands of poor Scotch-Irish began their New World careers as indentured servants. From 1725–1728, only one in ten could pay his own way from Ulster to America. But the great shining reward waiting for the Ulsterman at the end of his several years work as a servant, was the opportunity to own property and freedom from religious and political restraints. Shipowners sent their agents through Ulster communities seeking indentured servants or settlers for great tracts of land. The system worked this way: In the 1730s, according to James Leyburn, William Beverley received 118,481 acres from the colony of Virginia and Benjamin Borden more than half a million. But before the patents were made final, these two men had to fill the land with settlers from *outside* Virginia. Thus their agents canvassed the countryside of Ulster. In all, it is estimated that one hundred thousand or more Ulstermen reached America as indentured servants.

Leyburn notes, "Even if one-tenth of the Scotch-Irish immigrants were, as Archbishop Boulter has said, in 1728, men of substance, the migration would have been unusual. What mattered, however, was not the property a man came with, but his qualities of character and self-reliance, his ambition to make good, his adaptability in crises. As pioneers, the Scotch-Irish proved their mettle."

They were a new kind of settler, the real pioneer, who brought strong convictions to America, including a love of whiskey and a love of liberty.

4

Of Pumpkins, Parsnips,
and Walnut Tree Chips

In the heroic ages our forefathers invented
self-government, the Constitution, and
bourbon, and on the way to them they
invented rye. Our political institutions
were shaped by our whiskeys, would be
inconceivable without them, and share in
their nature. They are distilled not only
from our native grains, but from our native vigor, suavity, generosity, peaceful-
ness, and love of accord. Whoever goes
looking for us will find us there.
—Bernard De Voto

To say that the drinking and the making of liquor came naturally with the American frontier would be an understatement. To the
colonists, suspicious if not deathly afraid of the "poisonous" water of
the New World, and faced with the reality of the rugged frontier,
strong drinks were a dire necessity. From the earliest days at James-
town, the colonists up and down the seaboard looked on alcoholic
beverages as essential for survival.

It was only natural, therefore, that brewing and distilling would
command an early and important role in the New World. On the ill-
fated Roanoke Island Colony in North Carolina, Thomas Hariot
recorded, "Wee made of the same (mayze) in the countrey some
mault, wherof was brued as good ale as was to be desired." The
Virginia Assembly in 1623 called on all newcomers to bring in malt
to brew liquor to tide them over until their constitutions became
accustomed to Virginia water.

Early Alchemists of the Middle East tried to create humans in their alembics, the first type of distillery pots, predecessors of the copper pot stills of Scotland, Ireland and America. (Bettmann Archive).

A handmade, six- to eight-gallon capacity copper still, reportedly used by Lord Baltimore to make his "drinking liquor." The distilling pot and the condensing apparatus are both in one unit. The cap or dome is hidden inside the large cup-like container at the top. Water was circulated in the cup, causing the vapors from the pot to condense in the still head and run off into the arm at the right. (Courtesy of the Mercer Museum of the Bucks County Historical Society).

Advertisement by a Philadelphia coppersmith and still maker, Francis Harley's Copper-Ware Manufactory and Store. The ad noted that the firm made stills with patent pewter worms ''calculated for the West India market,'' as well as ''stills for fruit, grain and turpentine distillation.''

This painting by William M. Davis, done in 1871, depicts cider making on Long Island. (The New York State Historical Association, Cooperstown, New York).

By 1625 two brew houses had begun operation in Virginia. Several years earlier, an Episcopalian missionary, Captain George Thorpe, had learned how to convert Indian maize into liquor and had set up a crude distillery at Berkeley Plantation on the banks of the James River. To a friend in London he wrote that he had found a way "to make so good a drink of Indian corn as I protest I have divers times refused to drink good strong English beer and chosen to drink that." Unfortunately, gentle and scholarly Captain Thorpe did not get to perfect his still, dying at the hands—the story is true—of drunken Indian scalpers on Good Friday, March 27, 1622.

While the Indian corn was destined to become the base for the true-blue American drink, the first spirits made and consumed in volume in America came from the fruits that grew wild and from the lush orchards that soon proliferated under the hands of the early day Johnny Appleseeds. Within a few years, "peares, apricocks, vines, figges," cherries, apples, peaches, and quince were flourishing across Virginia and Maryland. By 1639, early settlers in Massachusetts were beginning to make wine from pumpkins, grapes, currants, elderberries, and parsnips. Indeed, it appeared there was no fruit or grain that was not "grist for the mill" to satisfy the colonists' desire for fermented and/or distilled spirits. Soon they were distilling ardent spirits from blackberries, persimmons, plums, whortleberries, sassafras bark, birch barks, corn stalks, hickory nuts, pumpkins, the pawpaw, turnips, carrots, potatoes, and small grains. As an old song went,

If barley be wanting to make into malt,
We must be content and think it no fault,
For we can make liquor to sweeten our lips
Of pumpkins, of parsnips, of walnut-tree chips.

Of all the fruits and grains available to the early settlers, peaches and apples, and particularly the latter, were the base for most early drinks along the seaboard. Colonists made "peachy" from peaches, "perry" from pears, and cider from apples. Apple trees were "prospering abundantly" in Massachusetts in 1691, John Josselyn wrote in his *Voyages*. Gerald Carson, in his light-hearted *Social History of Bourbon*, noted that "soon every New England home had an apple orchard for making cider. Hard cider was part of the scene at every barn raising, wedding and town meeting." Even John Adams, one of the early leaders in pushing for temperance reform, drank a large tankard of hard cider every morning on arising, right up to the end of his life.

New Englanders "frosted" their cider by leaving a jug outside on a freezing night, then draining off the alcoholic essence. This they called "applejack." Further south, applejack was the designation for apple brandy. "Virginia drams" was another term for apple or peach brandy. Another fruit brandy, "applejohn," also gained fame in New England, so much so that it was said applejohn and hard cider built the stone walls of the region, a gallon per rod of wall.

In every colony, breweries and distilleries sprang up, most of them on individual farms. The stillhouse—usually a windowless log cabin —became an important and useful appurtenance on many a plantation in the South and on the farmsteads of Pennsylvania, Maryland, Delaware, New Amsterdam, and New England. These were not elaborate—merely large enough to take care of family and friends and to make enough to provide libations and treats for special work, like the raising of a barn and the shucking of a crib full of corn.

"The use of liquor [during colonial days] was universal," noted Hewson L. Peeke in his *Americana Ebrietatis*. "A libation was poured on every transaction at every happening of the community . . . John Barleycorn was a witness at the drawing of a contract, the signing of a deed, the selling of a farm, the purchase of goods, the arbitration of a suit . . ." When death struck a community, everyone quit work and gathered at the house of mourning, watching day and night with the dead until interment. The family would have a table of liquor on hand, and the spirits circulated freely.

Ardent spirits also contributed to eighteenth century democracy. "Treating" by the candidates drew out the voters as did nothing else. George Washington learned his lesson well after suffering two defeats for the Virginia House of Burgesses (in 1755 and 1757) when he neglected to "swill the planters with bumbo." In a third election, in 1758, he provided the 391 voters of Frederick County, Virginia, and associated other people with 169 gallons of rum, wine, beer, and cider, and won by collecting 310 votes to his opponent's 45. In paying his expense account of thirty-nine pounds, and seven shillings —of which thirty-four pounds was for liquors—he wrote, "I hope no exception were taken to any that voted against me but that all were alike treated and all had enough; it is what I much desired."

Another basic role of spirits in the early days of the colonies was as medicine. Settlers drank spirits to prevent malaria and to speed the recovery of anyone taken ill. "Whiskey was to the pioneer what tranquilizers, stimulants, disinfectants, vitamins, rubbing alcohol, and anesthetics are to us today," Harriette Simpson Arnow, a native of the Cumberland River country of Tennessee, has written, "The newborn got weak toddy at birth, the mother had it stronger, the father straight, the old and cold bathed their limbs in it . . ."

During the years leading up to the Revolutionary War, rum became *the* distilled drink of Colonial America. In addition to "raw dram," which was straight rum, there was "stonewall," a combination of rum and hard cider. (Perhaps this is where the expression "stoned" originated). "Blackstrap," a combination of rum and molasses, was a staple of the colonists. Casks of rum stood right alongside salted and dried codfish in every country store. "Bumbo"—rum, sugar, water, and nutmeg—rose to high popularity. "Mimbo," bumbo minus the nutmeg, was only slightly less popular. In the 1600s, another rum drink boomed to widespread acceptance in the interior—"mamm," made of rum, water, and sugar. In the cheery atmosphere of the taverns, many rum-drinkers pulled the fiery, cherry hot loggerheads from the big fireplaces, and dipped them, sizzling, into their tankards of "flip"—a rum-beer combination to which sugar or syrup was sometimes added.

By the early 1700s, the colonists were consuming twelve million gallons of rum a year. At first, rum came from the Caribbean. But almost overnight, rum distilleries rose in great numbers across New England, launching the nefarious three-cornered syndrome of rum, molasses, and slaves. New England shipowners hauled rum to the Guinea coast, using it to buy slaves from the African chiefs. The ships transported the blacks to the West Indies (where they were needed in the cane fields) and traded them for molasses. Then the ships made the last leg back to New England brimming with molasses to feed the rum distilleries. By 1750, out of the Boston area alone, there were a thousand vessels engaged in the rum-slaves-molasses triangle, and the sixty-three rum distilleries in Massachusetts were consuming fifteen hundred hogsheads of molasses annually.

Despite its ascendancy, "the good creature," rum, began losing ground to the increasingly popular corn and rye whiskey coming from the American frontier. In addition, England began passing acts to force the colonies to buy their molasses from the English rather than the French and Dutch islands in the West Indies. Finally, the American Congress in 1808 outlawed the trading of slaves—which knocked out the vital link in the three-cornered trade triangle.

Meanwhile, throughout the colonies, the pioneers had been perfecting the distilling of corn. By the 1750s, according to North Carolina historian R.D.W. Conner, "distilling had come to be considered one of the chief industries of the colony." A western North Carolinian of the same period wrote in his will: "I leave the still for the benefit of the family whilst my wife keeps house with the children." In Westmoreland County, Virginia, William Rust willed his "still, worm and tub" to a son.

It is about this point in time that we rejoin our friends, the Scotch-Irish from Ulster.

Down the Great Valley of Pennsylvania and Virginia, through the 1730s to the 1770s, rolled one of the greatest movements of people in American history, people who were destined to change the drinking habits of the American continent, and more important, play an important role in wresting the wilderness from the Indians and waging the War of Independence (which would come to a head partly over such issues as the rum and molasses trade).

While many of the Scotch-Irish immigrants lingered in eastern Pennsylvania, and still others filtered across the forbidding Allegheny Range to the Shawnee lands of southwestern Pennsylvania, the great horde of newcomers from Ulster headed to the wide open Southwest, the great American frontier of Virginia, the Carolinas, Tennessee, and Georgia. Between 1720 and 1775, some two to three hundred thousand Ulstermen got off ships at the Delaware River ports of Chester, New Castle, and Philadelphia, and most of them swung down the verdant Great Valley of Pennsylvania, continuing into the Valley of Virginia—today's Shenandoah Valley.

In Pennsylvania, they went as far west as possible until they reached the province's boundaries (which also happened to be the formidable Alleghenies), then swung in an arc to the southwest. Rows of pack horses and red, white, and blue Conestoga wagons, their horses flying brightly colored ribbons, with tiny bells swinging and tinkling like Santa's sleigh, crunched down the Indians' old War-riors Trail, which became the Great Philadelphia Wagon Road. From Philadelphia, the road ran west to Lancaster County, crossed the Susquehanna River to York and Gettysburg, swung almost paral-lel with the Allegheny Range, crossed the Potomac into the Shenan-doah Valley of Maryland and Virginia, and then plowed like a straight furrow down the eighty-mile-wide valley between the Al-leghenies and the Blue Ridge ranges. From Winchester in northern Virginia, the road went up the Shenandoah Valley, across the upper waters of the James to the Roanoke River, then down the Roanoke southward through the Blue Ridge, crossing the Dan River, and still further southward to the headwaters of the Yadkin River in what is now Forsyth County, North Carolina. (The road extended on through Charlotte, North Carolina, to Camden in South Carolina's sand hills, and eventually to Augusta, Georgia.)

The Scotch-Irish raced southward along the route, bypassing many Germans, most of whom quickly settled in the upper valleys of Penn-sylvania and Virginia. Soon Ulstermen began hop-scotching over fel-low Ulstermen. It seemed as if they had a repugnance to remaining put. Most of them would make at least one and sometimes two and three moves in their lifetimes. And each new generation moved fur-ther into the frontier.

Like Daniel Boone, who kept moving on to avoid being hemmed in by civilization, the Ulstermen poured into western Virginia, and then into North and South Carolina. Many went into north Georgia for the cheap (and often free) land. Still others crossed the Cumber-land Gap, shortly after it was opened by Boone, into Kentucky. This became the Wilderness Road branch off the Philadelphia Wagon Road. By this route, thousands of hardy frontiersmen followed Boone deep into the Cumberland Plateau. Many went down the Hol-ston and Watauga Rivers into east Tennessee.

By the time of the Declaration of Independence, the Virginia val-ley was well populated, and North Carolina's back country had sixty thousand settlers. Anson, Orange, and Rowan Counties, North Caro-lina, which in 1746 had less than a hundred fighting men, had blos-somed to at least three thousand by 1750, "for the most part Irish Protestants and Germans, and dayley increasing." North Carolina Governor Tyron reported that in 1765 alone, more than a thousand immigrant wagons passed through Salisbury. Neighboring South

Carolina had eighty-three thousand people on its backwaters—around three-fourths of the colony's white population. (In 1766, Charles Woodmason, a minister of the Church of England, toured South Carolina's interior and found it settled "by a set of the most lowest, vilest crew breathing—Scotch-Irish Presbyterians from the north of Ireland." He severely criticized the South Carolina Legislature for spending money to bring in 5,000 Ulstermen "solely to balance the Emigrations of People from [seaboard] Virginia who are all of the Established Church.")

On the frontier, the Ulsterman was indomitable. Although he was to move time and again, he seemed to feel, for the first time in his long and bitter struggle against the tyrannies of past centuries, that he was really a free man.

His deep craving for land and his insensitiveness to others led him to clash head on with the Indians, who deeply resented his continuing incursion into their sacred territories. The immigrant Protestants grabbed frontier land and belligerently dared anyone to dislodge them. In Pennsylvania, "audacious and disorderly" Ulstermen swarmed onto Conestoga and Gettysburg tracts that had been reserved for the Penns, declaring it "against the laws of God and Nature that so much land should be idle while so many Christians wanted it to labor on and to raise their bread." Pennsylvania provincial officials time and again had to settle up with angry Indians who were dispossessed of their land by the eager Ulstermen. Pennsylvania proprietors tried to adopt the practice of "quit-rents," which enabled them to retain land possession by requiring annual payment of a few cents an acre. But the Scotch-Irish, remembering their troubles with the rack-renters of Ulster, would not stand for it, and forced the proprietors to sell. A statement by a mountain man in later years reflected the sentiment of practically all the Ulstermen: "I hain't a-goin' to rent. I'll own some land if hit's only a house-seat." Many refused to allow warrant surveys required by the colonial governments, driving off the surveyors by force.

The settlers had a point, actually more than one. They felt they were entitled to ownership after clearing and planting wilderness land. But they mainly felt they were justified in their cause because they were being used as a buffer to protect the tidewater planters against the Indians.

Constance Lindsay Skinner pictured the frontiersman who

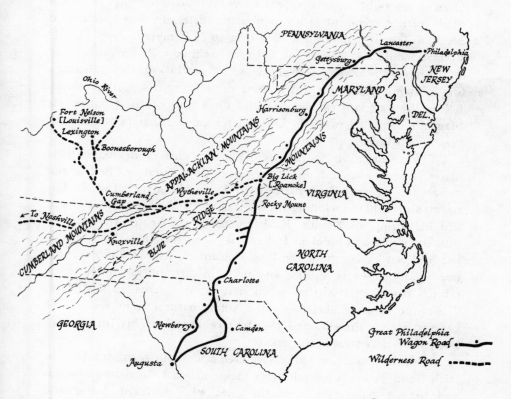

PENNSYLVANIA

Lancaster

Philadelphia

Gettysburg

NEW JERSEY

MARYLAND

DEL.

Ohio River

Harrisonburg

Fort Nelson [Louisville]

Lexington

Boonesborough

APPALACHIAN MOUNTAINS

MOUNTAINS

Cumberland Gap

Wytheville

Big Lick [Roanoke]

VIRGINIA

To Nashville

CUMBERLAND MOUNTAINS

BLUE RIDGE

Rocky Mount

Knoxville

NORTH CAROLINA

Charlotte

GEORGIA

Newberry

Camden

Augusta

SOUTH CAROLINA

Great Philadelphia Wagon Road

Wilderness Road

Drawing by Tom Hill

emerged as "a type of man who was high-principled and narrow, strong and violent, as tenacious of his own rights as he was blind often to the rights of others, acquisitive, yet self-sacrificing, but most of all fearless, confident of his own power, determined to have and to hold." The self-confidence spilled over to his prayers, when an Ulsterman would ask, "Teach me, O Lord, to think well of myself."

Wherever the Ulsterman went, he took his whiskey. Pennsylvania's Dr. Benjamin Rush put down some disparaging descriptions of the fellow Presbyterians he had observed on a tour of the frontier. He blamed what he felt were the Ulsterman's indolent habits on the ever-present still-houses:

"The quantity of rye destroyed and of whiskey drunk in these places is immense, and its effects upon their industry, health and morals are terrible." Rush blamed whiskey-making for all of the Ulsterman's troubles, including his quarreling ways, his unkempt farms, and his stump-filled fields. Rush compared the Scotch-Irishman to "the barbarous and indolent Indian; he plants little more than maize, lets his livestock run wild and lives a disorderly life. He loves spirituous liquors, and eats, drinks, and sleeps in dirt and rags in his little cabin." Rush observed that when civilization catches up with him, "he cannot bear to surrender up a single natural right for all the benefits of government, and therefore he abandons his little settlement and seeks retreat in the woods."

Yet the opposite could also have been said about the tough Scotch-Irish—and Teddy Roosevelt made the point: that the most ambitious and bravest Americans were the ones who ventured deeper and deeper into the frontier. "That these Irish Presbyterians were a bold and hardy race is proved by their at once pushing past the settled regions and plunging into the wilderness as the leaders of the white advance," he asserted. "They were the first and last set of immigrants to do this; all others have merely followed in the wake of their predecessors . . ."

What Rush did not acknowledge was that whiskey-making had a very practical purpose for the Ulsterman. A settler's first job on arriving in the wilderness was to clear enough land for his cabin and then get in a crop—usually corn, which was easy to produce with only a hoe. Food wasn't a problem because the forests abounded with wild game of all sorts and the rivers were full of fish. What the settler needed was a cash crop to enable him to pay his taxes and thus retain his precious property—usually a few hundred acres. This was where his whiskey-distilling became an extremely important adjunct to his farming. With his whiskey, he had "legal tender" to pay his taxes and obtain the few necessities that he could not make himself—such as salt, nails, and cloth. Many Scotch-Irish had brought along their copper worms and small pot stills slung under their ark-like wagons, or on their pack horses. Some, however, brought only a knowledge of how to build a rig, and some, not even that—they quickly learned from one of their neighbors.

The fact that the settler was locked within the fastnesses of great mountain chains was another reason why it was almost inevitable that he would turn to whiskey-distilling. For although he could produce from forty to sixty bushels of corn per acre (and sometimes more on rich bottomland), it was virtually impossible for him to get ground cornmeal or flour to markets on the seaboard. He could easily and economically convert his corn or rye into spirits, however, and then with a pack horse, transport the liquid equivalent of twenty-four bushels of corn. H. F. Willkie, in his *Beverage Spirits in America*, explained the general economics of the situation: "There were no roads in the new territory, and most of the trade was by pack-horse. It cost more to transport a barrel of flour made from the grain which was the principal product of that region than the flour would have sold for on the eastern markets. If the farmer converted the grain into whiskey, a horse, which would carry only four bushels in solid form, could carry twenty-four bushels in liquid form. Practically every farmer, therefore, made whiskey."*

The frontiersman found "whiskey farming" sensible, no different, say, from turning corn into pork or, as in the case of his compatriots in New England, harvesting syrup from maple trees.

By the mid-1700s, columns of steel blue smoke poured from hundreds of stills over the six-hundred-mile backcountry along the Appalachian Mountain chain. "Where there's smoke, there's bound to be whiskey," was the favorite expression of the time. The people on the frontier became hard drinkers, and understandably so. Out in the

---

* The yield from rye distillation was a gallon of whiskey for each 1½ bushels of grain. One pack horse could carry two eight-gallon kegs of whiskey, one strapped across each side, or the equivalent of 24 bushels of grain. In its solid form, corn would bring only twenty-five cents a bushel. The horse, therefore, could carry only two dollars worth. But with whiskey, which was worth at least one dollar a gallon, his payload rose to a minimum of sixteen dollars.

wilds where each family had its own plot of land—many averaging three hundred acres—unencumbered by the pressures of society such as had existed in the towns of Ulster and even the frontier "settle-mints," the rules of sobriety were quickly forgotten. The frontiersman worked hard to carve out the wilderness for himself and his family, and worked without letup for weeks and months at a time. When it came time for pleasure, he entered it with great gusto and energy.

"When we had a corn-shuckin', a log-rollin', a house-raisin', or any such frolic," recalled a frontiersman about his youth, "the whiskey just sloshed around like water. . . . Whiskey! I should say so!"

Edwin Tunis, in his *Colonial Living*, noted that when a community building job was completed, everybody celebrated with an all-night dance, feasted on potpie and got drunk on homemade whiskey.

Thus emerged the American frontiersman—a dogmatic Presbyterian, a hard drinker and a contentious cuss who carried his long Pennsylvania rifle with him at all times. Perhaps he was proudest of his ability with his rifle with which he could "knock the eyes of a squirrel out at a hundred yards." Such feats of marksmanship were not uncommon in community shooting contests, the prize being "kags of whiskey."

The Scotch-Irishman also was intensely loyal to his new homeland —patriotic to the core. It was said that not a single Tory—a "loyalist" to the crown—could be found in the backcountry.* "It was Patrick Henry and his Scotch-Irish bretheren from the western counties that carried and held Virginia for Independence," wrote the historian Charles A. Hanna. Indeed it was the homogeneous Scotch-Irish up and down the colonies who held the Patriot cause together. New York's sentiment was heavily loyal to the crown, and other areas were in the neutral corner. But not so among the Scotch-Irish.

---

* While the Scotch-Irish from Ulster—basically of Scotch Lowland extraction— filled up America's Appalachian interior, a colony of Scot Highlanders settled along North Carolina's "lowlands" around Cape Fear, Wilmington, and Fayetteville (which was first called Campbelltown). The heavy immigration of Scot Highlanders to the North Carolina coast began in 1746 when, following their defeat at Culloden, they were pardoned by the king in exchange for pledging allegiance to the crown and emigrating to America. Many of these Highlanders retained their fealty to King George throughout the American Revolution. Just as their Ulster counterparts in the interior, the Scot Highlanders brought with them to North Carolina their love of whiskey and their ability to make it.

The near half-million Ulstermen from Pennsylvania to north Georgia stood as a man in favor of freedom and of independence from the monarchy which they had come to despise. Their sentiments and their role in the Revolution were a continuation of their resistance to British policy that began in Ulster. King George III roared angrily that the resistance of the colonies was a "Presbyterian war."

Led by people like Patrick Henry, who let his position be known loudly and clearly, the Scotch-Irish swung the backcountry Dutch, French Huguenots and Palatine Germans to the Patriot cause—all of these groups had similar backgrounds of religious and personal persecution. The Declaration of Independence by the Watauga Association in 1772 in east Tennessee was "the first ever adopted by a community of American-born freemen," according to Teddy Roosevelt. This was followed by the Declaration at Abingdon, Virginia, in January 1775, where the pioneers resolved never to surrender. On May 23, 1775, after the declaration of war in April, the flag of a new and independent nation, Transylvania, was raised at Boonesboro, Kentucky. This was followed by the Mecklenburg Resolves in North Carolina on May 31, 1775. The citizens of Mecklenburg County (Charlotte) resolved to "desolve the political bands which have connected us to the Mother Country" and declared themselves "a free independent people . . . under the controul of no power other than that of our God & the general government of the congress, to the maintenance of which independence civil & religious we solemnly pledge to each other our mutual cooperation, our lives, our fortunes, & our most sacred honors. . . ." Lord Cornwallis was later to call Mecklenburg "the hornets' nest of the Revolution."

The experience of the frontier, it would seem, was just the training the settlers needed to become the saviors of the new nation. Having become tough and lean on the frontier, they were also sharp-eyed wizards with their Pennsylvania "squirrel rifles." In the course of the Revolution, they also learned about guerrilla warfare in fighting the Tory-led Indians.

The British strategy in squelching the Revolution was to attack the colonies from the coastal cities and to use the Indians against the Patriots on the frontier. The Indians didn't need much persuading. Their hatred for the Ulstermen was already fierce, and they entered into battle with great and energetic viciousness.

For eighteen years, before, during, and after the Revolution, the borders of the frontier ran with blood. While the Ulstermen with their land-hungry ways undoubtedly helped ignite the flame of Indian terror, they plunged into battle to win, and win they did. In north-west Virginia, Andrew Lewis, a young Scotsman of Augusta County, had recruited a band of riflemen in 1756 and carried the battle against the Shawnees. In 1774, Lewis' "long knife" marksmen decisively defeated Chief Cornstalk at Point Pleasant, pushing the Shawnees beyond the Ohio River, and leading to the swift settlement by other pioneers of western Virginia and Kentucky.

In 1776, while 435 Patriots were weathering the shells of the Royal Navy from behind palmetto logs at Charleston, South Carolina, 210 raggedy frontiersmen in the Watauga area of east Tennessee—led by "Nolichucky Jack" Sevier and Isaac Shelby—repulsed a screaming band of Cherokee Indians, led by Dragging Canoe and Oconostota. After this, Sevier took his riflemen on the offensive and became famous for his winning campaigns, leading his men with the cry, "Here they are! Come on, boys!"

In battles from Georgia to Virginia, the frontiersmen, noted Samuel Tyndale Wilson, "swept in retributive wrath upon the Tory-led Indians, and dealt them such a blow as extorted from them an unwilling but at least a temporary peace." At the same time, the Tories living on the frontier were either driven out or forced to take the oath of allegiance to the Confederation.

The mountain fighters became Washington's favorite troops. He had learned of their bravery and marksmanship in leading a company of them against the French at Great Meadows in 1754. When the Continental Congress picked Washington as commander-in-chief, Morgan's Riflemen and Nelson's Riflemen from the frontier were his first volunteers. They brought with them their own rifles, the long, flint-lock weapons developed by the immigrant German gunsmiths of Pennsylvania.

While the frontiersmen in the main fought the "Rearguard of the Revolution" against the Indians, they earned their greatest laurels at the Battle of Kings Mountain in South Carolina. It happened in the fall of 1780, at the low point of the Revolution, when Washington had said, in exhaustion, "I have almost ceased to hope." Lord Cornwallis had captured Charleston and had begun a march through South Carolina into the "hornets' nest" of North Carolina. But the frontier worried him, and he sent a force of a thousand Tory militia and one hundred crack Rangers, commanded by Major Patrick Ferguson, to protect his western flank and to rally the Tories.

Ferguson threw down the gauntlet to the "over-the-mountain" backcountrymen around the Cumberland Gap and marched his army deep into North Carolina's Piedmont foothills, at the base of the Blue Ridge Mountain range. He sent word to "Nolichucky Jack" Sevier, now a colonel, that if the frontiersmen did not halt their opposition to the crown, he would march his Tory troops over the mountains, hang the frontier leaders and lay waste the country "with fire and sword." Major Ferguson was to rue the day that he made the threat.

The frontiersmen at the headwaters of the Holston, the Nolichucky, and the Watauga Rivers took Ferguson's warning seriously and sent an urgent call throughout the backcountry for volunteers. The response was electric. Roused to fever pitch, volunteers came pounding in on their horses from the waters of Cumberland, Virginia, from the Saluda and Savannah in Carolina, and the valleys of Watauga. On September 25, more than one thousand of them gathered at Sycamore Shoals on the Watauga, near the present Elizabethton, Tennessee. They looked like the Daniel Boone prototype, wearing buckskin shirts, breeches and gaiters dyed with walnut juice, their long hair tied behind in a queue, covered by brimmed hats. And they were in an angry mood. The crowd was swelled by 400 tough fighters who came in a long march from Virginia, under Colonel William Campbell.

Each man brought his own rifle, a bag of parched corn, a blanket, and a knapsack. Rev. Samuel Doak, a Scotch-Irish preacher from Watauga, gave the suddenly formed army a rousing pep talk. Recalling the story of Gideon's Army, he called on the men to carry as their battle cry, "The sword of the Lord and of Gideon!"

The following day, they began their chilly trek over the six-thousand-foot high Appalachian Mountain range, some riding horses and some marching afoot in snow up to their ankles. Five of their six leaders were Presbyterian elders.

A week later, safely through the mountains, they plunged southward toward Major Ferguson, who apparently had had second thoughts and had already started a slow retreat toward Cornwallis' forces in Charlotte. On October 6, word came that Ferguson was in the vicinity of Kings Mountain. The Patriot force, now made up of nearly eighteen hundred men, rode and walked through the night,

keeping their precious flint-locks dry underneath blankets, knap-
sacks, and shirts. They reached the mountain on October 7. Although many were tired, they were also eager to plunge ahead into
battle. Colonel Isaac Shelby declared, "I will not stop until night, if I
follow Ferguson into Cornwallis' lines." Ferguson, from his commanding position atop a Kings Mountain ridge which rose sixty feet
over the heavily wooded plateau, sent down words of defiance, declaring he would not be dislodged by "God Almighty and all the
rebels out of hell."

As the clouds began to lift, 900 hand-picked frontiersmen surrounded Kings Mountain and began the ascent on foot. Just before
leaving, Colonel Benjamin Cleveland of Wilkes County, North Carolina, one of the ten Patriot leaders,* addressed his troops:

> My brave fellows, we have beaten the Tories already, and we
> can beat them again. They are all cowards; if they were not, they
> would support the independence of their country. When engaged
> with them, you will want no word of command from me. I will
> show you how to fight by my example. I can do no more. Every
> man must be his own officer, and act from his own judgment. Fire
> as fast as you can, and stand your ground as long as you can.
> When you can do no better, run; but do not run quite off. Get
> behind trees, and retreat. If repulsed, let us return and renew the
> fight. We may have better luck the second time than the first . . .

Crouching and running up the gentle wooded hillside in open
formation, Indian style, the frontiersmen opened fire. "The mountain
appeared volcanic," declared an eyewitness. "There flashed along its
summit and around its base, and up its sides, one sulphurous blaze."

As the mountain men neared the crest, Ferguson rode back and
forth on his horse, blowing a silver whistle. His troops mustered two
bayonet charges which temporarily drove the attacking frontiersmen
partway down the hill. But the mountaineers, taking Cleveland's
advice, did not run far, and hid behind trees and rocks. They quickly
counterattacked and soon had the entire crest surrounded. Fer-

---

* The Patriot leaders were of Irish, Scotch, Welsh, English, French, and German
ancestry. Colonels Isaac Shelby, Charles McDowell, John Sevier, Benjamin Cleveland,
and William Campbell were referred to as Presbyterian elders. Their opponent,
Major Ferguson, was a Scot.

56

guson's silver whistle went silent as he and his horse plunged to the ground, struck by at least eight volleys. Within an hour, the frontiersmen had control of the entire mountain, with an amazingly small loss of only 28 killed and 62 wounded. The enemy losses were 224 killed, 163 wounded and 716 taken prisoner. Nine of the Tories who had terrorized the countryside were subsequently hung from an oak in nearby Rutherford County.

It was a stunning victory for the Patriot forces, giving a shot of "corn whiskey spirit" to the discouraged continental armies and to the American people. The battle delayed Cornwallis' northward advance, and the renewed American resistance completely demoralized his campaign of 1781. Sir Henry Clinton, Britain's commander-in-chief in North America, said the defeat at Kings Mountain "was immediately productive of the worst Consequences to the King's affairs in South Carolina, and unhappily proved the first Link of a Chain of Evils that followed each other in regular succession until they at last ended in the total loss of America."

George Washington called Kings Mountain "proof of the spirit and resources of the country." Said Thomas Jefferson: "That glorious victory was the glorious annunciation of that turn in the tide of success which terminated the Revolutionary War with the seal of independence."

And all of it accomplished by men whom Ferguson had called "backwater men . . . a set of mongrels." They were men who, "without orders, without pay, without commission, without equipment and without hope of monetary reward," struck a decisive and eloquent blow for the entire country.

Such was the manner of man who was bringing pure corn whiskey into being throughout the backcountry! Distracted temporarily from his still-house while defending his hearth against the British and the Indians, he would soon resume his quest for a true American drink. And he wasn't far away from finding it, either.

5

The Excise Years

Corn whiskey was a common man's best
money crop.
                                —Pioneer from
                                Appalachians

He smote the rock of the national resources, and abundant streams of revenue
gushed forth.
                —Daniel Webster, praising the fiscal
                acumen of Alexander Hamilton

GOOD old "Monongahely rye," a strong, full-bodied whiskey,
was coming on strong across the western frontier of Pennsylvania
during the final days of the Revolutionary War, its fame spreading
back east to Philadelphia, and even down the Ohio and Mississippi
Rivers. In Philadelphia, it commanded a dollar a gallon, and was
recognized as hard currency much more stable than the continental
dollar. Easily divisible, and constantly increasing in value as it aged
in oaken kegs or sloshed around on a trip over the mountains or
down the Ohio River, it was indeed the frontier farmer's greatest
bank balance. He could easily barter his whiskey for the necessities
of life—for salt, at five dollars a bushel, or nails, at fifteen cents a
pound. With enough whiskey, he could buy a farm.

Every fall, the farmer-distillers of the Monongahela River country
around Pittsburgh would put together mule trains and traverse the
Alleghenies via the rutted Forbes Road. Strapped across the back of
each animal would be two eight-gallon kegs of whiskey, twenty-four
bushels of grain in liquid form, 128 pounds in all (since each gallon
was equal to eight pounds of corn). No wonder that practically every

58

farmer became a "whiskey grower," converting his surplus grain into spirits.

Stills made by the coppersmiths of York, Lancaster, and Philadelphia proliferated on the frontier. Particularly in southwest Pennsylvania. By 1790, of the 2,500 known distilleries in operation in the thirteen states, 570 were concentrated in the four counties around Pittsburgh, 272 in Washington County alone! Hugh Brackenridge, the famed Pittsburgh lawyer of the era, declared the still was "the necessary appendage of every farm, where the farmer was able to procure it." A complete copper still and worm was literally worth a 200 acre farm within ten miles of Pittsburgh. Although not every farmer could afford a still, there was at least one in every settlement, with from six to thirty families sharing its output.

The Pittsburgh area had filled up rapidly following the defeat of the Shawnees by the Scotsman Andrew Lewis at Point Pleasant in 1774. Thousands of settlers poured in from Pennsylvania's Cumberland valley west of Philadelphia, "the seedplot and nursery of the [Scotch-Irish] race." A West Virginia historian described the Ulstermen's onrush as "the flying column of the nation . . ." Many of the new settlers came down the Valley of Virginia on the Great Philadelphia Wagon Road, then threaded their way back up northwest via Braddock's Road along the Potomac and on across the Allegheny Mountains. The area in which they settled was part of Virginia, and it drew the settlers because, unlike Pennsylvania with its speculators, land in Virginia was cheap.

By 1790, around seventy thousand settlers—English, Scotch-Irish, German, and Welsh—were living in the verdant "over the mountain" country along the rippling Monongahela. But the living was rough. The threat from the Indians was always present, and carving farmland out of the wilderness took steady perseverance. The westerner had to fight the Indians for his own self-interest (and self-preservation), and he resented strongly being cast as a shield to the people back East.

But whatever friendship he had toward the East turned sour when the new American Government ruled that the frontier Pittsburgh territory, originally part of Virginia, actually belonged to Pennsylvania! Overnight, the farmers who thought they had gotten their land cheaply from Virginia, found themselves saddled with huge mortgages, owed to the land speculators of Philadelphia. Thousands of settlers, who were lucky if they ever saw as much as twenty dollars cash in a year's time, were furious.

Then, on top of this startling bit of news, came word that the Secretary of the Treasury, the Federalist Alexander Hamilton, had devised a new scheme to pay off the country's twenty-one million dollar war debt: he would tax whiskey distilleries and whiskey production! The shock waves reverberated through the backcountry, riveting the frontiersmen with rage.

Instead of receiving the appreciation due its soldiers for their heroic role in the fight against England, the West found itself confronting a discriminatory excise on its whiskey! Why didn't the federal government open up river trade with the Southwest via the Ohio and Mississippi Rivers? Why didn't it build some good roads to the eastern markets? No. What it planned to do was equivalent to a slap in the face.

Albert Gallatin, destined to become Jefferson's great Secretary of the Treasury, spoke out strongly against the excise. "We are . . . distillers through necessity, not choice, that we may comprehend the greatest value in the smallest size and weight. The inhabitants of the eastern side of the mountains can dispose of their grain without the additional labor of distillation at a higher price than we can after we dispose labor upon it."

Despite the West's protests, Congress paid no heed and on March 3, 1791, voted Hamilton's proposal into law. As amended later in an attempt to mollify the westerners, the tax was set at seven cents per gallon of liquor produced, or 54 cents per gallon capacity of each still. Adding insult to injury, the law also offered rewards to "informers" who would spy and report on unregistered stills.

In the U.S. House of Representatives, Georgia's James Jackson blasted the "odious, unequal, unpopular, oppressive" tax, and shouted his fear that "the time will come when a shirt shall not be washed without an excise." Indeed rumors circulated across the frontier that the excise next would be laid on spinning wheels and on newly-born males. Pennsylvania's House of Representatives denounced the excise measure as "subversive of peace, liberty and the rights of citizens . . ."

In the Monongahela country, reaction was even more strident. Incidents began to occur. A gang from the Mingo Creek settlement, dressed in women's clothes, captured the excise revenuer for Washington and Allegheny Counties at Pigeon Creek, sheared off his hair, and tarred and feathered him. The deputy marshal persuaded an unsuspecting cattle drover to serve the warrant in the case, and the poor drover was stripped naked, tarred and feathered, tied to a tree, and robbed of his horse.

Meanwhile, down the Ohio River in Kentucky, the federal inspector, Thomas Marshall, father of the future Supreme Court chief justice, announced his determination to enforce the law. In *The Kentucky Gazette* of March 17, 1792, he inserted this notice:

Some of the stillers, I am informed, pretend to say that they are taught to believe that the excise is not to be collected in this district. From whence they derive their information I cannot conceive; but do hereby inform them that the collectors will shortly be with them in order to collect it.

The distillers hung Colonel Marshall in effigy, cropped the ears of his collectors' horses, slashed the collectors' saddles, and destroyed their papers.

Back in western Pennsylvania, black-faced gangs broke into the homes of excise collectors and ripped down their excise notices.

All the while, nobody in the western Pennsylvania "survey" was paying the excise or registering his still.

General John Neville, the inspector in charge of the survey that covered southwest Pennsylvania, joined the collector for Washington and Allegheny counties to visit "obstinate" distillers. They didn't get far before they were chased by a mob of sixty irate farmers. The gang subsequently dropped by the home of an excise-paying distiller, one James Kiddoe, peppered his still with bullets and attempted to set fire to his log still-house.

The leader of the gang, John Holcroft, referred to the episode as "mending" Kiddoe's still, and described his "menders" as "Tom the Tinker's men." The term became the rallying cry of the protesters, who "mended" the stills of several distillers who were complying with the excise laws. Soon papers began appearing throughout the region signed "Tom the Tinker."

To all good citizens:

You are hereby advised that it has been resolved to take all legal methods to obstruct the operation of the iniquitous and oppressive Excise Law. You are hereby warned to have no fellowship with such as accept offices under it, and to withdraw from them every assistance of whatever sort; to withhold comforts of life; to refuse to sell or to buy the labor of, or to employ as laborers any and all persons who accept such offices.

By Order of the Committee,

Tom the Tinker

The old "liberty poles" of the revolutionary period reappeared, calling on the people to rise up against the new tyranny. Colorful streamers fluttered from the poles, bearing such inscriptions as EQUAL TAXATION AND NO EXCISE, and NO ASYLUM FOR TRAITORS AND COWARDS.

President Washington offered a two-hundred dollar reward for the capture of excise opponents. Few people in the Monongahela country dared to offer leads. The situation reached a fever pitch in 1794 when the U.S. District Court at Philadelphia issued warrants against seventy-five distillers who had not registered their stills, most of them whiskey-makers in the four Monongahela-area counties.

On the morning of July 15, General Neville and Federal Marshal David Lenox served four of the writs, and just before noon, galloped up to William Miller's farm at Peter's Creek to serve the fifth writ. Lenox unrolled a long summons ordering Miller to "set aside all manner of business and excuses and appear in proper person before the judge of the district court of the United States at Philadelphia, August 12." Miller exploded in fury and refused to accept the summons. He said afterward, "I thought 250 dollars would ruin me; and to have to go [to] the federal court at Philadelphia would keep me from going to Kentucky this fall, after I had sold my plantation and was getting ready. I felt my blood boil at seeing General Neville along, to pilot the sheriff to my very door."

Meanwhile, a crowd of angry neighbors, who had received or would receive similar summonses, charged toward Lenox and Neville, firing blasts as they ran. Fortunately, the marhsal and the inspector had fast horses.

Arriving back at his mansion on the Chartiers Creek, the general, fearing attack, sounded the alarm among his eighteen slaves and servants, whom he kept supplied with arms in case of attack from Indians. His home, "Bower Hill," was a magnificent, two-story frame building, considered the finest residence in the West. It was wallpapered, had fine furniture, carpets, four looking-glasses, an eight-day clock, a Franklin stove, china, glass, and silverware.

Shortly after daybreak the following morning, a band under John Holcroft surrounded Bower Hill and ordered the general to give up his commission and turn over his official papers. Neville refused. Firing broke out. The volleys from the rebels were answered by blasts from the slave cabins. Holcroft and his men withdrew, with five wounded.

Overnight, Neville got reinforcements—soldiers from the Pittsburgh Militia. At the Mingo Creek church, angry volunteers in turn swelled Holcroft's force to five hundred men. They were put under the command of James McFarlane, a former Revolutionary War officer. In the morning, they marched again to Bower Hill.

This time, the general—apparently sensing a disaster—hid in a nearby thicket and watched the developments. He was lucky that he didn't stay inside.

An Army major named Kirkpatrick was in command of the troops in the mansion. He rejected the rebels' demand they be allowed to search the house for papers.

"Then we fire!" the insurgents declared.

McFarlane, leading his men up the hill, was struck down and slain. The rebels said he had come into the open because of a flag of truce they saw flying at Bower Hill. Now infuriated, the band of "white Indians," as they called themselves, set the outhouses afire, including the Negro cabins, and poured volley after volley into the main house. The Army major surrendered his defending force. The triumphant rebels ransacked the building, rolled out barrels of rye whiskey from the cellar and, in a drunken orgy, sent the beautiful mansion up in flames.

McFarlane's funeral at Mingo Church stirred the whiskey men even further. David Bradford, a rebel leader who wanted to be president of a new state, spoke at the funeral and condemned "the murder of McFarlane." Many of the mourners muttered that they should march on Pittsburgh and burn down its excise offices. Their mood was reflected by the epitaph they carved on McFarlane's tombstone, which read:

He fell . . . by the hands of an unprincipled villain in the support of what he supposed to be the rights of his country.

Some days later, the Mingo Creek Militia—bolstered by several thousand like-minded and armed militiamen from the other counties—did indeed mount a march on Pittsburgh. The air crackled with revolution.

The immediate objective of the march was Braddock's Field—about eight miles south of Pittsburgh on the banks of the Monongahela at its confluence with Turtle Creek. At this spot, in 1755, Britain's Braddock suffered a crushing defeat at the hands of the French. The people of Pittsburgh became panicky, particularly after a whiskey rebel rode through the streets swinging a tomahawk.

As the sun set, Pittsburghers hastily buried their silver and locked up their daughters. Nobody got much sleep. Women were in tears. Messengers pounded into town to warn that the community would be reduced to ashes unless certain citizens were banished—such as Major Kirkpatrick, General Neville's son Presley, and other supporters of the excise.

The next morning, a detachment of worried Pittsburgh citizens rode out to greet the 5,000 rebels, with the aim of assuaging and pacifying them. The lawyer, Hugh Brackenridge, atop the lead horse, had a white handkerchief fluttering from his riding whip. He asked if his group could "join" the protest. They were welcomed warmly.

The commander for the occasion, "President" David Bradford, with the assumed rank of major general, cantered around the grounds reviewing the troops atop "a superb horse in splendid trappings, arrayed in full martial uniform, with plumes floating in the air and sword drawn." He barked out orders up and down the lines and stirred up the crowd with a continuing harangue against the Federalists in Philadelphia. A pall of smoke soon covered the field as marksmen "shot at the mark" and fired volleys into the air to express their hostility. It reminded many of the battle with Braddock on the same spot thirty-nine years before.

"On to Pittsburgh" they marched the next morning. Pittsburghers met the throng at the town limits, bearing whiskey and wagonloads of dried venison, bear meat, hams, and poultry—all designed to discourage a rampage through the city. Brackenridge contributed four barrels of his best whiskey. "I thought it better to be employed in extinguishing the fire of their thirst, than of my house," he said.

Seventeen hundred of the rebels were mounted and the line of march was two and a half miles long. Across the Monongahela on the cliffs overlooking Pittsburgh, crowds of women cheered the "invaders." The rebel soldiers twirled their hats on their rifles and shouted, "Huzza for Tom the Tinker!" "Down with the Excise!"

The rebel rank-and-file were ready to put the torch to the town, but their leaders managed to keep them in check. The line of marchers turned down the main street, and then back out to a plain east of town, where they enjoyed still more liquid hospitality, courtesy of the people of Pittsburgh. The threat of serious violence was passed. The town's efforts had worked.

Several ferryboats were pressed into duty to take the foot soldiers back across the Monongahela. The mounted troops forded the stream. By nightfall, only a few hundred rebels remained. From the hillside, flames leaped out in an eerie glow as insurgents, in partial realization of their intentions, put the torch to Major Kirkpatrick's barns. Despite this incident, Bradford boasted of "a glorious revolution accomplished without bloodshed."

Certain citizens of Philadelphia—particularly George Washington and Alexander Hamilton—were not smiling over the ominous turn of events. At Hamilton's urging, President Washington called on the governors of Maryland, Virginia, Pennsylvania, and New Jersey to draft armies for the job that lay ahead. Some thirteen thousand troops, including 11,000 infantrymen, were put on the alert by the four governors, awaiting one last attempt to settle the issue without marching.

Despite the gravity of the situation, there were light moments. *The Pittsburgh Gazette* of August 23, 1794 ran a satire in which the Army of "Captain Whiskey" declared itself ready to lay down its life for its favorite drink:

> Brothers, we have that powerful monarch, Capt. Whiskey, to command us. By the power of his influence, we are compelled to every great and heroic act. . . . We the Six United Nations of the White Indians . . . have all imbibed his principles and passions. . . . Brothers, you must not think to frighten us with fine arrayed lists of infantry, cavalry and artillery, composed of your water-melon armies from the Jersey shores; they would cut a much better figure in warring with the crabs and oysters about the Capes of Delaware.

"A Jersey Blue" answered the declaration, declaring in turn that "the water-melon army of New Jersey" would be coming over the mountains soon with "ten-inch howitzers for throwing a species of melon very useful for curing a gravel occasioned by whiskey."

Washington sent commissioners to Pittsburgh, and it was agreed to hold a referendum asking the anti-excisers to submit to the new law by pledging oaths of allegiance. Those who signed would be pardoned for past offenses. But the Westerners resented the oath, and the percentage of people who signed was far from overwhelming. Washington, under pressure from Hamilton, felt no other recourse was left to him: he ordered the troops to march. Virginia's 3,300 troops rendezvoused at Cumberland together with Maryland's 2,350 soldiers while Pennsylvania's 5,200 militiamen gathered at Carlisle, on October 4, and reviewed the Pennsylvania and New Jersey "right wing." Washington's arrival was greeted with the ringing of the town's bells and the lighting of the courthouse. Washington rode on to review the Virginia and Maryland troops at Williamsport, Maryland, and at Fort Cumberland and Bedford, Virginia.

The two wings of the army—commanded by "Lighthorse Harry" Lee, governor of Virginia, with legal counsel provided by Alexander Hamilton—converged on the Youghiogheny River near Budd's Ferry. Camps were set up at the mouth of Mingo Creek, at Washington, at West Newton, at Elizabeth, and about five miles from Pittsburgh.

Meanwhile, in Monongahela country, as the government's forces swelled, the ranks of the rebels became contrastingly thin. Some two thousand insurgents quickly disappeared from the area—among them, John Holcroft and most of the ringleaders. Many fled down the Ohio River into Kentucky and beyond. Those who elected to remain lived to regret it.

On November 13, 1794, in the midst of winter, the federal troops across the four counties dragged rebel suspects and witnesses from their cabins during what became known as the "dreadful night," and forced them to run without shoes for miles in the severe cold. The "Jersey Horse," a New Jersey cavalry unit charged with the objective of arresting the "whiskey pole gentry" in the Mingo Creek area, tied them back-to-back for a trek to the stockade. One man who went into convulsions was tied to a horse's tail and dragged along behind. The men were then shoved into a pen in the snow and rain, and were kept away from a bonfire by the soldiers' bayonets. During succeed-

66

ing days, many more suspects were arrested and their stills were ripped out of furnaces.

But the "war" ended quickly. Just three weeks after arriving, most of the troops began the march back to Philadelphia, carrying with them seventeen haggard, ill-clad prisoners, who were driven by foot across the ice and snow. It took a month to cross the Allegheny Mountains. Arriving in Philadelphia on Christmas day, the troops followed a circuitous route so everyone could get a glimpse of the frontier yahoos wearing INSURGENTS signs on their hats. Some twenty thousand Philadelphians turned out to watch the triumphal entry of the troops, who rode with swords raised high. Their ragged captives were spaced two abreast between mounted cavalrymen.

The trials were an anticlimax. All but two of the seventeen were acquitted. Washington subsequently pardoned all who were not under indictment or sentence, and eventually he pardoned the two found guilty. So the Whiskey Rebellion, which started with such a roar, ended with a whimper.

The rebellion cost 1½ million dollars to squelch—much more than the total excise collected in a year's time. But the effort apparently had the effect that Hamilton desired: it gave credibility to the power of the federal government.

But men did not stop making whiskey during the excise years. Indeed, the rebellion helped set the stage for the beginning of America's widespread distilling activity, for it pushed whiskey-making deeper into the West and South . . . into Kentucky and down the Appalachians into the Carolinas and Georgia. Many a Mononga-helan lashed his still onto a pack horse and headed for the promised land, where a man could carry out "stillin'" to his heart's content away from the prying eyes of the exciseman.

Soon almost every farm down the Appalachians and into Kentucky and Tennessee had a still of some type. While most stills were copper pots, whiskey was also sometimes "made in a log," which H. F. Willkie, in *Beverage Spirits in America*, described as an eight to ten-foot poplar log "which was split, hollowed with an adze and a copper pipe run from one end to the other. The halves were joined, beer poured in at the top, steam sent through the pipe, and alcohol was taken off through another pipe." Many farmer-distillers had two copper pot stills, a large one for the first run, usually 150 to 200 gallons, and a smaller one, around 50- to 80-gallon capacity, for the second, since less volume was required for the doubling run.

Even George Washington took up whiskey-distilling at Mount Vernon during this period. His farm manager, a Scot named James Anderson, knew how to build a distillery and how to operate it, so Washington had one of his unprofitable farms converted to the growing of rye and had Anderson build a five-pot distillery. Construction began in 1797 near Washington's mill on Dogue Creek, about three miles from his mansion. The first year's operation netted eighty-three pounds, plus 155 gallons of whiskey leftover in storage. Washington also distilled brandy from peaches, persimmons, and apples. La-Fayette, on a visit from Paris, was astounded by the "swift authority" of the Mount Vernon spirits.

Meanwhile, the booming "Southwest"—today's southeastern U. S.—which had been made relatively safe through an agreement with the Cherokee Indians in 1775, lured many people from Pennsylvania and northern Virginia down the Great Valley. The key event laying the groundwork for the mass onrush, was Daniel Boone's pioneering work in the late 1700s opening the Cumberland Gap trail through the towering Appalachians near the point where Kentucky, Tennessee, and Virginia converge. Bolstered by plenteous "kags" of corn whiskey from his home country along the Yadkin River in North Carolina's Piedmont plateau, Boone and thirty axemen had slashed the Wilderness Trail through to "Kaintuck."

Kentucky also was being invaded from the north by ever-increasing numbers of people looking for a spread on which to settle. From western Pennsylvania, families floated down the Ohio River on handmade flatboats and barges, "arks" and "broadhorns" (sporting cattle horns on the bow), their farm gear—including pot stills, millstones and tub mills—stacked on the decks alongside the cattle and horses.

Many more came by land via the southern entrance, tracing Boone's footsteps from North Carolina, crossing the headwaters of the Holston, the Clinch, the Watauga and Powell Rivers, and going through the "gap" into the Wilderness Road. Many continued on up the Boone Trace. Weary and worn, yet highly excited, they came in on foot, hauling their belongings on pack horses. Others would follow in the years after, coming in Conestoga wagons stashed with kitchen utensils, their precious axes, farm plunder, hand looms—and whiskey stills.

In *Flowering of the Cumberland*, Harriette Simpson Arnow described the important place of whiskey in the lives of these pioneers. "Stills came with the first settlers to the Cumberland. Old Johnnie Boyd who came in the Donelson convoy is said to have been the first distiller; Frederick Stump, another first settler, was not far behind; and by 1799 there were for the less than four thousand people in Davidson County, sixty-one stills. All things on the Cumberland— the Scottish background of many of the settlers, the fine corn-growing soil, the abundance of firewood, plenty of white oak for barrels and the ease with which whiskey could be stored or shipped as compared to many farm products—contributed to the manufacture of corn whiskey." *The Kentucky Gazette* in 1796 gave detailed instructions on proofing whiskey strength:

> Take half a pint of spirits in a cup or tumbler, take a small quantity of clean cotton, lay it as light as possible on the surface of the liquor; if your spirits be good proof, the cotton will sink immediately to the bottom; add a little water to it and the cotton will rise.

In 1794, the British gave up their northwest posts and in 1795, Spain signed Pinckney's Treaty, allowing Americans to ship their whiskey and other products down the Mississippi. These developments added considerably to the Kentucky and Tennessee boom. In just two months of 1795, upwards of thirty thousand people crossed the Cumberland River into middle Tennessee. Soon, twenty-ton barges were plying the Tennessee River from east Tennessee, loaded with barrels of frontier spirits—destination, New Orleans. (In 1796, Tennessee achieved statehood, her first governor being "Nolichucky Jack" Sevier, victor over the Tories at Kings Mountain. Sevier's Kings Mountain compatriot, Colonel Isaac Shelby, became the first governor of Kentucky, which achieved its statehood in 1792.)

Meanwhile, across the "southwestern" frontier deep into Virginia, the Carolinas, Georgia, Kentucky, and Tennessee, the great common denominator was corn. It provided hoecakes and hominy for the settlers, feed for the hogs and horses and, perhaps most important, the base for the settlers' favorite drink. Moreover, corncobs could be used as fuel and shucks to fill a mattress.

Getting the corn ground presented a problem, but the frontiersman wasn't long in meeting the challenge. "Grist" mills sprung up on many a stream, alongside waterwheels. But even before the grist mill, which required stone millwheels, the frontiersman created crude "tub mills" by carving turbines from long sections of tree trunks. Such a mill, run by water power and grinding only a few bushels a day, was described by a mountain man of the early 1800s:

> When a man lives on a branch or a prong of the creek, whar the water's lasty and thar's a right smart trickle all the time, he puts him in a tub mill, and lets the water grind fer him.
>
> Ye take a log and hew it till hit's kindly like a tub with a long spindle rising right out'n the midst of it. Run your water in a trough so it'll hit right in the tub and as fast as hit turns o' course the spindle turns too. Then ye fasten your grindin' stone on the top o' your spindle, and thar's your mill. Of course ye make a roof and walls and put a floor in, and thar's a letle room for grinding, up above the tub. The spindle goes up through the floor.

Looking back on it, it seems a miracle that the people on the frontier came up with such contraptions. But the mountain people were ingenious. They had to be. "We didn't have no money to buy the tricks and fixin's they had down in the settlements," recalled an old-timer. "And we couldn't ha' brung them in hyer, noway. There ain't no roads scarcely yit, and 'twas worse back in them days. A man could fetch jest what he could pack in on his horse—or on his back, like as not."

In some cases, the earlier mountain settler ground his corn by pounding it in a hollowed-out tree stump, with a wooden pestle "sweep mill." He would tie the pestle to the top of a nearby sapling, which would spring it back up after each lick. The tapping sounds enabled many frontier families located a good way apart to "keep in touch."

The water-powered grist mills which followed became one of the real milestones of Appalachian Americana. Like the still-house, the grist mill became a community landmark and a center of activity. "Well before the Indian Wars had ended," noted Mrs. Arnow, "middle Tennessee settlers were risking their scalps to go to the mill. . . ." Former Tennessee governor, Robert L. (Bob) Taylor, recalled that when he was a barefoot boy in the early 1800s, his grandfather's old grist mill "was the mecca of the mountaineers. They gathered there on rainy days to talk politics and religion, and to drink 'mountain dew' and fight."

In the fall of 1798, 177 rebellious Kentucky distillers were indicted by a federal grand jury for failure to register their stills and pay the federal excise. Among those convicted was the Reverend Elijah Craig, a Baptist preacher credited by many writers with being the discoverer of bourbon whiskey—and likewise defrocked of this honor by many others. Whether he was or was not the father of bourbon, Craig was typical of the spirited, independence-minded immigrants who were swarming into the interior. A hellfire-and-brimstone evangelist (whose only major compromise apparently was his hankering for a drink or two in the morning and a hot toddy at night, "for the stomach's sake"), Craig came with the tide of newcomers from Virginia, some twenty years earlier, via the Wilderness Road and the Boone Trace. He came seeking the religious freedom denied him in Virginia, where he was slapped in jail for preaching his convictions. And he came to Kentucky with a wooden still and two French burr millstones in his wagon. (His brother, Lewis, was also a preacher who felt the sting of persecution from the colonial government in Virginia, but he continued to preach through the grating of the Spottsylvania County jailhouse.)

In 1781, Preacher Elijah set up a grist mill at Royal Spring in what is today Scott County, Kentucky. He was an enterprising old gentleman and before long his waterwheel was also turning the gears of a sawmill and a "fulling mill" (which made cloth), and his surplus corn and rye meal were going into a cluster of white oak mash barrels and eventually into his burnt brown copper pot still.

Many unknowing historians have even credited the good reverend with being the first whiskey-maker in Kentucky, but they are far from the mark. Numerous stilling operations—including that of Kentucky Governor Shelby—were ahead of him. Still others want to give the colorful parson credit for discovering the charring technique for barrels used for storing and aging whiskey. (Charred oak purges the clear booze of many of its impurities and gives it an amber color, plus a smooth oak-flavored bouquet and "body." Today, charring is a federal requirement for the maturing of bourbon.) The story goes that Craig one day just happened to use a barrel that had been accidentally burned on the inside and subsequently discovered its lubricious effects on alcohol. Other accounts attribute the charred barrel to early coopers who burned straw inside new barrels to clear them of rough edges, splinters, and bacteria. Still others say that barrels were burned originally to clear out the rank odor of fish or molasses. (Barrels previously used to store salted fish will "kill" a batch of mash, as distillers soon discovered. A modern-day maker says the best used barrel for whiskey mash is one that has previously held pickles!)

The excise years were drawing to a close. In 1800, a significant year for whiskey men everywhere, but particularly for those on the southern and western frontiers, Democrat Thomas Jefferson, with the great support of the democratic peoples of the West, won an overwhelming victory over the Hamiltonian Federalists and became President. One of Jefferson's early objectives was eliminating the "infernal" whiskey excise which he felt was hostile to the genius of a free people. Craig and his fellow whiskey men across the West and South celebrated the repeal which came on June 30, 1802. The Lexington Light Infantry "paraded and fired seventeen vollies of musquetry," the Kentucky *Gazette* reported: "The bell rang a joyful peal—the bonfire blazed—shouts rent the air. . . ."

So the frontiersmen at last were free from the excise. And except for a three-year imposition of a tax following the War of 1812, they had a relatively long era without visits from gaugers, excisemen, and collectors. During this happy period, they refined their distilling, as well as their drinking. Old Ebenezer Hiram Stedman, a Georgetown, Kentucky, papermaker, recorded the expanding popularity of the western whiskey in his letters to his daughter.

> Every Boddy took it. It ondly Cost Twenty Five Cents pr. Gallon. Evry Boddy was not Drunkhards. . . . A Man might Get Drunk on this Whiskey Evry Day in the year for a Life time & never have the Delerium Tremers nor Sick Stomach or nerverous Head Achake . . . One Small drink would Stimulate the whole Sistom . . . It Brot out kind feelings of the Heart, Made men sociable, And in them days Evry Boddy invited Evry Boddy That Come to their house to partake of this hosesome Beverage.

By the year 1819, New Orleans alone was receiving more than two million gallons of whiskey a year from up the river in Tennessee, Kentucky, Ohio, and Indiana.

Tennessee itself was turning out more than 800,000 gallons in a year. And its stills—typical of those across the Appalachians from Virginia to north Alabama—were small ones. Distilling remained very much of an individual effort. Mrs. Arnow noted that "for the small farmer up river, the still continued for generations to be movable equipment housed at best in a shed or not at all, with pouring of water and mash done by hand. In most of the pioneer stills . . . the smell of whiskey was so strong—none needed any advertising."

At the same time, skilled distillers were highly sought craftsmen. In 1825, the following ad appeared in the *Farmer's Friend*, at Jonesboro, in far northeast Tennessee:

Wanted immediately, a first rate distiller. A young man without family, who understands the art of distilling corn and rye mixed, and all rye. He must be a man of sober habits. To such a one constant employment and good wages will be given.

6

The "Revenue" Goes to War

Come out and tell me who ye be. Fer if
ye be one of them damned revenuers, I'll
mince yer shivering slats with the contents
of my barker.

—Anonymous mountain man

COMMENCING with Thomas Jefferson's removal of the excise
in 1802, the golden era of American whiskey as a tax-free agricultural enterprise and frontier cottage industry (with the exception of
three years following the War of 1812) lasted for sixty years. The
honeymoon came to an end in 1862 when Congress—in desperate
need of money to pay for the Civil War then being fought—reimposed the excise.

The Act of July 1, the basis for our present tax system, created the
office of Commissioner of Internal Revenue, and imposed taxes on a
variety of items, including distilled spirits. On March 3, 1863, the
position of Deputy Commissioner was added, at which time three
"detectives" were authorized to help deter, detect, and punish tax
evaders. Their job, in other words, was to "protect the revenue"—
thus they became "revenuers."

From the imposition of the tax in 1862, the excise on distilled
spirits rose from twenty cents a gallon in 1863 to $2 in 1865 (to
$10.50 today). In 1868 Congress passed the Act of July 20, which
set forth the use of stamp taxes on liquor and tobacco, bringing the
liquor/tobacco tax system substantially to its current form.

Whiskey-making didn't skip a beat in Appalachia with the new
1862 law, however. In fact, if anything, it expanded a bit, particularly in the Confederate States, since, at the time, they weren't af-

74

fected by the law. The activity, though, did not receive universal
Confederate approval. In Georgia, Governor Joseph E. Brown asserted in 1862 that the copper used in the stills over his state would
"make many a battery of six-pounders, to be turned against the
enemy." He told of one county alone in which about seventy stills
were "constantly boiling and consuming more grain than was necessary to feed the whole population of the county."

To conserve the precious grain, Brown issued a proclamation
(later backed by a law passed by the State Leglislature) outlawing
the use of corn in the manufacture of whiskey. But according to
Georgia historian E. Merlton Coulter, "The thirst of Georgians, out-
running the power and ingenuity of the law-makers, soon broke out
in the erection of illicit stills which began the distillation of such food
products as molasses, sweet potatoes, pumpkins, peas, and dried
fruit."

The following year, the General Assembly counterattacked with a
law which, Coulter related, "forbade the distillation of all the articles
of food legislative wisdom could enumerate. But even so, Governor
Brown with all the power of his government was never able to put
down the whiskey-makers."

On the basis of this situation, typical of whiskey-making affairs
across the South, a case could be made that whiskey-distilling might
have had a dampening effect on the South's ability to wage war. On
the other hand, its corn whiskey may have given the Rebels the
courage they needed to fight the industrialized North.

In any case, following the Civil War, when the effect of the federal
excise against whiskey took effect across the South, many southern
whiskey-makers tried to comply with the law establishing the so-
called government distilleries (technically they were not government
stills but rather were government-regulated) subject to federal taxes
and the visit of revenue agents about once a month.

In Dawson County, Georgia, a nineteen-year-old German gun-
maker from Pennsylvania settled in a spot called Centerville, bought
himself a farm, put up a still and got a government license to operate
it. He did so well, he eventually had three stills operating simultane-
ously. His grandson remembered the operation:

"Granddaddy had a name for making good likker. Sold you any
amount you wanted to buy. He'd ship it in wagons and on the railroad, mostly to Atlanta and to Tennessee. He put most of it up in five-

gallon kags and his name and address, Centerville, Georgia, were burned in on the barrel with a brandin' iron. He also shipped some in big five-gallon stone jugs, about a quarter of an inch thick and hard to break. Granddaddy had 50-gallon turnip pots. All copper. Cap was tapered like a cork top. He run it, then doubled it back. That second run got all the fusel oil out. Cooked the headaches out. Granddaddy made his whiskey around a hundred ten. He wouldn't drink anything under a hundred. He never used a chaser. Said if whiskey's too mean to drink straight, it's too mean to drink. He aged his whiskey in barrels and it'd turn reddish color. That took a lot of the fire out of it. Smoothed it out. Aged corn whiskey wouldn't hurt you. It'd make you drunk as a hoot owl in just a little while. But you didn't have no bad hangover."

There were hundreds of regulated distilleries on individual farms around north Georgia and in other Appalachian states after the Civil War. "Government inspectors" came in every month at an appointed time and inspected the mash, the supplies, the still and the whiskey—and the books, to see if the operator was paying the proper amount of tax.

But many of the "government" stills, it turned out, were operating legally only by day (and sometimes only on the day of the inspector's visit) and shifted to illicit operations at night and for the rest of the month. And even greater lawbreaking was taking place deeper in the hills, by fulltime illicit distillers—and with it came many of the characteristics that have become typical of the moonshine life.

In 1877, revenue officials ran a survey and learned, to their amazement, that several thousand illicit stills were operating in the coves and ridges of Appalachia. The new commissioner of Internal Revenue declared in his report for 1876–7:

I can safely say that during the past year not less than 3,000 illicit stills have been operated in the [mountainous southern] districts named. These stills are of a producing capacity of 10 to 50 gallons a day. They are usually located at inaccessible points in the mountains . . . and are generally owned by unlettered men of desperate character . . . armed and ready to resist the officers of the law. Where occasion requires, they come together in companies of from ten to fifty persons, gun in hand, to drive the officers out of the country. . . .

The revenue's toughest job at first was breaking the area's iron curtain of secrecy. Practically everyone in the mountains either made whiskey or sympathized with or feared those who did. Few dared to become a "reporter"—an informer—for fear of having his stock slaughtered and/or his barns and homes burned. Numerous such reporters disappeared, presumably assassinated.

The life of an informer in any close-knit community would ordinarily be hazardous, but under the "code of the mountains," these Judases were treated with special contempt and disapproval. In 1889, in Pickens County, Georgia, twenty-seven moonshiners formed their own klan-type, hooded order to intimidate informers. Called "The Honest Man's Friend and Protector," the order adopted a ritual and a disguise—a black gown that extended to their knees, and a black hood, with slits for the eyes. Their records were kept in a hollowed-out black gum tree by the clerk of a local church. The pastor, it was reported, was a member "in good and regular standing." They held their meetings on Sundays and signed their oaths in blood. Each member of the "HMF&P" received the name of a suspected "reporter" in the area, and took on the job of conducting counter-espionage against that individual. During subsequent weeks, the moonshine night-riders set fire to three homes. Eventually, seven of the gang were brought to trial, convicted of arson and sentenced to prison terms at Brushy Mountain, Tennessee.

An old-time moonshiner in Union and Towns Counties, Georgia, told me how he and his "stillin' " colleagues gave an informer the scare of his life in 1939.

This feller—we called him "Coon Rod"—lived at Gum Log. Once when his house burnt down, we all went in and made up money and built him back a house. And, fact of the matter me bein' a carpenter, I did most of the work.

A couple years later, Deputy Sheriff Virge Kelly was offering a $75 reward to anyone reporting a still. "Coon Rod" came over to Blairsville one day and got to drinking and decided to go see Virge and claim $75 by leading him to our still.

There was eight of us working that day. We had 80 sacks of sugar and we had run two runs on our copper still. Seven of us got caught. The only one that got away was my daddy. He had on his clean clothes and hadn't really got started to work.

Some of our friends came over to the county seat and made the boys' bond. About dark, we all got to drinking and someone said, "Let's go over and git Coon Rod." I said, "I said, "It suits me."

Coon Rod lived alone then in a lumber camp shack a few miles back in the mountains. We went in about 10:30 at night and got him down from the top bunk. We told him, "Come down, Coon Rod, we come atter ye . . . and don't be all day gettin' your britches on." There was six of us. I was the driver.

We went out to the harness room and got a rope and tied it around under Coon Rod's arms where he couldn't get out, on through his overall bib and tied it to the bumper of my car. After we started driving, Coon Rod would run, trying to keep up, and he'd give out and fall down and drag. The mud would pot up in his overall bib. He really hollered and took on. I stopped the car and let him rest a while and then drove on. We done him that-a-way about a couple of miles. I got sorry for him and put him in the car. He sat on Jack Smith's lap. Jack slapped him around.

We went over to our house. Luke Jones was about to shoot him with his '38 special. He cocked it and put it right in Coon Rod's face. I just reached over and put my thumb between the hammer and the bullet. He snapped it over my thumb and led me all over the house that way. We dog-piled Luke and took his gun away from him. Somebody said, "Let's just take him to Murphy and put him on a bus."

They hauled their captive across the state line into North Carolina and gave him a bus ticket to his home. But "Coon Rod" broke loose and ran to the police. Eventually the moonshine group was tried on kidnapping charges in a U. S. district court and received sentences of one to two years apiece.

They "built their days" [in prison] and came back, and there ain't been too much reporting around here since. I was lucky to get off with six months in the CCC camp—what I called the "peckerwood army."

Since informants were so scarce (although revenue men offered a ten dollar reward for information, a sizeable fee in 1880), the revenuers sometimes followed "smell and smoke" to ferret out stills. Another method was to scour the countryside, following to its source water from which a horse refused to drink. Since horses will not drink water containing still slop, the raiders would know there was a still upstream.

But revenuers learned early of the difficulties of tromping around unguided in the "infested territory." The first sign of a foreign face would cause mountain "younguns" to scoot across the ridges to the still-houses. The women, meanwhile, would pull down their "blowing horns"—those curving, high-sounding cow horns used by fox hunters—and after one blast, another would answer in the next cove, and soon the whole region would resound like Gideon's Army on the march. Deputy Internal Revenue Collector Joseph L. Spurrier recalled a trip into the east Tennessee mountains in the 1880s:

> The moonshiners found out I was in the mountains before I fully knew the fact myself. And the way they spread that information would do credit to a long distance telephone. The first man that heard of me blew a horn. I think he had a certain number of toots for my name. The horn could be heard three miles, and everybody within hearing took up the alarm till the echoes were awakened by the sound of the horns. In an hour after the first blast people one hundred miles away knew that Spurrier was on a raid. I didn't get a dog's chance to seize a distillery.

Some of the early revenuers became undercover agents, posing as peddlers. They would haul their goods into a neighborhood on a wagon and then peddle the wares on foot, taking plenty of time to investigate still-house setups. Another ploy was to pose as cattle and fur buyers. Before long, the mountain people became suspicious of all such buyers. Even the children laughed in their faces, and pulled down the blowing horn.

Before the return of the excise, the still-houses of the southern Appalachians were placed conveniently in sight of public highways.

But with the reimposition of the tax, the stills were shifted deep into the forests and mountains, away from prying eyes. Usually very rude structures, the typical still-house was made of round logs, rarely had more than one door, and was without windows. It was generally chinked and daubed with mud to keep out the chilly winter blasts. In addition to the pot and worm and mash barrels, the room would have a rough built-in bed in one corner, and a skillet and coffee pot.

The early moonshiner chose his still site with great care. The first requirement was a good stream of cool water—preferably soft water free of minerals such as iron, which will ruin a run of liquor. Next was the requirement of seclusion, where no one ever traveled or thought of traveling. Naturally this would be a considerable distance into the mountains away from any inhabited neighborhood. Usually the site was in a deep hollow covered on both sides with a heavy growth of mountain laurel or timber, with hills high enough so the smoke would be absorbed by the atmosphere before reaching the summit.

John Wyatt, a federal revenuer who worked Kentucky in the late 1800s, recalled a picturesque still-house in Pulaski County:

It was constructed of the very roughest of wood, hewn in the crudest of style, ten feet high and not more than three times as long, and twice as wide. Built in the entrance of a cave, shadowed by overhanging trees and dense growth of briers and bushes, at the base of two high mountains, a stream of cold water trickling by, and you have it. There for years, moonshine whiskey was distilled and had the discovery not come about most peculiarly, there is no telling how long the butternuts [moonshiners] would have operated. In the dead of winter, the sheep of the surrounding country sought this spot to feed on the refuse matter and also to protect themselves from the Borean blasts between the hills. These tracks betrayed the butternuts.

Former revenuer George W. Atkinson recalled another type of still-house which usually was found in Kentucky in the 1880s—the subterranean cavern. These caves were usually entered by a slight decline, but some went straight into the ground, and the bottom could be reached only by a ladder. Atkinson also found stills in cliffs along rivers or large creeks, with water being pumped from the stream below. Cliff locations were considered specially desirable, because of the difficulty of access they presented to revenuers. Atkinson declared that two courageous men in a cliff still-house "could keep off almost any number of raiders who might attempt to attack them from below."

Atkinson's description of the distilling atmosphere in the late 1800s is very informative:

> Doubling Day at a moonshine distillery is almost as important an event to the mountain community as the coming of a circus to the small boy in the towns and villages. Usually moonshiners, when grain is plenty and the weather is not too hot, make from two to three doublings in a week. During the two weeks preceding Christmas, their stills are run day and night and they, therefore, double every day, or rather every night, as the doers of dark deeds prefer darkness rather than light.

Just about the most famous story in moonshine folklore concerns the revenuer who tried to bribe a mountain boy to take him to his pappy's still. The story has cropped up in so many versions from so many states, all the way from Arkansas to West Virginia (and told for a price ranging from fifty cents to five dollars), that it is probably the result of a pulp writer's fertile imagination. The most colorful version was the one from the Arkansas Ozarks, as told by Isaac Stapleton, a historian of Arkansas moonshining. According to Stapleton, a revenue man was scouting among the hills of western Newton County, looking for a wildcat still. A bark of a hound attracted his attention to a little shanty up on the side of the mountain, half-hidden by scrub-timber and grapevines. He climbed the steep hillside, and saw a small boy:

> "Where is your father?"
> "Oh, Pap's up there making moonshine."
> "Up where?"
> "Up yander under the bluff."
> "And where is your mother?"
> "Ma's up there helping Pa."
> "Sonny, I will give you fifty cents if you will take me up there where your father and mother are."
> The boy held out his hand.

"No, no, I will give you the money when we get back," the agent said.

"I will take the money now," said the boy, "for you ain't coming back!"

Atkinson recalled a young revenuer who marched into the mountains dressed in rough homespun, carrying a grip filled with iron cement, which he sold for ten cents a bottle. He visited eleven still-houses, got the names of all the operators, drew a map of the entire area, and came out without ever having been suspected!

Fishing and hunting also proved for a time to be successful decoys. Atkinson and another agent walked into Kentucky's Cumberland mountains with their fishing tackle and shotguns, camping conveniently near a cluster of still-houses. They fished and hunted by day and prowled around the still-houses by night.

The revenue man, faced with the problem of penetrating a closed community to arrest men who were not criminals in an ordinary sense, thus became a character in his own right within the world of illicit whiskey-making.

One of the colorful revenuers of the era was John Wyatt. As deputy U.S. Marshal in Kentucky, Wyatt waged a relentless campaign against moonshiners in the mountains of Kentucky, carrying a fat and worn pocket-book filled with warrants.

During the holiday week in 1877, Wyatt and five assistants, armed with Henry rifles, swept through suspected areas of Magoffin and Breathitt Counties. Arriving at Death Hollow, a known site of "wild-cat" stills, they were led by the unmistakable, sour odor wafting from the mash pots. With their hatchets, they hacked the red hot pot, dumped the bubbling, milky-looking mash into an adjacent stream, and smashed the wooden fermenters. Thirty to forty mountain men —with rifles in hand—popped up on the rim of the cove. Wyatt gathered his little band in the log still-house and prepared for a shoot-out. The bearded moonshiner leader, Levi Patrick, laid down his rifle and met Wyatt halfway, then reached a reconciliation. The moonshiners invited the entire Wyatt group to spend the night, and the following day threw a magnificent barbecue. It turned into a rip-roaring, jolly affair, with the fellowship enlivened by keg after keg of "mountain dew." Wyatt and his men "left rejoicing"—but without any prisoners, apparently part of the deal.

Such peaceful coexistence soon ended, however. Between 1877 and 1881, the Internal Revenue stepped up its enforcement, and its officers seized almost five thousand stills and made eight thousand arrests through the moonshine states. But the effort was costly. During these years, twenty-nine agents were murdered on moonshine raids, and sixty-three were seriously wounded. As many if not more illicit distillers met the same fate.

A pitched battle was fought between government forces and moonshiners on August 23 and 24, 1878, in the Cumberland mountain country of Overton County, Tennessee. The Revenue force of ten men was commanded by Deputy Collector James M. Davis, a moonshine raider with a strong record. Standing six-foot-two and one-half inches tall, Captain Davis was a large-boned, muscular 210 pounds. Possessing the attributes of the southern woodsman, he had much of the shrewdness, cunning, and daring of the Indians, whom he much admired. He virtually lived in the woods and was intimate with nearly all the bypaths and deep recesses of the Cumberlands. A companion described him as "a man of the very best quality of nerve . . . and withal a dead shot." Yet despite his rough appearance and expertness with a gun, he was gentle and kindhearted.

On this particular mission, according to Atkinson, Davis and his men found lodging at the home of 102-year-old James Peek, nine miles north of Cookeville. But no sooner had they tied up their horses than they found themselves surrounded by a yelling, gun-toting mob of moonshiners led by Campbell Morgan, the monarch of the moonshiners in Tennessee and reported to be, "next to [Lewis] Redmond of South Carolina, the most notorious moonshiner in America."*

Three of Davis' men were wounded, one critically, before nightfall. The next morning, finding they were surrounded by the guns of one hundred mountaineers, Davis took his seven unhurt men into an adjacent two-story log building then under construction and climbed to the second floor where the logs had wide cracks between them, not

---

* Lewis Redmond was idyllized in the *New York Herald* in the 1870s as the Robin Hood of the Mountains. A part Indian with "hawk-like eyes and raven black hair," he indeed was the King of the Moonshiners in western Carolina. He shot and killed a deputy marshall and was subsequently cornered and shot down at his cabin on the Little Tennessee River in Swain County, North Carolina. But he survived and lived to be eighty-seven. A fraudulent paperback in 1879, reputed to be his true life story, added more luster to his fabled reputation.

yet chinked with mud. The cabin served as an excellent blockhouse. Captain S. D. Mather, commissioner of the U. S. Circuit Court, and a member of Davis' force, recounted the event:

Firing was opened upon as early in the morning and was kept up all day. Our ammunition, being scarce, we shot sparingly. We had no water and but little to eat; still we held out to the end and did the very best we could. . . . About sundown, it seemed as if there were a thousand men around and about us, judging from the bugles, the yells of the demon moonshiners and the balls they were pouring into the walls of our block-house. The night that followed was almost pandemonium itself. Sunday morning dawned with armed men in sight of us in every direction. . . . The roads were barricaded with fences and large poles on top, which made the beleagurement complete. But it seemed that no one desired to pass, as the whole country had joined the moonshiners, or were in sympathy with them. To us the situation was gloomy and desolate. . . . About 10 o'clock it began to rain and we caught a small supply of water. During the rain they fired at us almost continuously, possibly to keep their guns dry. Now and then we saw a chance to get in a shot and promptly put it there.

This was the condition of matters when, late in the afternoon, some gentlemen came from Livingston, the county seat, having learned of our situation, to see if something could be done to bring about an honorable peace. They had hardly explained their mission when two of the moonshiners sent in a note asking permission to confer with the Government officers, whom they had been besieging for two days and nights. We consented to their coming in and they did so promptly. They at once proposed to go, with the delegation from Livingston, to Campbell Morgan, the generalissimo of the besiegers and if possible, have the attacking party disperse. They went, and shortly after returned with a message from Morgan, that if we would petition the President of the U.S. and the Federal Court to pardon all their offenses up to date, they would let us go on our way, but under no other condition would they remove the embargo which they had placed upon us.

We responded we could not control the action of the Federal Court and would therefore promise nothing . . . that we had plenty of ammunition and that reinforcements were on the way. . . .

The delegation again went to Morgan, who stated that he had heard that Capt. Davis intended to kill him on sight and that he [Morgan] had organized this forcible opposition only in self defense. He also said if the Govt. had a warrant to serve on him and would put it in the hands of someone other than Davis, he would promptly give himself up and would do everything in his power to correct the evil ways of his neighborhood and this should be his last resistance to Unit. States authority.

This last proposition was acceded to and Morgan and his men, some 25 in number, left their stations on the hillsides, filed past our fort, and went their way. They all looked like determined men and we know, to our sorrow, that they are fighters from the hills.

This episode did not end the history of Davis and Morgan.

Morgan—the grand sachem of the Cumberland mountain moonshiners—had stills in both Tennessee and Kentucky. Son of a Presbyterian clergyman, he developed as a young man "a wild and reckless nature and soon passed beyond the control of his father." A latter-day Daniel Boone, he stayed in the outdoors, hunting, fishing, and trapping. He was well-educated, and soon became the recognized leader of the moonshiners with whom he associated. For years he operated an illicit distillery in Jackson County, Tennessee, in a deep hollow shrouded by dense woods. His still-house was built for battle, with portholes on every side, and double-lined doors.

Morgan seemed invincible, and for years officers were reluctant to attack him in his lair. However, Capt. Davis, several months after their hillside battle, determined that he would go after him, and he led a cadre of his best officers into the hills near Gainesboro. Morgan was ready, and had his own army within his "fort." When the Davis party started closing in, Morgan shouted out that if they came any nearer, his men would kill the last one of them. Shortly, he thrust his rifle out one of the portholes and fired. His barrel was shattered by a volley of ounce balls from eight of the officers. He thrust out another rifle, and it was shattered, also. In the meantime, Davis' men began pouring a tremendous volley of shots into the still-house, while Davis and Morgan fired at one another through the same porthole.

At last, Davis fired an ounce ball into Morgan's right arm. The moonshiner surrendered in pain.

After being taken prisoner by the federal government, Morgan sat

85

down and wrote the Commissioner of Revenue in Washington, Green B. Raum, asking for clemency in return for his promise to give up his illicit whiskey business.

General Raum's reply read thusly:

Treasury Department
Office of Internal Revenue
Washington, D.C.,
November 18th, 1878

Campbell Morgan, Esq., Gainesboro, Tenn.:

Sir: I am in receipt of your letter of the 9th inst., in which you give an account of the difficulty which occurred in April last, at the time of the seizure of your distillery.

I must compliment you upon the ingenuity displayed in presenting yourself as an unoffending citizen, peaceably pursuing his avocations, and the officers of the United States as violators of the law. It is obvious, from your own admissions, that the internal revenue officers would not have visited your premises if you had not been engaged in violating the laws of the United States and defrauding it of its resources. By your act, your distillery had become forfeited to the Government, and you had subjected yourself to the penalties of fine and imprisonment. Under these circumstances the officers were entirely justified in entering upon your premises. . . .

To me it is a matter of extreme regret that it is necessary, in the enforcement of the laws of the United States, that officers should go around ready to defend their lives against assault and to meet force with force. In this free county of ours every citizen should have such a love of the Government and its laws as to cheerfully give obedience to their provisions, and not be found engaged in defrauding it of its revenues, or forcibly resisting, with fire arms, the officers engaged in the enforcement of the laws. . . .

You say that you never intended to violate the spirit of the law and you invite an investigation of your character for truth, honesty, sobriety, industry and peace. It is not necessary to discuss the question of your intentions. They are to be judged by your acts; and the establishing of an illicit distillery and operating it for years, as you admit, without paying tax upon the produce, is conclusive evidence that you not only intended to violate the letter but the spirit of the law. Without having a knowledge of your character for truth, sobriety and industry, I deem it unnecessary to discuss it. I leave it to your sense of right whether a man can be considered honest who defrauds the Government of its revenue, or peaceful who, with arms in his hands, resists the enforcement of the law.

There is no disposition to enforce the law in a vindictive spirit, but, on the contrary, I am very desirous of inspiring the people with respect for the law and a disposition to observe it. The difficulty in your case is that, not satisfied with resisting the officers some months ago, you assisted in besieging them for nearly two days and nights, in which affair three officers were wounded.

I am glad to know that you have determined to abandon the business of violation of the law, but I am not advised of any reasons that would warrant a pardon in your case.

Very respectfully,
Green B. Raum, Commissioner.

The commissioner's letter may have had an inspiring and rehabilitative effect on Morgan. For the first time he appeared to see the government's side of the moonshining problem. In any case, after serving out his prison term, he applied for a job as a revenuer—his knowledge of the business, after all, was considerable—and got it. For a number of years, he served under and alongside Captain Davis, his former adversary, and a close friendship developed.

In May of 1880, Davis was assigned to go into northeast Georgia to squelch a widespread complex of moonshine operations—particularly in Towns County, around Hiawassee.

The word was that the " 'shiners" there, headed by the "king moonshiner," had resisted all suppressive efforts by the local law. Davis said he would undertake the mission on one condition—that he be allowed to take along Campbell Morgan. This he was allowed to do, and the two woodsmen rode their horses more than one hundred miles northeast from Atlanta into the Georgia mountain country.

Well into Towns County, they were struck by the apparent absence of any men. The area bore the hallmarks of poverty—poor livestock, old-fashioned farming implements, worn out lands, much of its topsoil having washed from the clear hillsides. They saw that sturdy mountain women, and not the usual menfolk, were doing the field work. Morgan pulled up to a woman cutting a furrow with an ox. "Where are all the men?" he asked.

"They are expecting you'uns," she replied, "and they are hidin' in the woods, or else watchin' for you at the still houses."

Davis and Morgan organized a squad of ten men to go against the "moonshine king," who had a reputation in the hills for once having forced twenty revenuers to free him. The 'shiner and his three sons were living in the woods, and would be informed of unwanted visitors by the blowing of horns by his wife and daughter, who remained in their home. Davis and his men hid around the home, and after the first night, at dawn, captured two men who emerged from the forest and were crossing a field to the house. They turned out to be sons of the "king."

The two sons, who were expecting brutal treatment, instead were handled with good humor and firm kindness. In a short while, they pointed out the location of their own still, which had been carefully buried. The people of the settlement for years afterward considered the discovery to have been the result of super-human detective work.

In time, the "king" himself surrendered. When the "terror of the mountains" showed up for a hearing before a United States commissioner in Blairsville, he turned out to be a diminutive, wizened old man. After reading the charges of illicit whiskey-making, the commissioner asked the old man, "Guilty or not guilty?"

"Guilty, if I am hung for it," he replied proudly. But he added, in a low voice, "I am through with this blockading business. It has given me a fame that I don't deserve. They talk about my resistance. Those twenty men turned me loose only when my three sons aimed their rifles from the bushes and demanded my release. That's the way I resisted the United States Government."

Soon Davis had the old man, Bill Berong, helping him, too. The "king" invited the captain to come back and visit him, promising to help him break up other illicit stills in Towns County.

As the squad galloped by on their way out of the county, a woman yelled from her door, "Look here, Mr. Davis, I don't want you to take all the men out of this county. We women can't get along without them."

Davis lost his life by ambush sometime later in Tennessee, while delivering a moonshiner to prison. It was near the spot close to a still where he himself hand once killed a whiskey-maker in a shoot-out.

No one was ever brought to trial for the shooting of Davis, a testimony to the "code of the mountains."

The stepped-up campaign of the revenue agents during the end of the 1870s, though it cost the Revenue ninety-two casualties, marked the beginning of the end for the moonshiner. It also marked the beginning of the all-out drive by the "Big Law"—the Revenue—against illicit whiskey-making, a drive that has gradually built up momentum until today the "Big Law" has become the bane of anyone who would defy the liquor laws of the United States of America.

7

Big Court Week and Uncle Amos

Judge: Well, sir! I want to know why it is that you, who look like an honest man, persist in pursuing this illicit whiskey business? I want to know whether, after the lenience shown you by this court, you expect to come back here any more.

Defendant: Why, bygosh, jedge, I didn't *come* here *this* time!

Judge: Well, then, how did you get here?

Defendant: They fotch me! Yes, sir, jedge, they fotch me! I didn't *come* here, jedge, and I never will *come* here, you needn't be oneasy about that.

—North Carolina trial

A federal judge asked famed western North Carolina blockader Quill Rose if it was true that aging improved corn whiskey.

"Your honor has been misinformed. I kept some for a week one time and I could not tell it was a bit better than when it was new and fresh."

—John Parris

IN the late 1800s and early 1900s most of the cases in federal courts in the Appalachians involved moonshining, and the trials afford a good opportunity to observe the manner of men who had elected to go into the distilling enterprise.

"Big Court Week" was possibly the most notable event of the year for the hill people, rivaling revivals and camp meetings. In the valleys, coves, and ridges for miles around, citizens would put aside their plows and Winchester rifles and mash sticks and head for the courthouse. There they would catch up on the news with their friends and kinfolks—and listen intently with hands cupped to their ears as the trial testimony unfolded.

The wooden benches in the courtroom usually were packed with the rough-hewn folk, who brought along plenteous plugs of tobacco and tins of snuff. The informal courtroom atmosphere was enlivened by volleys of tobacco juice arching to the brass spittoons along the walls and aisles.

Henry Wiltse, who put down his experiences in a little book published in 1885, described the sort of men who were on trial. The average moonshiner of the era, he said, would be dressed in homespun, had long hair, an unkempt sandy beard, and smelled of the mountains, of the leaves and wood soil that permeated his clothing. Meal and still beer often could be seen caked on his shirt. He wore no coat or vest, unless the weather was cold. He usually had no suspenders or only one (a "gallus"), and in lieu of suspenders would wear a leather belt or an old piece of rope. He was somewhat above average height, inclined to be slight in proportion to his height, and somewhat stoop-shouldered.

Despite their rough appearance, uncultured background, and limited knowledge of the ways of the world, many of the moonshine defendants—they usually referred to themselves as blockaders— exhibited a natural knack for common sense. Often, they appeared in court as their own counselors, defending their cases with humor, shrewdness and, on occasion, amazing success.

For example, there was the Baptist preacher who was brought to trial for illicit distilling and for trafficking in mountain dew. As his name was called, he arose from his seat among the lawyers to declare, "Your honor, I am the man." His confident, commanding bearing immediately attracted the attention of the audience. Feeling in his pockets for his glasses, he discovered, to his apparent surprise, he had left them at home. He looked up at the bench and declared: "Jedge, I see you are a man about my age, will you be kind enough to loan me your specks for a few minutes?"

Grins spread through the audience at the boldness of the old parson. While everyone enjoyed a laugh, including the court and the bar, the judge dispatched a bailiff with his eyeglasses to the defendant.

Holding up the glasses, the preacher-moonshiner rubbed them intently with a threadbare handkerchief, then declared:

"Jedge, them's might' nice looking specks. They are yaller and look as though they mout be gold. Are they gold or brass, jedge?"

By this time, the courtroom was in near hysteria, with people elbowing one another in great merriment.

The preacher, meantime, remained calm, composed, and intent. Finally, he picked up a book and began to look it over with deliberateness. Again he turned to the judge:

"Jedge, these is fine specks, but they are a little too young for me; and I'm sure I wouldn't a-thought so, seein' as how you are so gray headed; but gray hairs is not allers a sign of age. There's my old woman. She's whiter headed nor you are, jedge, and she's ten year younger nor me, so you see that's no sign."

A new outburst of laughter forced the judge to rap his gavel for order.

"Now, jedge, if you will let me see what you say agin me in your warrant, I'll tell you what I've got to say about it."

To this the audience applauded enthusiastically.

The solicitor brought out the indictment, and the old parson read it through, tossed it onto the table and made the following statement to the court:

"Jedge, that paper says I carried on the business of a distiller, and the business of a retail liquor dealer, when I tell your honor that I did no such thing. My business is farmin' duren the week days, and preachin' on Sundays, and now I would like for you to tell me, when I have spent all my time as I've been tellen you, how I could carry on them two other kinds of business what that paper says I do? [Laughter.] If I do all that, Jedge, I must be an unusual kind of man, mustn't I? [Laughter.] Now, I tell you what I have done—no more, no less—and I am tellen of the truth, too. I just made two runs last fall and one run of peppermint in Jannywary, and in them three runs I didn't make over thirty gallon in all, and it was for medicine, too. One of the gals in the neighborhood was sick with the breast complaint, and another one was down with the yaller janders, and I wouldn't of made the runs I tell you about if it hadn't been on their account. Now them's the facts, as God is my jedge."

A thundering applause roared through the courtroom as he took his seat.

The judge asked the old moonshiner if he were lenient with him on this, his first offense, whether he would stop making whiskey illicitly. The parson indicated he thought he could stop. The judge fined him one hundred dollars, and court costs, lenient for a well-heeled whiskey-maker.

One of the most colorful moonshiners to grace a federal court during the post Civil War period was Amos Owens, widely known as the "cherry bounce king" of Rutherford County, North Carolina. Owens' "bounce" formula was a generous portion of his finest corn whiskey, with a few dashes of sourwood honey and cherry juice added, the juice, so it was said, having been trod from the cherries by the bare feet of his beautiful daughters, in true Old World style.*

A rotund, red-faced, leprechaun of an Irishman, whose high-pitched "whiskey tenor" voice commanded the awe of his friends and foes, Owens was the epitome of the Appalachian moonshiner of the 1800s. He was a hard-drinking, defiant, freedom-loving outdoorsman who believed it was his God-given right to turn his fruit and grain into "legal tender" brandy and liquor without being hamstrung by a "dad-burned" federal excise tax. In this regard he, like others, was carrying forward the traditions of his blockading predecessors who had been contemptuous to a man of any attempt to restrict their "inalienable rights" to make a livelihood from their land, so long as their activities did not interfere with the rights of their neighbors.

As with most pioneer farmers of the eighteenth and nineteenth centuries, particularly in the Appalachians, Owens had no reason to consider his "diversification" into whiskey-making as anything illegal or immoral. He reasoned the land was his, the corn and the cherries and apples were his, the copper pot still was his. Moreover, he had suffered near starvation in a Union stockade as a Rebel prisoner. Arriving home deathly ill before the end of the war, he found his

---

* Here is how the Junior Service League of Johnson City, Tennessee, described "Cherry Bounce" in its compilation of east Tennessee recipes, *Smoky Mountain Magic:* "To one gallon of white spirits put two quarts of water and five to six quarts of wild cherries. Wash cherries and put in jug with alcohol. Corn cob stopper in jug. After they stand three months, drain off liquor and strain it well, sometimes twice. Make a thick syrup with one and one-half pounds white sugar and water and boil until ropy. Add the syrup to liquor from jug to taste."

only slave had been freed by the enemy. Then "why in tarnation," he reasoned, should he share the yield from his blockading labors with Washington? He vowed he'd not pay a cent of excise tax.

Yet, despite his angry defiance, when accosted at his still by federal agents, he never attempted to run, never tried to escape from imprisonment and, typical of practically all corn whiskey producers of his era, always showed up in court on his own when summoned.

Picture this, a recollection of Owens by Lee Weathers, former editor of the Shelby, North Carolina, *Star*:

> Uncle Amos was a household word in these parts before the turn of the century. I remember having seen him once as a child when my family lived near the Seaboard depot. . . . Owens was sitting in a passenger coach, riding to Charlotte for his fourth trial in Federal Court for making and selling moonshine liquor and refusing to pay the revenue. . . . He was a jovial passenger, wearing a high beaver hat and a Prince Albert coat. A pair of homemade leather suspenders held up his baggy trousers. Everybody seemed to know Amos. He greeted his friends and moonshine customers with a grin, admitting that he might be sent back to Sing Sing* in Ossining for a 'post graduate course.'

"Yep, I reckilect plenty 'bout Amos," an old-timer told the *Asheville Citizen* in 1933, "but I'm afeered it's not what could be printed. There warn't but *one* Amos! His likker? Now *that* was a drink for you. Why, with one swig from a jug of Amos Owens' cherry bounce, ary man in the state could lick this depression single-handed."

In his early trials, Owens often won acquittal, "for the roars of laughter he evoked prejudiced even stern justice in his favor." Even while on trial, Amos would proudly defy his captors by stationing one of his cronies from Cherry Mountain right outside the courthouse with a wagonload of whiskey, the spirits being covered by sweet potatoes and chestnuts. A usual load was "20 bushels of 'taters and 40 gallons of corn whiskey." By the time his trial was over, he would have in hand more than enough cash to pay off his lawyer *and* his fine.

* A check with federal officials at the Ossining (now a New York state correctional institution) did not reveal any records of Owens having been incarcerated there. It is possible he was sent to the federal prison in Albany, New York. However, the U.S. Bureau of Prison records go back only as far as 1910.

James M. Davis, *left*, Revenue man, and Campbell Morgan, *right*, Tennessee "moonshine monarch" of the late 1800s, who fought one of the most violent battles of the excise years, and ultimately became good friends. See pages 83–89.

Amos Owens, Uncle Amos, "cherry bounce" king, one of the great moonshiners and party givers of the Appalachians. See pages 93–106.

This still was located in Franklin, in far western North Carolina, near the Smoky Mountains. The still is a copper pot; it and the flake stand are on the left, the mash barrels are on the right. Again, the site is hidden in dense "laurels." (Library of Congress photograph).

This photo of the arrest of two whiskey makers in the Appalachian mountains was probably made in the late 1800s when the Revenue launched an all-out war against illicit whiskey operations across the Appalachian South. The still was relatively small—probably 30 gallons in capacity. The cap is off. At the left is the wife of one of the moonshiners. (Library of Congress photograph).

Moonshiners in the U.S. Annex of the Atlanta (Georgia) jail in the late 1800s.

A member of the north Georgia Moonshine Klan, the Honest Man's Friend and Protector. See page 77.

When whiskey was legal.

When whiskey was illegal. One of the unique whiskey containers that came out of the depression was the "Carrie Nation" flask, made in the shape of an axe, in honor of the famed saloon-raider of the era. This flask is on display at the Barton Museum of Whiskey History, Bardstown, Kentucky.

Federal Judge Robert Payne Dick took a great liking to the spunky little blockader. But he wearied of Owens' continued appearance in court for defiance of federal liquor laws.

"Uncle Amos," the judge declared at one trial, "I want to tell you something. You've given this court lots of trouble."

"And jedge," Amos replied in his near falsetto voice (apparently a result of having drunk his over 100-proof corn liquor "neat" for years), "Jedge, I want to tell you sump'n. This hyar court's give *me* lots of trouble, too!"

On a subsequent occasion, back in the same court, Amos was sternly rebuked.

"Amos Owens, stand up," Judge Dick ordered. "You have stiffened your neck and hardened your heart again, against the majesty of the law. You have made whiskey and sold the same. Why do you persist in your lawless course? Look at me . . . I am sixty years of age, was never drunk, and have never incurred the woe of putting the bottle to my neighbor's lips. What have you to say, why the sentence of the law should not be pronounced upon you?"

"Waal, jedge," Amos warbled, as he winked to the crowd, "you've missed a durned lotsa fun if you hain't never made, drunk nor sold no likker." Then he added the following intriguing remark: "As to what I have to say about a sentence? Jedge, do you know what the gov'nor of North Caroliny said to the gov'nor of South Caroliny? Waal, jedge, them's my sentiments."

For many years, I had heard this expression about the famous conversation between the two unspecified governors, but nobody could tell me what was really said. Some people told me it was a fictitious "bit of malarky," meaning, "To hell with you, too." Others said it was merely a cliché to indicate that nothing really was said. But *The Atlanta Constitution's* "Action Line" came through magnificently. The answer?

"It's been a long time between drinks!"*

It was a patently ironic comment for a notorious liquor-maker to make to a federal judge preparing to pass judgment on him! Judge

---

* *Action Line* said: "The story is almost legend and goes back to the 1840s when J. M. Morehead was governor of North Carolina and James H. Hammond was governor of South Carolina. According to Phil Grose, writer/researcher for the present Governor, John West, of South Carolina, the story goes that Morehead and Hammond got into a heated argument one day. Evidently wearied by the debate, Morehead turned to a servant and said, 'It's been a long time between drinks.' It has become a cliché now referring to any drawn-out ordeal."

95

Dick didn't find the response a bit funny, and sent Amos up to the federal pen for a year and fined him twelve hundred dollars.

During his fifty-odd year career of "stillin,' " Owens' notoriety for squeezing out great corn whiskey and fruit brandy spread far, despite the limited communications of the time. His greatest fame obviously rode on his cherry bounce, known in backwoods hamlets and saloons across the South and as far as the Mississippi River, where bartenders kept a few jugs in the luxury paddle wheelers that plied the river from Cincinnati to New Orleans. Amos invited folks to an annual cherry bounce celebration every second Sunday in June, when the black-heart cherries were ripest. People would ride in on their horses and mules and in their wagons and buggies, pulled by oxen and mules. Hundreds would also come on foot by a narrow dirt road whose deep ruts circled the sides of Cherry Mountain to the remote table-like mountaintop.

M. L. White, a Polkville, North Carolina, school teacher who "wrote up" Owens' life under the pen name "Corn Cracker," waxed extravagant when picturing the mountain scene:

Amos owned Cherry Mountain which was 3,000 feet above the level of the sea. From here was a most enchanting view of the mountain scenery that is called the 'Switzerland of America.' From here could be seen Shelby, Rutherfordton, King's Mountain, with a view of the mountains of Georgia, Virginia and Tennessee. Here could be breathed the pure air of heaven, and here as pure limpid water as ever gurgled from the bosom earth rippled down the delves of the mountains. Here grew the famous cherry trees, some three feet in diameter, and are found nowhere else, that yielded every June a crop of fruit remarkable for its size and flavor. Here was found the ideal honey-producing flavors of poplar, chestnut and sourwood, and here was the ideal range for the cattle of a thousand hills. The home of the cow, honeybee, pure water and invigorating mountain air, and not excelled on earth for the fruit tree and the vine. Amos said here would he build a castle like the baron of feudal times, and here should be the land of milk and honey, peach and honey, and the abiding place of cherry bounce.

A more down-to-earth description of the festival was given by Owens' granddaughter in Shelby:

The family would cook for a week beforehand, barbecuing pigs and cooking chicken and ham and beef and all kinds of vegetables. People came from miles around. They paid 25 cents per plate. They danced and drank for as long as the food and drink and money lasted. Some would get so drunk and carried away they would dance in the nude. One man caught his daughter and her escort in this way and made them marry. Some would ride their mules through the dance hall. People wrote their names across the walls. You couldn't find a spot as big as your hand on any of the walls because they were filled with names and addresses scrawled on them.

Amos was a genial host to his throng of merrymakers. While one group would be dancing in the barn-like hall to the sound of a fiddle and the pat-pat-pat of the fiddler's foot, another cluster of people would be eating the food that was spread on the groaning tables. Still another group might be watching or participating in the boxing contests, which often developed into rough brawls. For the guests who passed out under the influence of the liquid beverages, the cellar was available to sleep it off.

"Gander-pulling" was one of the diversions Owens offered to his guests. Cruel though it was, gander-pulling, which came from England, was one of the most popular diversions among mountain people in the 1800s, and Amos made sure that his ring was equal to any. The object, brutal to say, was to break the gander's neck and pull off the head. Amos plucked the feathers from a gander and strung him up by his legs onto the branch of a tree, just high enough so that a rider coming by would have to stretch to reach the head. Then Amos took a gourd of goose grease and spread it liberally all over the gander's head and neck. The gander, meanwhile, was squalling and clacking all the while as he swayed to and fro in wait for the first rider. When Amos fired his long squirrel rifle, the contest began. As a rider swung by on his way for the gander, Amos would pop the horse's rump with his rawhide whip, making it more difficult to grab the gander.

During the next hour, the crowd would yell, "He's a *gone goose!*"

97

At the end, the winner would proudly bring the head to Amos to claim his prize. Amos, meanwhile, had collected twenty-five cents an entrant from the competitors and was therefore able to give the winner a good prize.

Amos offered still other amusements, such as cockfights and dog fights. All for money, of course. Amos was about as close with his money as were his Scotch-Irish neighbors. After the celebration had ended and the crowd had pulled out, Amos would pile his "take" into half-bushel baskets, lash the baskets onto the back of a mule and ride across the mountain and bury them. He always carried his shotgun and threatened to kill anyone who followed. No one ever dared.

Before his death, the old man commissioned "Corn Cracker" to write his biography. The fifty-five-page pamphlet was printed in 1901, the type having been set laboriously by hand, a letter at a time. The booklet carried a Lincolnesque picture of Owens, wearing his high silk beaver—a gift of an admiring federal judge. It also contained a picture of Owens' Cherry Mountain home, which he described as being "three stories long and one story high." Pictured in the yard is a large copper pot still with Amos proudly standing by in shirt sleeves, smoking a corncob pipe. Although it is written with a great deal of flourish and long-winded ambiguity, occasional paragraphs stand out, shedding light on the old man's experiences.*

Owens was born around 1822, on Sandy Run in Rutherford County, Kentucky. His father was said to have been a ne'er-do-well. His grandfather was a native North Carolinian and a patriot of the Revolution, having been among the corn whiskey-making, mainly Scotch-Irish sharpshooters from the hill country of the Carolinas and Tennessee who, with their long Pennsylvania rifles, challenged and defeated Ferguson's Redcoats and Tories at Kings Mountain. Five miles from Owens' home, nine of the surviving Tories from Kings Mountain were strung up and hung at what became known as the "gallows oak."

---

* I am indebted to one of the present-day owners of Cherry Mountain, Kenyon Withrow, for providing me a mimeographed reproduction of the biography. Mr. Withrow, a retired federal crop-insurance official who is now happily engaged in his great love of tracing family histories, owns an 800-acre farm in a beautiful valley adjacent to Cherry Mountain as well as a summer home on top of the mountain itself (as do several other local citizens). He serves as one of the hosts at the annual Second Sunday in June Cherry Festival, in memory of Amos—minus the strong cherry bounce.

98

Here's how White described Owens' early life.

"Except for a rugged, well-knit frame, a constitution like board-inghouse butter, digestion like the bowels of a threshing machine, there was nothing especially unbearable about the youth of Amos Owens. He was strong, active, an unerring shot, and, while peace-able, would fight desperately when aroused. Amos was unlettered, having never attended school but a few days."

At age nine, he was hired out as a "hewer of wood and drawer of water" (a good term straight out of Ireland of the 1700s), a job he maintained for thirteen years. In 1845, he bought 100 acres of land near Cherry Mountain, but the severe drought prevented him from producing much of a crop. Perhaps this is the reason he turned to making whiskey and brandy. In any event, his biographer relates that in 1845—with the use of a "turnip-type" copper pot still—Owens began converting his corn, cherries, and apples into liquor and brandy. At that time, of course, there was no federal excise tax on whiskey or on distilleries.

Now a property owner, Amos was ready to settle down and get married. He courted Mary Ann Sweezy from a neighboring moun-tain. When he got ready to pop the question, he rode over to "Old Man Sweezy's," where he found the bewhiskered gentleman pulling "sucker" shoots from his tobacco plants. Sweezy called out for him to "light and look at her saddle," which translates into "get out and set a spell."

"Hain't got time," said Amos. "Where's Mary Ann?"

"She's gone atter walnuts to dye some cloth. What's up?"

"Nothing much. We're aimin' to marry this evenin'."

"Marry, the devil!" the old man exhorted.

"No, jest his daughter," said Amos, grinning. "I hain't no notion to marry the whole family."

The bride-to-be appeared, bareheaded and barefooted, with her walnuts. She ran in and put on her homemade shoes and "wagon-cover" bonnet and climbed onto the horse behind her man. Leaving her father standing in his tobacco patch with his mouth agape, the two galloped off in search for a justice of the peace. Amos rewarded the J.P. a quart of his finest apple brandy and a coonskin. Both of these items were valuable and "legal tender."

Around 1851, at age twenty-nine, Amos had put aside enough corn whiskey and brandy profits to buy Cherry Mountain itself. He acquired 100 acres in one tract and 140 in another. Amos quickly got to work and "caused the mountain to blossom as a rose." He grew fine corn, wheat, and oats and was especially proud of his giant cherry trees growing wild on the mountainside. The fruit of all of these, of course, could be turned into spirits.

When the Civil War erupted in 1860, thirty-eight-year-old Amos joined the Confederate Army's 16th North Carolina Regiment. His action was in contrast to that of many other moonshiners further west: in far western North Carolina, Tennessee, and Kentucky, many joined the Union forces. Owens fought with the Rebels in Virginia's Blue Ridge valley and mountain region and also at Mannassas and later joined the 56th North Carolina Regiment, fighting subsequently as a sharpshooter in the siege of Petersburg.

Following the war, during which the federal government reimposed excise taxes on all whiskey and on distilleries, Amos "registered a blood red oath that this tax he'd never pay."

From atop his 3,000-foot high mountain stronghold, with the help of a telescope, he could spy on the revenuer coming from afar, those much-hated "red-legged grasshoppers," as they were called by Zeb Vance, onetime governor of North Carolina. Despite his lookout, Amos got caught on numerous occasions, but never fled.

Altogether during his career of illicit whiskey-making, Owens had nine distilling outfits destroyed and served three terms in the penitentiary.

In 1890, the revenuers arrested him for the fourth time, for the same old offense, and again he was taken before Judge Dick—this time in Charlotte. Now sixty-eight, white-haired, and his back bent with age, Amos' appearance evoked apparent compassion in the heart of the judge.

Asking Amos to stand up, Judge Dick recalled that he had sent him to the pen on three occasions. "You are said to be a man of noble impulses and many worthy traits of character. Your gray hairs should be a crown of glory instead of a badge of infamy. Amos, I can't but believe there are deep and hidden well-springs of good in your nature, and ere I am called to the bar of just God, I shall appeal to the generosity of your better nature. Amos, man to man, will you cease to violate the laws of our country and be an outcast of society?"

An intense hush pervaded the courtroom.

The hardened look of defiance faded from Amos' face, his biographer reported, tears welled in his eyes, his rugged frame shook with feeling. In a voice choking with emotion, he said:

"Jedge, I'll try."

"The effect was electrical," recalled biographer White. "All the judicial dignity in the state could not have restrained the rapturous yell that rose from the audience, packed to overflowing. The sight of the audacious moonshiner, who had hitherto seemed to have a demoniac spirit that no man could tame, weeping with contrition at the bar of justice, and the dignified judge in tears, convinced all present that 'a touch of nature makes us all wondrous kind.' "

The lawyers present, the newsmen, and many others, "including a red-legged grasshopper," shook Amos' hand.

"Then and thereupon, the lawyers of Shelby, Charlotte and Rutherfordton 'chipped in' and bought Owens a fine beaver top hat and a pair of gold-banded eye glasses," White reported.

His granddaughter said that he always had said he would make moonshine all his life and that when he died, he would hang a coffee pot on the corner of the moon and keep on making it.

But Uncle Amos returned home and, as far as history records, never again fired up his still.

In his advancing years, Amos "got right with God," so the story goes, and became a devout member of the church.

He died quietly in his nineties in his "three-story"-long castle atop Cherry Mountain.

8

John Barleycorn's Death and Resurrection

> Preacher: You have a fine country up here, but you have the roughest roads I ever saw. I don't see how it is possible for you to haul over them even the necessaries of life.
>
> Mountaineer: Well, it is pretty hard. But the worst part is that since we have this prohibition law, they make it so mean that you cain't hardly drink the durned stuff after you get it hauled.
>
> —Story told by the late Judge Felix Alley, Waynesville, North Carolina
>
> The pride of the calling has departed. Moonshining, once a gentleman's avocation, is now a business.
>
> —Francis Pridemore

AT 12:01 A.M. on January 17, 1920, protestant church bells rang out across America, celebrating the beginning of Prohibition.

In Norfolk, Virginia, an appropriate funeral service was held for John Barleycorn and 10,000 "mourners" turned out to hear evangelist Billy Sunday give the old boy a final sendoff.

Old Demon Rum, it appeared, was being put to rest from shore to shore, never again to rise. The victim's "body," ensconced in a twenty-foot casket, was drawn by horses and accompanied by twenty jovial pallbearers. In the pulpit, Billy Sunday danced a jig and

102

preached a rip-roaring funeral sermon in honor of America's collective climb aboard the Water Wagon.

"Good-bye John," Sunday intoned. "You were God's worst enemy, you were Hell's best friend. The reign of tears is over. The slums will soon be only a memory. We will turn our prisons into factories and our jails into storehouses and corncribs. Men will walk upright now, women will smile and children will laugh. Hell will be forever for rent."

Sunday's histrionics did not have much lasting effect, and his predictions proved to be woefully inaccurate.

By 1930, the Federal Prohibition Enforcement Bureau estimated that 800 million gallons of illegal booze was coming out of illicit distilleries and gin mills across the country or coming illegally across the borders with millions of gallons being converted from industrial alcohol.* Ships brimming with tanks of whiskey anchored just outside the three-mile limit up and down the east coast, bearing booze for pickup by rum runners. People boiled up whiskey on their tiny "alky cookers," and the moonshiners in the South had dollar marks in their eyes for the first time and ran their stills overtime to meet the big demand, not only for the "fruit jar trade" around their communities, but for the big markets up north.

Actually, Prohibition wasn't very new to the people of the South. They had had comparable laws for a number of years before the Volstead Act came into being. Georgia voted out whiskey in 1907. Alabama, Mississippi, and North Carolina went officially dry in 1908, followed the year after by Tennessee. Virginia joined the "drys" in 1914, West Virginia in 1917. Indeed, these states could have given the nation a lesson on the effects of Prohibition. They were noted for their tendency to "vote dry and drink wet." As Will Rogers was to declare, "If you think this country ain't dry, just watch 'em vote; if you think this country ain't wet, just watch 'em drink. You see, when they vote, it's counted, but when they drink, it ain't." A politician declared that Mississippi, which remained legally dry longer than any other state in the Union after the repeal of National Prohibition, would remain dry "as long as its citizens can stagger to the polls to vote." (Mississippi ended total Prohibition in 1966.)

---

* The Bureau of Internal Revenue had set up a Prohibition Unit to combat illegal liquor traffic, and in 1930 this enforcement unit, with many of its officers, was shifted from the Bureau to the Department of Justice.

II: THE HISTORY

A North Carolina newspaper told a visiting reporter: "I reckon we're what you'd call drinking prohibitionists. This paper, for instance, is dry in policy and principle, but"—and here he pulled a bottle from his desk—"how about joining me in a little shot of corn?"

By the time the United States entered World War I, there were twenty-six dry states. At least they prohibited the saloon and the retail liquor traffic. They did not, however, prohibit the *manufacturing* of liquor. After all, whiskey-making was a major industry, particularly in the South. North Carolina, for instance, had 733 licensed grain distilleries in 1895 and more than 1,300 legal fruit distilleries, turning out well over a million gallons of whiskey and brandy a year. The illicit industry was even bigger (much bigger!)—a situation that held true throughout most of the Appalachian Southeast.

While many of the preachers and the women sincerely wanted the states to end the whiskey traffic, the southern politicians had other motives in supporting dryness. Whiskey, you see, made the Negro assert himself.

W. J. Cash, in his *The Mind of the South*, noted that, as the politicians saw it, "Cuffey [a colloquial synonym for Negro], when primed with a few drinks of whiskey, was lamentably inclined to let his ego a little out of its chains and to relapse into the dangerous manners learned in carpetbag days—to pour into the towns on Saturday afternoon and swagger along the street in guffawing gangs. . . . It seems genuinely to have been believed that to forbid the sale of legal liquor, and so presumably to force up the price of the bootleg product, would be to deprive him of alcohol altogether and so make it easier to keep him in his place. Certainly the argument was much used in winning over the hard-drinking poor whites."

But there was considerable wet sentiment in the South—mainly among the moderates and the realists who wanted to see liquor remain legal but controlled. In 1907, Captain Swift Galloway of Greene County told the North Carolina House of Representatives that he was upset by the rising dry sentiment:

There is an era of fanaticism upon this country, that came here along with the epizootic, the trippe and hog cholera. It came here from the Puritans who landing at Plymouth Rock, who first got on their knees and then on the aborigines. I sometimes feel like wishing that instead of their landing on Plymouth Rock, Plymouth Rock had landed on them. They tell me that in some sections of this State you have laws which make a man a criminal if a certain amount of liquor is found in his home and that a . . . upstart policeman has a right to break into that sacred home, to find out if he can find it. I do not hesitate to say that if I lived in a community of free men who would submit to such tyranny, I should want to get an occasional furlough and get relief from outraged feelings by brief visits to hell.

In 1909, the Tennessee legislature debated the merits of Prohibition. And while the Volunteer State was, like Kentucky, one of the major whiskey-producing states of the nation, the populace ironically wanted to stamp out the liquor traffic. A west Tennessee legislator, Caruthers Ewing, made an eloquent appeal in behalf of whiskey:

> In this sad hour when so many . . . are raving and rioting against the use of intoxicants, I desire to go on record as favoring the stuff. It may be driven from the haunts of men and exiled from the homes of those who love and long for it, but wheresoever it may be driven I want it to know that I entertain for it the liveliest affection and will never permit it to go unused and neglected, if I can avoid it. It has been my fortune to know its virtues, to feel its exhilarating embrace, to yield the response of blood and brain to its amorous touch, to learn its glory and its grief. . . . Intoxicants, discreetly used, have lightened many a burden, silver-rimmed many a cloud, dissipated many a friend of care, made roseate many an unhappy hour and converted many a wail of woe into a 'rippling river of laughter.'

> I have heard much in my time from Reformers who neglect their own business to attend to the business of their neighbors. They think that they are entitled to speak by the mere claim that they never took a drink. I have no more respect for the temperance preachments of a man who never was drunk than for the legal opinion of a man who never practiced law. The man who knows naught of the glory and the grief that lurks in a jug is not qualified to harangue about the liquor habit. It takes a man who in his time has enveloped much booze and beer, who has felt the sad

sagging of the knees, who has doubted the stability and damned the billowing of the firm set earth, and yet felt within his brain the ectasy of universal dominion.

Despite Ewing's impassioned appeal, Tennessee went "bone dry" that year, just as the nation itself did ten years later, in 1919, with the passage of the Eighteenth Amendment, followed by the Volstead Act (1919), which added the necessary enforcement teeth that took effect on Jan. 17, 1920.

While the wealthy and the well-to-do had been able to store up plentiful supplies of booze for the dry spell, the rank and file were not so lucky. But they were not to be denied. They wanted a taste of the forbidden fruit, and were prepared to go to almost any length to get it. While the average citizen had been relatively temperate before Volstead, he became a guzzler in the new environment. "A working-man has to buy a drunk to get a drink," reported the Wickersham investigative committee, formed by President Hoover to study prohibition law enforcement. "He buys a half pint of liquor and he is afraid he is going to lose it, or be arrested, or it will leak out of his pocket, and he drinks it all at one drink."

Up-and-coming bootleggers and gangsters were standing in the wings, ready to fill the need.

The director of the Prohibition Enforcement Bureau, General Lincoln C. Andrews, and his beleaguered agents were faced with a full-scale, nationwide war. The general estimated in 1925 that a half-million Americans were tied into moonshining or bootlegging in one way or another. His agents captured 172,537 stills during that year alone! Between 1921 and 1925, still seizures totaled 696,993. But for every still seized, General Andrews estimated nine remained undiscovered!

In many areas, particularly in the South and Middle West, criminal gangs set up elaborate moonshining and bootleg networks, forcing farmers to run stills for them. Around San Antonio, Texas, the Stephens Gang—with immunity guaranteed through payoffs to the police and Prohibition agents—operated twenty-three combined stills and "cutting plants," in the latter portion of which they increased the volume of booze with adulterants and water. The gang quenched the alcoholic thirst of a wide swath of Texas people—hardy pioneer types who grew up on strong, homemade liquor.

106

While the Prohibition era gangsters didn't really get very far in attempting to control the tough breed of Anglo-Saxons in the traditional moonshine belt of Appalachia, they did offer them a lucrative market. And they persuaded many a mountain whiskey craftsman to go north and put his expertise to work manufacturing booze in the big cities, where the demand was insatiable.

In addition to these professionals, amateur distillers popped up everywhere. One gallon portable stills—which could be operated on a cook stove—sold like hotcakes for six and seven dollars. Magazine articles explained in detail how to sweat the spirit out of a peck of cornmeal. In Birmingham, a moonshiner was caught fermenting garbage in preparation for a run. Americans bought out an old U.S. Department of Agriculture bulletin which told how to produce whiskey by boiling cornmeal mash (properly fermented) in a teakettle, when capturing the steam in a bath towel. Stores in many cities offered distilling supplies including copper tubing, cooking pots, crocks, yeast, malt, cornmeal, charred kegs, and the like. Corn sugar came on the market at five dollars a hundred pounds, and it soon became the prime ingredient in moonshine across the country. Of all bootleg products, however, the hottest item was probably the "peripatetic bar"—a slim flask designed to fit into a man's back pocket.

Across the country, in speakeasies and "blind pigs," moonshine emerged with some odd-sounding names noted by Herbert Asbury in his book, *The Great Illusion*. On the waterfront in Philadelphia, "happy sally" and "jump steady" were the favorite drinks for a time, along with "soda pop moon" which, spiked with isopropyl alcohol, paralyzed the tongues of its victims. Baltimore citizens imbibed "old horsey" and "scat whiskey." "Goat whiskey" gained fame in Indiana and South Dakota. "Jackass brandy," made of peaches, created a stir in some sections of Virginia, causing intestinal pains and internal bleeding—all for a mere four dollars a quart. Around Washington, D.C., and in adjacent areas of Virginia and Maryland, "panther whiskey" gained fleeting fame, as did "old stingo," which some Washington bootleg entrepreneurs put into bottles bearing an Old Lewis Hunter Rye label.

In the South, "blue john" became a popular moonshine in Alabama, Tennessee, and Georgia.

In the black ghettos of Chicago, Washington, and New York's Harlem, "nigger gin," a low grade moonshine, sold for ten to fifteen cents a drink, but it was "awful tastin'." Kansas City "speaks" sold another nasty drink, "sweet whiskey," made by boiling potassium nitrate. Southerners visiting Chicago eagerly bought "yack yack bourbon," moonshine spiked with burnt sugar, iodine, and other adulterants.

While there were a few instances where the whiskey produced was fair to good, industrial alcohol converted to beverage alcohol (or not really converted in many cases) was about the worst. In order to discourage citizens from imbibing the illicit booze, Prohibition officials added denaturants to industrial alcohol to make it undrinkable —such additives as sulphuric acid, wood alcohol, iodine, and soft soap. When the bootleggers got hold of it, they were incapable of really recovering it properly. Most did not have the machinery to accomplish it. And some didn't even try. In many cases they came up with an even more poisonous mixture by adding embalming fluid, rubbing alcohol, iodine, wood alcohol, glycerine, and creosote. Henry Lee, in *How Dry We Were*, declared that lethal beverages such as Jamaica ginger and industrial alcohol, "deliberately poisoned by government policy with such ingredients as aldehyde, pyridine, benzine, nicotine, mercury and other additives, blinded, paralyzed or killed thousands of drinkers." In 1928, drinks containing wood alcohol killed hundreds of people—sixty in New York City alone. "Smoke"—wood alcohol "rectified" by being strained through newspapers—left hundreds of victims unconscious and blinded in New York's Bowery.

Just about the most horrible drink appearing during the Noble Experiment was "jake," an almost ninety per cent alcohol fluid extract of Jamaica ginger with wood alcohol added, which literally paralyzed its victims in the hands and feet. "Jake paralysis" victims walked with a goose step, their feet flopping around out of control. "Jake" was dispensed by drugstores for around fifty cents for a two-ounce bottle and was prescribed for stomach disorders. But drugstores procured it by the barrel load (on permits from the Prohibition Bureau), and it was grabbed up by thousands of eager imbibers, who drank it with ginger ale or soda pop. In 1930, the Prohibition Bureau estimated more than fifteen thousand people had been paralyzed by the drink across the country, five hundred in Wichita alone.

While "jake" was devastating, there were many other moonshine concoctions that merely gave their consumers a very rough time. In the Southwest, "sugar moon," distilled from a sugar beet base, gave an awful hangover. So did "American whiskey," made in Mexico from cacti and potatoes and smuggled into the U.S. where it was given an artificial flavoring and color.

In some areas, excellent whiskey came from moonshiners. Kansas turned out a top-rate corn called "deep shaft," which was manufactured in the shafts of long-unused coal mines in the southeast Kansas "Balkans" region. Travelers would pick up charred, ten-gallon kegs of "deep shaft" and throw them into their rumble seats for aging. Underground stills in the coal mining areas of Ohio turned out "Straitsville stuff" while in nearby Indiana, street salesmen hawked "red eye" for two dollars a pint.

Prohibition was such a farce that United States Senator James A. Reed, one-time mayor of Kansas City, offered his recipes for "pumpkin gin" and "applejack" right on the floor of the Senate. For the first, he said, you pluck a ripe pumpkin, cut a plug from the top, and gut it of its seeds. Then you fill it with sugar and seal in the plug with paraffin. Thirty days later, he said, you could open it up and pour out a scrumptious "pumpkin gin," really a type of wine. This was very similar to "pumpkin wine," then popular through the Midwest. Instead of filling the pumpkin with sugar, however, farmers poured in hard cider, moonshine, or wine, along with raisins, and sealed it up for a month.

In northern New York State, summer residents poured alcohol over ripe black cherries and left the mixture alone until the following summer. They called it "cherry dynamite."

As a poet at the New York *World* put it:

Mother makes brandy from cherries;
Pop distills whiskey and gin;
Sister sells wine from the grapes on our vine—
Good grief, how the money rolls in!

America was on a drinking binge, and to hell with where it came from! Even perfume, hair tonic, anti-freeze and canned heat found a ready market. Doctors sold books of prescription blanks for three dollars a sheet, enabling druggists to dispense whiskey as medicine, for five dollars.

In this atmosphere, the traditional old corn whiskey-maker of the Appalachian mountains underwent a tragic degradation—degenerating from the skilled craftsman with great pride in turning out a fine, wholesome, full-soul product, into a greedy, money-grabbing entrepreneur. Not all of them, of course. Many of the old-timers refused to bend to the new morality and retained their small pot stills, their pride, their patience, and their neighborhood clientele. But they were pushed aside in the outside market by thousands of others, particularly the younger men who, with a knowledge of the rudiments of "stillin'," succumbed to the lure of the fast buck.

Even the method of distilling underwent a vast transformation, to speed up and boost the volume of production. By this time, someone in the hills had already invented the "thumper" keg, which eliminated the time-consuming second distilling step. The thumper, usually fifty gallons in size, is placed between the cooking pot and condenser, and filled with beer. Hot vapors sent bubbling up from the pot through the thumper beer produce a second distillation in the keg along with a rhythmic thumping sound. The resulting whiskey is thus double distilled on only one run. Next, a new type of still was put into operation—a "steamer," which enabled the illicit distillers to boost production tremendously. The steamer sends hot vapors through one or a series of pots of fresh beer, providing very efficient distillations. Many of the early steamers were "stack steamers"—two or three metal drums welded together. In some isolated areas, the groundhog still came onto the scene—giant metal cylinders that enabled a man to produce two or three hundred gallons of whiskey a day and to ferment and distill in the same giant pot.

But the big revolution in making illicit whiskey came with the discovery that sugar could be substituted for most of the grain meal, reducing the production period by three-fourths. Along about this time, corn sugar began coming out of the Midwest by the thousands of tons. Corn growers of Iowa, who had been supplying the legal distilleries, merely diverted their sugar into the illegal channels. They were chastised by evangelist Sam Jones, who told them they should "stop raising hell and raise hogs."

For only $5 worth of sugar—100 pounds worth—the moonshiner could turn out ten gallons of high proof 'shine, selling for $20 to $40 a gallon, or for a total of $200 to $400. By cutting the booze with water and adulterants, a $5 investment would be parlayed into $300 to $500.

In Kentucky, moonshiners started speeding up fermentation by dumping chunks of carbide into their fermenter boxes, which heated the mash but left a deadly chemical residue. Other adulterants that helped to provide the proper bead included sulphuric acid, olive oil, soapwort, lye, and buckeyes.

Two moonshiners of this era got into a quarrel, according to the Asheville *Gazette News*, and one revealed in court his partner's recipe for a liquor called "temperance tipple." It went like this: "Take one bushel cornmeal, 100 pounds of sugar, two boxes of lye, four plugs of tobacco, four pounds of poke root berries and two pounds of soda. Water to measure and distill." This was said to yield 14½ gallons.

The prohibition period marked the beginning of the decline and fall of corn whiskey as a fine art in Appalachia. It was a tragic period of ignoble acquiescence by a high-spirited, self-reliant people who traditionally had displayed an amazing nobility of spirit and character.

Francis Pridemore, a one-time corn whiskey-maker in the West Virginia hills at the turn of the century, was appalled at what he found when he revisited the scene of his stilling career.

Sadly, Pridemore concluded that a skull and crossbones should be placed in every bottle of whiskey coming out of his home region. "The pride of the calling," he said, "has departed. Moonshining, once a gentleman's avocation, is now a business."

Even in the hills of the Arkansas Ozarks, the temptation snared many an honest man. Vance Randolph noted that "such prices as these [twenty dollars a gallon] allow the illicit distiller to make enormous profits, and have tempted many men into the moonshining game who would never have considered such a thing in pre-prohibition days. It is mighty hard for a man to work from daylight to dark, hoeing corn which sells for seventy-five cents a bushel, or cutting stovewood at one dollar and fifty cents a cord," when he could make ten times more for less work.

Almost half the 2,200 prisoners in the Federal Penitentiary in Atlanta were there on liquor charges. In one western North Carolina county alone, several hundred persons were indicted for making and selling whiskey. Most of the violators, who got the traditional year and a day behind bars, came home and promptly went back into the business. Some took less than twenty-four hours to fire up their coppers. This dispatch was printed in a Birmingham, Alabama, newspaper on April 21, 1921:

CLANTON, Alabama—Ocie Mims, who pleaded guilty to the charge of having whiskey in his possession in county court yesterday, and who asked the mercy of the Court and promised on his honor that if he were given the lowest fine he would never deal in whiskey again, was found distilling yesterday afternoon before county court had closed.

Sheriff Gore heard that he and his brother were working at the still, and immediately rushed his deputies, who found the still in operation. As soon as the Mimses saw the sheriff and deputies they ran, but were apprehended by Joe Gore, a deputy, who had to use violent treatment before he could take the men in charge. When the deputy caught Ocie Mims, Watson Mims tried to cut the deputy with a knife. Just at this time, Tom Mims, the father of the boys, came running up, and he and J. L. Easterling, a deputy, wrestled for several minutes before Easterling took Mims in control.

"I have seen many raids," said Deputy J. M. Curlee, "But I have never seen one like this, for the whole family came running to the scene, some praying, some cursing and crying, and in the meanwhile each deputy and the sheriff wrestling with a man."

Claude Baker, who lives in that community, is accused of reporting the still, and last night his house, together with all the possessions of the family, including wearing apparel, was burned. Traces of kerosene used on the house were found. Mr. Baker was not at home at the time his house was burned, as he had heard threats had been made.

The traditional whiskey areas of the Southeast boomed and became famous. One was the "golden pond" area of southwest Kentucky, located on a wild plateau between the Tennessee and Cumberland Rivers. Equally famous was Cocke County in east Tennessee. Thousands of gallons of "silver cloud" distilled white whiskey rolled out of Cocke each night in souped-up cars carrying it to Asheville, Knoxville, Nashville, and points north. Another famous area was Franklin County, in the Appalachian foothills of southwest Virginia: Sherwood Anderson estimated the county's whiskey men turned out 3½ million gallons of illicit booze during a four-year period. One of the favorite sources of corn whiskey for Washington politicians was Signal Mountain, Tennessee, reached by a winding, steep W Road just outside of Chattanooga. One of Signal Mountain's colorful old distillers shipped his whiskey in ten-gallon charred kegs in wooden boxes marked "books." An acquaintance recalled that "the railroad agent would call and say, 'you better come down here, your books are leaking.' People back then were honest in their dealings."

Many non-traditional areas also began to produce moonshine during the Noble Experiment. Down in the Mississippi bayous, isolated islands became the hideaway for many stillin' operations. Rosedale, Mississippi, was particularly noted for its output during the 1920s.

At Hells Hole, South Carolina, on the coastal plain, Prohibition agents raided the "king of the South Carolina moonshiners," seizing eleven stills and 1300 gallons of liquor. (Shortly afterward, the Prohibition Enforcement Bureau hired the distiller as an undercover agent!) On North Carolina's coast, in the Dare County wilderness, moonshiners set up thirty steam distilleries, turning out 50,000 gallons a week. Amazingly, the product was rated an excellent whiskey, being gently flavored by the juniper brown water of Mill Tail Creek. Most of the output, properly colored, ended up sold as bonded liquor in Baltimore.

In California, prohibition agents chained and padlocked a giant redwood tree in which a moonshiner had carved out a room for a still! In Texas, the farm of Senator Morris Sheppard, the framer of the Prohibition Amendment, was found to have a moonshine rig on it, producing 130 gallons of booze a day. In New York, a destitute black was hauled before Judge John C. Knox, charged with running a moonshine still in Harlem. The defendant told about his old aunty's forty-acre cotton farm in South Carolina which she was operating with the help of only a fifteen-year-old boy. The judge sentenced him to South Carolina! The appreciative defendant told the judge: "If I ever see New York again, even on a road map, I will overlook it."

At 3:32½ P.M. (Mountain time) on December 5, 1933, the Great Hypocrisy came to an end when the repeal delegates, meeting in Utah's state capitol building, and hearing the news of Ohio's decisive vote for repeal, voted officially to ring down the curtain with the ratification of the Twenty-First Amendment.

Yet, while the "alky cookers" and rum runners and the speakeasies and the "blind pigs" went the way of the buffalo, the old-style illicit southern moonshiner did not become extinct. Instead, with his states retaining "local option"—i.e., remaining dry—he continued to flourish, although not at the level of affluence he had attained before.

But the fine art of corn whiskey had about had it. The old-timers who had inherited the pride of corn liquor craftsmanship from their forefathers were dying out, and their sons weren't buying the old ways. A much more commercialized moonshining was to be the wave of the future in Appalachia. It would be a long time before the scars of Prohibition would be erased from the hills and valleys and flat-lands of the Southeast. Up to the time of Prohibition, whiskey-making had been a form of defiance, a grand game of hide-and-seek against the federal agents. Now it was becoming a deadly serious business—an organized criminal business that was bound to have tragic consequences.

Students of the mountain people and their mores are agreed that Prohibition turned many otherwise honestly-motivated but ignorant folk into greedy gangsters. Prohibition brought to the mountains more whiskey-making, less dependence on farming, more drunken-ness, and a distortion of the mountain man's traditional philosophy of self-reliance. Then, with the Great Depression coming right at the end of Prohibition, the traditional moonshine country of Appalachia degenerated into America's worst "economically depressed" area, and its people soon began accepting federal welfare doles with few qualms or hesitation, a striking shift from their earlier, long-standing tradition of independence.

To the agents of the Treasury Department, the Prohibition years were the beginning of an era when people learned to have disrespect for the law.*

"We as a nation haven't recovered from it to this day," declared a top official of the Bureau of Alcohol, Tobacco, and Firearms, "and I don't think we ever will."

* With the repeal of National Prohibition in 1933, the Bureau of Internal Revenue organized the Alcohol Tax Unit. The ATU eventually became the Alcohol, Tobacco, and Firearms Division (ATF) of the Internal Revenue Service. In 1973, the ATF was pulled from the IRS and established as a distinct bureau of the Treasury Department.

III

THE LIFE

You just lay there by the juniper
When the moon is bright
And watch them jugs a-fillin'
By the pale moonlight.

Mountain Folksong

9

From Pure Corn
to (Almost Pure) Sugar

A man just back from a trip to the
north Georgia mountains showed us a
gallon of what he called pure doubled
and twisted corn liquor. Said he: "Why
it's so pure you can even smell the man's
feet in it who plowed the corn at laying-
by time last summer!"
—A. C. Jolly, Georgia humorist

NOW that we have an understanding of the art and history
of whiskey-making, Appalachian style, we will take a closer look at
the people themselves—the men and women and young folks who
have lived the moonshine life in its various stages. In this chapter, we
will hear the stories of two Georgia ex-moonshiners, each of whom
represents one of the two past eras of corn whiskey: the pre-Prohibition period of "pure corn," when the distiller took personal pride in
turning out a whole-souled product he wouldn't mind sharing with
his best friend; and the era of corn-sugar whiskey commercialization
that came during Prohibition.

Our first interview is with John Henry Chumley, of Dawson
County, Georgia, a silver-haired old gentleman who is now in his late
eighties. Mr. Chumley (which is his real name, by the way), granted
me an interview in 1971 at the ancient, weathered building he had
lived in for many years. It was situated, until it burned in 1972, on
the heavily-wooded banks of the Amicalola River, a cold north
Georgia stream noted for its clear, swift current, its depth (although
it is not very wide), and its speckled trout.

117

III : THE LIFE

During part of the interview, Mr. Chumley walked beside the swirling stream and showed us a covered bridge nearby, put together with wooden pegs, which his father helped build following the Civil War. Later, he settled down in a swing on his porch, and reminisced about the "good old days" with obvious relish:

Mr. Chumley, when were you active as a moonshiner?

"I done most of my makin' from the time I was eighteen years old—that was in 1905—until I was thirty. I married in '17. Before then I didn't do anything else but make moonshine—straight corn liquor. I made lots of it doubled and twisted, and thumped lots of it—just regular old thumper liquor, you know."

You used practically all corn, didn't you?

"Yes, all corn. It didn't do to put no sweetenin' on it. Not then, we didn't. It'd be too lively and foamy."

Where did you get your cornmeal?

"You could get all you wanted for about seventy cents a bushel. They shipped it in, from Atlanta and everywhere into these towns in two-bushel sacks. Most people that made liquor would buy 100 bushel—fifty sacks. They'd keep a stash of meal hid. You couldn't grow corn as cheap as you could buy it. Hauling and all, your meal didn't cost a dollar a bushel. Anybody that knowed how to make liquor could get three gallons to the bushel anytime. If he just got $1 or $1.50 a gallon, he tripled his money, you see. That was good money then, $1 a gallon."

Did you sprout any of your corn?

"You sprouted the corn and dried it. That made your malt. You'd get your malt corn from just anybody in the country and you'd swell it . . . put it in a barrel and pour water on it and swell it until it was about to sprout and then you'd drain that water off and cover it up real good. It'd sprout in about a day or night, about two inches long. Then you'd pour it out on a wagon sheet or something and then you take it to the grist mill and have it ground like cornmeal. There was grist mills all over the place. Most of 'em was water mills."

And then you put it in your mash?

"Oh, yes! Put that on top of your beer. Put it on and stirred it in real good, and does it work . . . whooooooooo! You could hear it, like meat a fryin', it was working so hard. I've made lots of it, a sight of it that-a-way, but hain't nobody around this country that I know of that lives that knows of how to make a doubling liquor now."

118

Did you have a copper still?

"Yeah, sure did. Pure copper. Everything was. Outlets and every-thing."

Did you make the still yourself right in the woods?

"No, I would hire somebody to make it. We'd go ahead and buy the copper—sheet copper—and we'd take it to a fellow who knowed how to cut 'em out and make the still. He'd charge about twenty or twenty-five dollars for making it. And you'd get the copper real cheap. On the average, the whole thing run about thirty dollars. That was a fifty-gallon still. Hardly ever anybody'd want one over fifty gallons. . . . I did build the furnace under the still. I can go back to them mountains now and just show you old furnaces that I built. The rocks are still there. What we'd do, we'd get soapstone rocks. We'd take an axe and hew 'em square. Then we'd get a bedrock four foot square, put it on top of the first row of rocks, and the copper pot cooker could set on top of the bedrock. You'd leave room back behind it about six inches wide so the fire could go back and then come back front around your still."

In other words, you built the fire under the bedrock?

"Under the bedrock, yeah, and the flames could come up over the bedrock from behind, and come around your still on both sides and come out the flue on the front. That fire would just lap its tongue out there."

What did you burn—hickory and oak?

"Used anything that came along. Lot of birch. These mountains full of birch, you know. Hit'd make a big racket . . . pop and crack, but it'd do the job for you."

Did your still ever get cut down by the law?

"Hardly ever did. I worked down there for several years and got cut only one time. The Law just come in there once in a while. Generally you'd get the news they was coming and slip off. Some-body would always let us know beforehand."

Did they catch you the time they cut your still?

"No, I outrun 'em. I made a 'foot bond' [a play on "cash bond"— he went free by running]. The reason I wuz able to get away, a feller come up on top of the hill and hollered, waved his hat and I knowed to go. There was another feller with me. He went one way and I went the other. We went lickity-split over them hills and hollers. They never did catch us."

When the law cut your still, did you rebuild it?

"No. I throwed it away, you know, and got another one. That's what we done when one wore out. You'd use it so long that the mash would stick on the sides. Even when you cleaned them up, they'd stick all the time. Give your liquor a scorched taste. Just wore out. So you'd get you a new still. For the mash, we used boxes, wooden, sloping boxes. We'd make the bottom of 'em about twenty-four inches square and the top would be three feet. They'd hold [enough for] four fifty-gallon stills full to the box. After a run, you'd put your pot-tail back in the boxes. Mash 'em back in, you know. This would give you sour mash whiskey. The first run would be sweet mash."

Did you make your mash boxes out of pine?

"No, we generally used poplar. If you used pine boxes, lots of folks wouldn't know it, but the first run that was run back in the boxes, that there alkihol would draw that rosin out and the liquor would have the taste of turpentine. We'd buy poplar lumber from a saw mill; a thousand feet of it at a time, and stack it up and let it dry a little before we built the box. Then when it got wet it would swell and be tight as a jug. Wouldn't leak a drop."

Did you have a still-house, a shack around your outfit?

"No, we put it right out, just like right out thar on the creek bank. Sometimes we'd put a shelter over it but the biggest part of the time we just had something to cover up the boxes to keep the mash from getting wet and the rest of the things was open. They got to where, before I quit, got to putting up big posts and putting a shelter up, but now it wouldn't be worthwhile, 'cause they'd [the revenuers] tear it down after you got it put up. Them moonshiners in the mountains wouldn't commence nothing like that now."

Was it pretty hard to get the corn up in there [Amicalola Falls] and get the whiskey out?

"No. They had plenty of mules and good wagons and they'd just come and haul it out. They'd just tote her on out to the road and up and were gone with it. We weren't scared. Didn't care. Never seed any law much then."

What did you put your fresh whiskey in—fruit jars?

"There was plenty of fruit jars, but nobody wouldn't fool with them. Too tedious. We put it in barrels—tens, fifteens, and twenties . . . fifties. The bootlegger'd come get it. They'd put it in one-gallon tin cans and pack it in their cars and away they would go. Once in a

120

while they'd come, maybe get as much as 100 gallons and get it in barrels and they'd bring barrels to exchange with us."

How often did you make a run . . . every day?

"Well, you see the way it was, you'd have enough boxes to know how many to run a day. If you run about four boxes a day, why you'd take sixteen boxes. That'd run you four days. By the time you got to set down and take a break, you would be back where you first started, ready to go again. There was never no stop, and there never hardly ever was but two of us working a still. The way we'd do, we'd set in of a morning, if we was a goin' to double it. We started out and first ran singlings. We would pour that up in the fifty-gallon barrel and strain it and keep it covered all the time. When we got the barrel full, we was ready then to make the doublin'. First we would wash our still out real good and clean and doub the [slop] arm of it real good in there so it wouldn't leak and then fill that pot full of them singlings. We'd put all the fire out but just a little, and then start it right slow, and just barely get it to boiling. When we'd see it was going to boil, we'd get that cap on there so it wouldn't lose none of our liquor. We didn't really want to get it too hot. It had to run slow. Didn't need it much over 170 degrees. The beer'd stick to the still if you got it too hot. Stick around the top. Did you ever taste liquor kinda scorched? The lower it was, the heat, the purer the liquor was. Anyway, when it sticks around the side, you have to keep stirring it until it reaches the boiling point before you put your cap on. You rub the sides of your pot every once in a while with a stir stick. It's a hickory stick with the end of it beat up like an old-fashioned toothbrush. You swab the side of that still . . . rub it and keep it clean. When it got ready to boil, we'd put on the cap and seal it good with rye paste, and weight it down with a rock, and would just get back and lay down and let that doubling run. Out of fifty gallons, you'd make about twenty—good and clean and clear as any spring water you ever seed. When the liquor came out, we strained it through fire coals which we put on top of flanigan cloth in a little copper funnel. When it went into the keg, it was just as clear as that water out there. It was real liquor. It was pure. And you could drink a pint of it and it wouldn't make you sick. It was better than this here old store stuff you buy now; you know, it's all called pure, but this red liquor, you know, it ain't pure."

Did you ever make whiskey out of sugar?

"Naw, I wadn't no hand to fool with it. That's all they make now. It's made out of sugar. It's quick, you know, and it makes much more in a day than you can get by running three or four weeks or a month with straight corn. You wouldn't make no money now the way times is now, fooling with just straight corn."

Did you ever drink much corn whiskey?

"Not much. But everybody kept a bottle in their hip pocket. Everybody nearly that you met out anywheres had a bottle in his pocket. They'd drink it like they do beer now. And it was pure liquor. It wasn't backins."

I guess corn whiskey was really the medicine of a lot of people.

"Oh, yes. The doctors back then in my day they'd tell people to get it and use it and they'd put up bitters and put up different things in it and they would use it and think it was good for them. Never did hurt them. Now if you was to get it and it was just kind of milky looking that wouldn't be no count."

Lots of homes in your day kept a bowl or pitcher of corn liquor on the table, didn't they?

"Well, some places they did. Generally they kept a quart or a half gallon setting up and if they needed any they'd just go get 'em some of it. People didn't drink very much of it then, you know, except just crowds getting out together and drinking. My wife told me just before she died about how you would meet people and they'd say 'you want a drink of liquor?' Just meet on the road, you know. They'd take a drink and go on about their business. You hardly ever seed anybody drunk."

It didn't give you any hangover?

"No. It wouldn't run you crazy. The way the stuff is now, you drink it and you don't know but what you'd be dead in ten minutes."

Could you tell me some of the other people that were prominent old-time moonshine makers?

"Well, they are all dead and gone. Ain't nobody round here now a living. Both of the fellows that worked with me have been dead a long time. I can't think of one that ever hope me make a drop of liquor that's a living."

Our second interview is with seventy-five-year-old Hubert Howell, a sprightly, smiling dirt farmer and onetime cattleman who block-aded in the southern end of Cherokee County, Georgia, only thirty miles or so from where Mr. Chumley spent his moonshining years. Howell's illicit liquor activity spanned the late 1920s and early 1930s (only a few years after Mr. Chumley got out of the business). But in that short interval, the era of pure corn whiskey had about disappeared and "sugar likker"—with grain the secondary consideration —had taken over. Also, by this time, as you will learn in the interview, the old copper pot still had about become passé, along with the painstaking, long drawn-out singling and doubling distilling procedure.

I interviewed Mr. Howell at his beautiful valley farm in Bartow County, Georgia, on three occasions. The last one, in the summer of 1973, in sight of his brightly colored one-acre flower garden. Adjacent was an equally luxurious vegetable garden, a grove of fruit trees, and a grape vineyard. Mr. Howell was working barefooted in his gardens when I arrived, and he graciously strolled back with us to his house for a stand-up taped interview in his garage.

Mr. Howell, when you started making liquor, was it made of pure corn?

"No, mostly of sugar. They just wasn't enough whiskey in pure corn to make anything on it. Now you could take five [100 pound] sacks of sugar and ten bushels of meal and make fifty gallons of whiskey . . . ten gallons out of every sack of sugar. Sometimes, you'd get twenty, if everything worked out right. But using pure corn only, you couldn't get much more'n a gallon of whiskey out of a bushel of meal to save your neck."

What kind of sugar did you use?

"We always used brown sugar. It's cheaper and it's got just as much or more liquor in it. We'd get our sugar from Atlanter. I bought a truck and ever night, I would take it down to Atlanter and load it up with three or four tons of sugar, you see. We paid $3 to $3.75 for a 100-pound sack of sugar."

Where did you get it?

"Not too far from downtown Atlanta. It was a half block off Decatur Street. Just a hole in the wall, run by a Jew. A policeman came by one night as were loadin' up our sugar. The policeman said, 'it goes out sacked up and dry and comes back sloshin' in a can.' The merchant said, 'No, no, no. This man runs a big bakery.' We got our barley malt there, too, at five bucks a sack, and our yeast cakes."

What kind of still did you have?

"During my active days, most people use these barbershop boilers, like a laundry boiler. Little five-, ten-horsepower boilers. Four men could handle them easy. We could pick 'em up and tote 'em. But I learned how to make a homemade steamer, a double drum steamer . . . two fifty-gallon drums welded together and laid horizontally in a furnace. We would make that furnace in the shape of a 'T.' That was my own invention. It would have rock walls in a 'T' shape. We'd use a hillside for the back side. We'd lay that long double drum down horizontally on the top of the 'T.' We'd put the fire in the front and the flames would go under and come all the way around and come out at the ends of the drums. The blaze went all over the drum, you see. We had a pressure gauge on the boiler. Fifteen pounds of pressure was all it would take."

Just how did your steamer still operate?

"We had copper tube connections from the double drum that ran the hot steam vapors first through a heater box, where we had the mash being heated up for the next run. Then it ran into the distilling pot itself. This pot was really two wooden barrels—stack barrels, they called it—one set on top of the other. On the bottom, we had a 100-gallon barrel that we took the head out of. We put a ninety-gallon barrel, with its head knocked out, upside down on top of the bigger barrel. Just set it down inside of it and sealed it up. That pot held about 140 gallons of beer."

Where was your pre-heater box?

"It was up higher. When it came time to fill up the pot again with fresh, hot beer, we had a hose there and we gravity-fed the beer into the pot. They give me a faar hose down at the faar house. They knowed what I wanted. We used the faar hose to deliver the mash and water. That kept us from having to tote it with buckets, you know. Most people toted mash in big old five-gallon buckets. But not us! We had a hand pump, operated by two men. We pulled the water out of the branch with that pump and hose, and we pumped the beer from the vats into the pot."

How did your pre-heater actually heat the beer?

"We had something like a double-wall copper condenser running through that box. The steam come out of the drum boiler into this condenser-like tube that was submerged in the next batch of beer being readied for the still. It was set way up high. From that heater box, the heated beer just emptied into the distilling pot."

124

It was a pretty efficient operation, wasn't it?

"Yes, when we emptied the distilling barrel and refilled it right quick with fresh hot beer from the heater box, we also had to empty the thumper keg of those feints and put in new beer in there. Sometimes we wouldn't hardly get the beer in there but a minute or two before that thing'd start thumpin . . . that quick."

So you had a thumper keg, a doubler, to give your whiskey a second distillation on the same run?

"Yes, and we fixed it up about the same way we did the distilling pot, as a stack barrel. For the thumper we had a sixty-gallon barrel, and on top of it, a fifty-gallon barrel. When that hot steam hits that beer, it just rumbles back through there. Sounds like somebody beating on a barrel with a hammer . . . BOOM . . . BOOM . . . BOOM. After it gets to thumpin' good, it simmers down and just sets there and quivers."

Did your vapor line then go to a condenser?

"Yes. Our condenser was a long, long copper worm and it laid flat in the branch. It was about fifteen feet long. It went fifteen feet up the stream, curved around and came back fifteen feet, went back up fifteen feet and came back. Those whiskey vapors would go through all of that, sixty feet of copper tubing, and sometimes the whiskey poured out real hot. I mean it would scald you! But we allus tried to have the whiskey come out cool. When it came out hot, it would evaporate on you."

Did your beer really get steaming hot for the next run in that preheater?

"I should say so. That still would hardly stop running whiskey. When you emptied the distilling pot, this other [pre-heated] beer was about to boil. You just emptied it into the pot from the heater box . . . and in not over two minutes, the thumper would go to thumpin' and the whiskey would start flowin' from the worm. You could make 400 gallons of whiskey a day on it—400 gallons in eight hours, easy."

You must have had a big crew working with you.

"Had seven men working for me. It took two men to take up the whiskey . . . to take care of the still. It took two more to look after the fermenters . . . the mash boxes. . . . Then it took four men to keep it faared up, to cut the wood with a crosscut saw and tote it. You put mules in there to haul it. Hardwood. But sometimes the men had to tote the wood from a quarter mile away. The hardest job we had was breaking the mash up with them old mash sticks. It took a *strong* back. And at a lotta still sites, we had to tote the sugar in on our backs and bring the whiskey out the same way. We'd bring it out in sacks—five one gallon tin cans to the sack, or forty pounds. We'd take two sacks out at the time and sometimes three sacks—fifteen gallons [120 pounds]. We were men, then, and we didn't mind totin' it. You'd tie two bags of sugar or meal and lay 'em on your shoulder and then put a bag of five empty cans on top of that. I told a lotta people I was branded Dixie Crystals on one shoulder and a meal brand on the other shoulder."

Did you ever strain your whiskey?

"No, because it bein' made with steam thataway, it never did puke. That's what you called it when it got that white [solid matter, meal, etc.] in it. That way you had to strain it."

Is steamer whiskey superior to copper pot double and twisted whiskey?

"Shore is. It's the best they are. It's never burned. Ain't got no burnt taste. Now, on these copper pots, you can't help but scorch the whiskey ever once in a while. Don't make no difference how careful you are, because you've got to empty that mash in that hot pot, you see, and before you can fill it up, it's going to stick and scorch. You've got to use what they called a toothbrush and rub those sides."

Did you ever use syrup for your sugar catalyst?

"Yeah, but I didn't like it. It made a funny taste. Lotta people swore by it, though. They loved syrup whiskey."

What did you catch your whiskey in?

"We'd use a Number 3 [galvanized tin] tub. Had two of those Number 3 tubs. Sometimes before we'd get the first tub emptied into the barrel, or in tin cans, the second tub would be full again."

What proof would it be?

"Ah, it'd be high. A hundred and sixty proof, sometimes higher. We'd add the weak backin's to it unless we had some special liquor we wanted for our friends to drink, then we'd add water. It would still end up a high proof—between 90 and 100, but it would be mild."

Did your customers like it, being mild?

"Most did, but we had a colored bootlegger in Atlanta, from Summerhill there, who told us some of his clients were complaining that

126

our whiskey wasn't strong enough . . . was too mild. The feller I worked with sent me to town to get five pounds of ground up cayenne pepper. He tied it up in a big sugar sack rag and threw it into the thumper. All we sold to this particular colored man was peppered that way. It'd make you sneeze just to smell the whiskey. Hot? Ooooooh, I say. They had to sleep with their feet in the bathtub, drinkin' that. We never did hear any more about the mild whiskey from that bootlegger."

What kind of mash boxes did you have?

"They were made out of old rough pine lumber. I'd go to the sawmill and pick out the lumber. I was always a goin' to do something about the house with that lumber [here he winked at his little joke]. They were sixteen feet long, three feet high, where you could reach over in 'em—and four feet wide. They helt a thousand gallons of mash. I made 'em just like a wagon box. That was another of my inventions. You could take them apart. I'd build the bottom and the sides and bore the holes in there—they were bolted together. I'd build 'em at the house and nobody wouldn't know what I was a doin'.

How many fermenters did you have?

"Had three, each holding a thousand gallons of mash. Fixed up one every day. That was a pretty good day's work. They kept us busy every day. You first put your twenty bushels of meal in the mash box. Then we'd take a big old hose leading from the boiler and pipe that steam into the mash boxes. That scalded and cooked your mash. You'd cook it in one evening. The next mornin', you'd go in there and break it up with a stir stick, thin it with water and put ten [100-pound] sacks of sugar, a 100-pound sack of barley malt and ten blocks of yeast—a block to each sack of sugar. Each block of yeast was about the size of a pound of butter. That's when it would really start rollin' and sloshin'. Sometimes before you left out, it was done rollin' like it was boiling, like it was trying to get out of there. Twenty-four hours later, it would be fermented and would be ready to distill . . . forty-eight hours altogether. It'd take about eight hours to distill that box, about all day. We made about 150 to 200 gallons of whiskey from each of the boxes."

So out of that first sweet mash run, you'd get ten gallons of whiskey for every sack of sugar?

"Yes, that's right, but on every run after that—sour mash runs—

we'd get twenty gallons of whiskey to every sack of sugar. You see we'd slop back—take the pot tail slop from the first run, and pump it back into the mash box. This formed the grain base for the next run of whiskey, and it was already sour. To that you'd add *twenty* bags of sugar. That doubled your sugar and doubled your whiskey. And you didn't have to put near as much cornmeal. You had another box of mash coming up fermented ever day. One one day and one the next. You'd get so taared of it you'd just lay off and quit for a while. You worked day in and day out. Then at night, I would take my old truck to Atlanter and haul back the supplies—the sugar, meal, malt, and yeast. Take me two and a half to three hours to make the round trip."

When your whiskey was distilled, you sold it to a local wholesaler, didn't you?

"Yes, to a country storekeeper, and he sold it to Atlanter and Rome, to the trippers who came in to pick it up. Lot of it, he'd store it in a private home that somebody lived in. But he'd built a cellar under the house, a secret cellar, and put them barrels of whiskey in there. When the trippers came up to his store with their truck or car, they'd turn the keys over to him and tell him how many gallons they wanted. In a few minutes, his car would be taken away to the secret stash. A while later, his car, loaded with whiskey, was returned and he would be told, 'You're ready.' It didn't take long. That was 'hot stuff.' "

Is that all you did, make liquor back then?

"When I was blockadin', I was farmin' too. Raised cotton and cattle and hogs. But in 1930, we sold a bale of cotton for twenty dollars, less than five cents a pound. It didn't pay the guano you put under it. You couldn't make nothin' on it. We would've perished. We would have suffered for something to eat if it hadn't been for that whiskey. Course we had gardens and hogs. But a feller can't live on that. Got to have bread and clothes."

Did you do pretty well by supplementing your income with liquor-making?

"So long as the market held. I sold most of my whiskey for two dollars a gallon. In the late '20s—when the liquor market was strong, I'd buy a new car sometimes every six months. Tear 'em up. They wouldn't be worth nothin' when I'd get through with 'um. Driving around on them rough roads, drive just like somethin' after me all

the time. Just as hard as I could go. It's a wonder I didn't get killed. I
liked a Chevrolet. I have owned Fords. I bought a '27, '28, and I
bought the first '29 car that come to this county. It was a long time
before airy another one come. That '29 was a six-cylinder. Up to
then, they was just four cylinders. And it had four-wheel brakes. I
turned it over in Floridey and tore it all to pieces. Swapped it for a
Ford. I didn't think I'd have enough money to buy enough gas to
crank that thing no more.''

You mean times got hard along about then?

"It got rough. In '33 [the end of Prohibition], the whiskey market
dropped and we made some whiskey for a while that we made only
ten cents a gallon profit on. We sold it for a dollar and ten cents a
gallon and it was costing us a dollar to make it and can it.''

Were you ever caught by the law?

"Never was. Not once.''

How did you manage that?

"When I would work at my still, I figured out a way to escape.
You know they always send up the holler two revenue men . . . great
big fat, pussle-gutted. You know, fellers that can't run. They come
up a holler. All you got to do is go down and meet 'em. They'll come
with their hands out to shake hands with you, you know, then you,
pop! [here he slapped his hands together], go by 'em just like that.
You're done and gone, you see, before these other officers that is hid
around up on the other hill can get down there . . . you're done out of
sight and *gone.* Yeah. Slick. Wallace Wheeler [a well-known ATF
agent] has raided a still that way, you know, and one man'd go this
way and one that way and he'd go and catch this one and handcuff
him to a tree and go back and catch the other'n! He was *that fast.* He
was the *only* man that could ever make me put all four of my feet on
the ground. Wallace Wheeler, yeah. He could run, but he couldn't
run fer. I got away from him *ever* time. I could *outrun* him. I mean,
just flat-footed outrun him and holler, 'Come on, come on, here I
am!' That'd make him mad, you know. Stay about a hundred yards
in ahead of him and whistle and holler, 'I'm right here, come on,
come on.' You'd get out of sight and wait 'til he tracked you up, you
know. Be out on another hill and holler, *'Hey! right up here!'* He'd be
all tired out. Atter a while, he'd just give up, get disgusted with me.
I've had 'em call me by my name, 'Hey Hubert, you need'n to run, I
know you,' but I didn't stop.''

At the end of the interview, Mr. Howell said there were hundreds of old still sites he could take me to where the old furnace rocks are still in place. But he was afraid to go during the summer time for fear of snakes.

"We'll go up there this fall," he told me, "when it gets cold enough to force snakes back in their holes. Don't forget now, come on up and we'll go out there. I can think of one right close to the lake [Allatoona]. The lake when it's high gets over it, but I think we can find it if the weeds haven't covered it over . . ."

10

The Moonshine Pockets

> Although the moonshiner existed everywhere in the mountains, his most noted retreat was the Dark Corners, on the eastern slope of the Blue Ridge. Where is this mysterious and dangerous region? . . . In a general way, it is over towards Hogback, across the South Carolina line. In course of time, one discovers the name to be generic.
>
> —Margaret Warner Morley

WHILE the practice of illicit whiskey-making was painted across the canvas of the rural South in continuing, bold strokes over the years, dozens of colorful patches of distilling activity have stood out—sometimes in relatively small communities such as Dark Corner, in South Carolina; Persimmon and Gum Log in northeast Georgia; Tobacco Road near Augusta, Georgia; and sometimes over entire regions such as Cocke County, Tennessee; Wilkes County, North Carolina; Franklin County, Virginia; Dawson County, Georgia; the Cumberland Plateau in south central Tennessee; and such regions as "Big Bend," along the Florida-Georgia line.

These areas had a lot in common—a longtime liquor-making tradition, a lack of economic opportunity, and a location relatively near metropolitan centers where the booze could be marketed easily and profitably. Most had two other key elements in their moonshine mix—a wild and woolly terrain, and isolation that afforded maximum security from prying federal eyes.

There were three former moonshine capitals of America, and a number of smaller, important "dark corners." Here we take a quick look at their history and character.

III: THE LIFE

DAWSON COUNTY, GEORGIA

Situated about fifty-odd miles north of Atlanta's Perimeter Highway, Dawson County was for years Georgia's undisputed corn whiskey capital, and during part of its history was the country's leader.

America's first Gold Rush occurred in 1828 at Dawsonville's near neighbor to the north, Dahlonega. But the veins didn't hold out very long and when the diggins' got low, the bold Scotch-Irish, German, English, and Irish frontiersmen who had pushed the Cherokee Indians aside to hunt for the precious metal had to find themselves another occupation. Many headed west and ended up in California. And many others plunged deep into the nearby hills and forests and went to making whiskey (which was second nature to most, anyway). Their primary market, reachable by a few days' journey with horse and wagon, was an up-and-coming little settlement called Terminus, located at the southern end of a state-built railroad. In 1847, Terminus (by then Marthasville) became Atlanta. It was a rough and tough "railroad town" with many more saloons than churches.*

In time, Dawson and her sister counties of Lumpkin, Gilmer, and Pickens—which anchor the southern shank of the Appalachian Trail—became Georgia's premier producers of corn whiskey. It was said that there was hardly a mile along any stream in the area that was not at one time "decorated" with a copper pot. Early in the morning, columns of smoke could be seen pouring into the skies from every cover, reminiscent of the smoke signals of the departed Cherokee.

By the early 1940s, Dawson and her sister counties in the foothills were pumping upward of a million gallons of whiskey a year into Atlanta. Stories were told of entire boatloads of sugar being bought

---

* Atlanta's first mayor, Moses W. Formwalt, twenty-eight, was a talented still-maker of French descent who had moved down from east Tennessee. Franklin W. Garrett, in his *Atlanta and Environs* noted that Formwalt's tin and copper business on Decatur Street was quite successful, "and Formwalt was soon selling tinware and copper stills over much of North Georgia." On election day January 29, 1848, when 215 ballots were cast in the mayor's race, some sixty fights broke out. Formwalt, four years later while serving as deputy sheriff of DeKalb County, was stabbed to death by a prisoner.

132

from Batista in Cuba and unloaded at Miami exclusively for the moonshine-makers of Dawson County. Down the kinky, narrow roads into Atlanta rolled a seemingly unending convoy of steel rear-springed Ford coupes, each loaded with around a thousand pounds of white lightning, encased either in one-gallon tin cans, five to an onion sack; or in half-gallon Ball jars, twelve to a six-gallon corrugated case.

Bootleg wholesalers from Atlanta often drove to Dawsonville to negotiate for loads of whiskey.

"What proof you want?" the moonshiners would inquire. (The market usually dictated the quality sought.)

"Just flash speed," the bootleggers often replied, meaning that when you shook the bottle, the bead would hang on top a bit and flash off. This would be around 85 proof.

Other responses were: "We want some with a good shake," higher proof; or, "Give us some with hoss eyes on it." Hoss eyes "was really tops," a tripper remembers, "say 150 to 160 proof."

This was a period when tiny Dawsonville still had only one telephone, a pay phone at a service station. The distillers had their own code for business calls, something like, "Is Nigger Jim buying any apples today?" The words moonshine or whiskey were never used. This was the case even in face-to-face conferences between the trippers and moonshiners. The favorite tripper expression was "stuff," i.e., "You got any stuff today?"

Today, whiskey-making has all but disappeared from Dawson County. Many of its skilled distilling artisans are either "building time" in federal pens or have already done so. Many more have hired out to the moonshine syndicates that have moved into other regions. But the problem, more than anything else, is that Dawson County and its neighbors in north Georgia are in the path of the urban juggernaut. Developers of second-home communities are gobbling up huge chunks of wild terrain, and the sturdy people of pioneer stock and their cherished corn whiskey traditions are being elbowed aside. Atlanta is even talking of perhaps building an airport in the area and has bought 10,000 acres as a possible site. The surviving old-timers are not happy. Among them is a quiet and gentle ex-maker of eighty-four years of age. "I'd shore hate to see that airport in Dawson County," he told me. "You couldn't hear yourself fart."

COCKE COUNTY, TENNESSEE

Of all the moonshine pockets in the Southeast, east Tennessee has the greatest image of them all—pure corn whiskey pouring from its copper pot and silver cloud stills on the side of the Smoky Mountain ridges, made by the hardy "Black Dutch" Germans, French Huguenots, and Scotch-Irish whose forefathers emigrated there in the 1700s and the early 1800s.

So many stories have circulated about the great east Tennessee distillers that it is difficult to sift myth from fact. In the early 1900s, a congressman from Memphis took the floor of the U.S. House to chastise a colleague from east Tennessee who opposed a proper apportionment of the liquor tax:

> Does not my friend know . . . that there is less tax paid and more whiskey drunk in his district . . . than in any other large similar sized territory in the United States? . . . A large majority of my colleague's constituents have not allowed an hour of daylight to pass since they were three years old without testing the quality of some character of exhilarating liquid . . . They have an economy where crops are often measured in gallons rather than bushels . . .

The heart of east Tennessee's traditional corn whiskey country is Cocke County, northeast of Knoxville. Cocke's whiskey-making was centered around the little town of Cosby, in the shadow of the Great Smoky Mountains. During and after national prohibition, train carloads and trucks full of sugar rolled into the area. The saying was: "The sugar comes in dry and goes out shakin'." Cosby moonshiners had a unique way of signalling the arrival of revenuers—dynamite blasts. The first blast, set off by the "lookout" on a road leading through Cosby into the hills, would be repeated by subsequent blasts further into the hills, giving the moonshiners plenty of time to "pull the copper."

Just before World War II, Ernie Pyle, the columnist, swung by Cosby and met a number of its moonshiners. "That day in the moon-

134

shining country gave me a new idea of honor," he wrote. "For one thing, most of the moonshiners weren't criminals at all. They were violating a law, of course, but as they said, how else could you make a living up there? And you don't find vicious criminals having genuine respect and friendship for the men who are sending them to the penitentiary right and left."

Taking Pyle on the tour was J. Carroll Cate, who, as the Prohibition era's chief of enforcement for the area, had arrested and sent to the pen hundreds of the Cosby violators. Pyle and Cate were invited to a fried chicken Sunday dinner by east Tennessee's former "moonshine queen." She told Cate, "Everybody always liked you up here. You played square with us."

I interviewed Cate in 1971 in Knoxville Hospital where he had just gone through major surgery, but he was happy to recall his days of law enforcement in Cocke County. He first went there during the early Prohibition years. "You wouldn't want to meet finer people," he said. "They were honest and honorable. Just poor people. I've turned many a widow woman loose and never made a report. I did it because if I had, her children would have had no food. But there were a lot of violators hauling whiskey out of there into Lexington, Kentucky; Asheville, North Carolina; and Johnson City, Tennessee." On one night Cate and his men captured twenty-eight cars. Most of the hundreds of violators he sent to the pen recieved sentences of a year and a day. When they returned to Knoxville after having "built" their time, many went to Cate's office and asked him for bus fare back to Newport.

Cocke County's days as the moonshine capital of America are long since over. The great majority of its people have turned from the risky pursuit of illicit whiskey-making, and now have jobs in the factories which have sprung up through east Tennessee with the coming of Tennessee Valley Authority.

WILKES COUNTY, NORTH CAROLINA

When the European-descended pioneers charged down the Great Valley of Virginia into North Carolina, one of their major stopping-off points was the Yadkin River on the eastern slope of the Blue

Ridge, in what is now Wilkes County. In addition to providing a rest stop for Daniel Boone on his way into Kentucky, Wilkes County developed into one of the largest corn whiskey production points in America. It is still a production point, although the output is considerably down from previous days.

Wilkes has made whiskey and brandy since 1750. The activity became big business in the '30s and grew to major proportions in subsequent decades. Near the end of World War II, Wilkes' younger blades began sporting little tags on their cars proclaiming their county "The Moonshine Center of America." Many of the older citizens resented the tags. But what really got them riled up was the visit of Vance Packard in 1950 and the article he wrote, which appeared in *American* magazine. Packard wrote flatly that Wilkes was, indeed, the moonshine capital of America, and he estimated that in 1949, a half million gallons of moonshine came out of the county, depriving the U.S. Treasury of 4½ million dollars. The revelation upset the U.S. House of Representatives, which launched a hearing. As a result, the Alcohol, Tobacco, and Firearms Bureau sent in a crew of thirteen investigators headed by Charles S. Nicholson, former special agent in Virginia. During their first month, the crew destroyed seventy-seven distilleries—big "Wilkes-type" steamer outfits.

With tighter enforcement, along with increased vigilance by U.S. Judge Johnson Hayes, a Wilkes native, the distilling business in Wilkes went into a decline. There is still illicit whiskey-making going on in Wilkes, but nothing like it was in the old days—such as in 1935 when one house yielded 7,100 gallons of white whiskey in a raid. The raid was the largest inland seizure of untaxed whiskey ever made in the United States.

THE SMALLER MOONSHINE POCKETS

The output of these colorful moonshine pockets never matched the huge volume of the "big three," but they contributed their share of both excitement and whiskey.

Just up the valley a piece from Cocke County in Tennessee sits Greene County, which claims to have been the place where sugar whiskey was introduced around 1913 by a copper pot craftsman who grew a handlebar mustache. The story goes that the old man and his colleagues carried out a daring experiment by adding fifty pounds of sugar to a bushel of meal in a fermenting barrel. When that ran off, they found that it had made about a case of whiskey—six gallons! Without the sugar they had been producing only two and a half gallons on a bushel and a half of meal. Still, so the story goes, the inventors were afraid to drink the "sugar likker" at first, fearful that it might kill them. One day fresh out of "drankin' likker," they started "teching" the supply of sugar whiskey and found that not only did it not hurt them, but it was downright delicious! The practice spread throughout the region. Little country stores soon began dealing in 100-pound bags of sugar for the moonshiners.

"Oh, law, yeah," declared Drifty Musser, as we will call the former country storeman. "I used to run a store in that Paint Creek section next to the North Carolina line there for twenty-two years. I've sold 200 bags of sugar a week—20,000 pounds." One little country store selling a million pounds of sugar a year! He recalled the sugar liquor originator as being a colorful character who was raised on the lower end of Paint Creek. "He never did get caught. He first moved in here about 1913. Lot of people made likker back then and made it on copper. He'd make all these stills for 'em. I bet there's been a thousand stills carried out off of Point Creek in the lower end where he'd made 'em."

Northwest of Greene County on the Virginia border—Sneedville, Tennessee—is the home of an olive-skinned race of people of corn whiskey renown called the Melungeons who some have said may have been survivors of the lost tribe of Israel. The word "Melungeon" is said to derive from the Afro-Portuguese *melungo*, meaning shipmate, or the French word *melange*, meaning mixture. One popular theory is that they were of Portuguese descent, having come from a band of shipwrecked sailors. Another speculation has them the descendants of Sir Walter Raleigh's colony at Roanoke Island which disappeared mysteriously in the mid-1500s. Still another theory considers them Phoenicians who may have found the Western World two hundred years before Columbus. Then there is the theory that they sprang from Hernando DeSoto's expedition of 1540 that reached east Tennessee.

137

In any event, the Melungeons—a name that the people themselves have never used, incidentally—came to have a reputation for making illicit liquor. At one time, so the accounts go, the tribe occupied the loamy, rich bottomland of the Clinch River, one of the primary routes of the pioneer settlers into Tennessee. During successive waves of immigration by whites pouring down the Clinch valley, the Melungeons were gradually forced onto the higher ridges, primarily Newman's Ridge, 2,400 feet above the river, where scratching out a living was difficult indeed. But for the tall, proud olive-skinned people, the ridge provided protection from the outside world and its prejudices. To survive, they began making corn whiskey, which they sold to the people in the valleys below. They also minted gold coins, which reportedly contained more pure gold than coins from the U.S. Mint.

Over the years, stories began circulating about the mysterious people on the mountainside, particularly about a 450-pound Melungeon nicknamed "Big Betsy," the she-devil queen. The hewn-log, six-room house where she lived is standing today on the ridge. One of the stories is that the queen—"Aunt Mahala" Mullins—became so heavy, due to a glandular disorder, that she was unable to walk and therefore didn't have to worry about being arrested for her bootlegging activities. The arresting officers couldn't get her through the door!

Here is how Henry M. Wiltse described Betsy in his book, *Moonshiners*, published in 1895:

Betsy is a moonshineress, and despite the vigilance and the bravery of Uncle Sam's gallant army of revenue officers, she will remain a moonshineress, no doubt, so long as she is able to pour a drop of liquor out of a keg or a demijohn and count the price of it.

She keeps open house all the year round, and extends to the officers as well as other people a cordial invitation to visit her whenever it suits their convenience. . . . She could not be taken out of the house without taking the roof off and hoisting her out with a derrick; and a derrick could not be taken there for the purpose, for she lives way up on Newman's Ridge, more than three miles from the nearest spot at all accessible with team and wagon. . . . During the greater number of her waking hours, she sits upon a low bed, resting her feet upon the floor, a cask of the 'contraband' always in reach, from which she supplies the necessities of any who honor her with their patronage.

She once sent her compliments to the judge, with the information that she would like to be arrested and taken to court, so that she might see him and something of the world before dying.

This gross woman (six hundred pounds gross) whose body measures nine feet in circumference, whose manners are as coarse as her physical organism; who violates law, defies officers, makes daily traffic of the 'dark beverage of hell,' is not without a spark of sentiment, a trace of those finer human impulses and aspirations which reach out toward the divine. Once every year, she causes her huge bulk to be transported to the cabin window, from which can be seen the graves of her five sons, every one of whom died tragically, and from this spot she watches the decoration of those graves with extravagance of beautiful wild flowers.

The story goes that at her death, her people removed boards from one end of the house reserved for a fireplace, wrapped her in quilts, and gently rolled her down the hill to be buried next to her kinfolk.

Although the prejudice against the Melungeons ended long ago, and intermarriage has taken place for many years now, there are not many Melungeons left in Hancock County, Tennessee. Perhaps 200 families, and most of them older folks. The survivors still carry on many of their mountain traditions, such as digging "sang" (ginseng roots) for the Chinese trade. But moonshining has virtually ended among them.*

A breed of moonshiner similar to the Melungeons—with a similar stoic passion about their calling—lived in the Big Bend region along the wide and meandering St. Mary's River on the Georgia–Florida border north of Jacksonville, not too far from the Okefenokee Swamp. There in the seclusion of the river swamps, the distillers would ply their trade, selling their output to the trippers from Jacksonville and Miami, at one time major moonshine markets. Many of

* Kermit Hunter, the famed historical writer, has put the Melungeon story into an outdoor pageant which is staged every summer at Sneedville, at the bottom of Newman's Ridge. But it does not attempt to solve the riddle of where the Melungeons came from, taking up the story in 1784, when "Nolichucky Jack" Sevier found them.

the swamp distillers also killed alligators and sold their hides, another illegal endeavor.

William R. (Tommy) Thompson, now one of the ATF's top officials and formerly chief of enforcement for the Southeast region, got his start as an investigator in northern Florida, working out of Tallahassee. He remembered the Big Bend area, covering the up-country regions in the counties of Nassau and Baker and Duvall, where the moonshiners would use a "still jigger"—a type of dune buggy—to service the stills. The jigger was never used on a public road, but was driven across the pig trails made by hogs, hunters, and timber workers. "The moonshiners would find a place for a still," Thompson remembered, "then they'd make a little road that would come parallel or right next to a public road, maybe only ten feet across. Then they'd bring in the still jigger." Thus they could transfer their sugar and supplies from a truck over to the still jigger and bring out the whiskey in the same way—and never use the regular road.

At the height of the Big Bend illicit liquor activity, in the 1940s, its output rolled down U.S. Highway 1 into Miami, then a big moonshine consumer. As in other cities, a large outlet was the metropolitan ghetto. The "bumper joints" in Miami's Negro sections dispensed moonshine by the drink, for thirty-five to fifty cents a shot, a common practice of the "shot houses" and "crack joints" in such areas.

"The moonshine queen" of Florida at the time was a hefty woman who ran a night club in Jacksonville called "The Come and Go." Rocking to raucous music, the customers of "Come and Go" were served up a combination of prostitutes and moonshine. The Queen, who went by an alias, Teresa Brown, was infamous as a whiskey runner, obtaining white liquor from the Big Bend moonshiners, and hauling it into Miami. Her arch nemesis was a sharp ATF investigator, Earl P. Carter, who took great delight in foiling her runs. Earl captured her on a number of occasions when she was speeding south with a "wet car." The last time she was caught, she was intercepted by agents just north of Miami, and her car was seized. On investigating, the officers found that Teresa had had the last laugh. The car had been registered in the name of—Earl P. Carter!

Investigators raiding the "queen's" home in Jacksonville found it was outfitted with copper tanks built into the ceiling, the pipes leading down through the wall to a faucet, which was hidden behind a piece of furniture. It was at this faucet that she filled her customers' orders. On one occasion, ATF agents, with search warrant in hand, raided the queen's living quarters, and found her wearing only a scanty apron, and nothing else. "They took her to jail *just that way*," recalled another investigator.

Dark Corner, located in the mountainous northwest corner of South Carolina north of Greenville, was a great producer of corn whiskey from before the Civil War through the Prohibition era. The area's days of blockading were recounted to me by an eighty-four-year-old retired preacher who grew up in the storied land. "There was more likker made, I reckon, around the foothills of Glassy Mountain and Hogback Mountain and Winding Stairs than all of South Carolina put together," he said. He remembered Dark Corner's other big landmarks—the Old Tugaloo Road (now State Route 414), and the Middle Tyger River.

Dark Corner got its name in an unusual way. An old mustering ground there, sort of a community green, was the site where old soldiers met once a year, had "dinner on the ground," and invited in speakers. At one such reunion, governor candidate Ben Perry—not the most popular candidate in the community—mounted the stump, a big two-wheel oxcart. Some devilish boys grabbed the oxcart tongue and rolled the candidate off into the woods. Perry took it good naturedly, brushed himself off and walked back on the green to declare, "Well, gentlemen, *this is the dark corner*." From then on, people referred to it as the Dark Corner of South Carolina, sometimes Dark Corners. Many people around Greenville were afraid to venture into the moonshine land, for fear of being attacked by the natives, or perhaps being captured by the feds on horseback, who were out hunting stills.

What helped give Dark Corner its infamous reputation was that its remote glens, and mountains, being on the border, were a natural refuge for criminals on the run. The most notorious figure to stop there was moonshine-and-murder fugitive Lewis Redmond, the "king of the moonshiners" in the Carolina mountains.

The old preacher remembered, "There was a blockade distillery on every branch up there then . . . making likker. . . . They made it and sold it by the wagonloads. I watched for 'em [as a sentry] when they'd be running off a run. I'd get way up on a hill and when I'd see those revenue officers—they rode horses, you could tell them from everybody else—I'd run and tell my people. They had little paths here and yonder and you couldn't hardly ever catch them.

"R. Q. Merrick was the leading revenue officer of Greenville County and my brother would keep him at his home of a night. Give him a good supper and breakfast. My brother reasoned that if the moonshiners went to shootin' the revenuers and runnin' 'em off, the federal people would just send more up in there. Those revenue officers weren't too bad. They'd come about once a month. If you'd be sort of nice, you know, they'd be nice. My brother, he was a big blockader, but he'd tell 'em, 'If nobody else don't ask you to stay with 'em when you're in our community, you come and stay all night with me.' "

The retired preacher remembered with pleasure how, as a twelve-year-old boy, he would drive a team of mules, pulling a covered wagon into Greenville with five five-gallon kegs of corn whiskey inside, plus a few clay jugs full. "My brother, he'd put me in that wagon and I'd drive it to Greenville. He'd come on by me in a buggy and meet me later down at the Greenville Livery Stable. The officers, they wouldn't hardly notice me, and they didn't bother me. It took all day to drive [the twenty miles] to Greenville.

"Wasn't many people that didn't drink that corn likker back then, but you hardly ever saw a drunk man. In Greenville, they didn't put a drunk man in jail. If someone got drunk, his friends'd just push his body up against the wall on Main Street there and when he got ready to go home, they'd just put him in the wagon and take him home. Well, he wasn't a doin' a thing. Just got drunk and went to sleep. They'd say, 'Where's he from?' 'Dark Corner,' they'd reply."

When he was fourteen, the youngster was converted to Christianity and went to college and became a preacher. His brother went into the ministry also and between the two of them, they began preaching the gospel among the poor people left in Dark Corner who had remained in whiskey-making. "One sermon up in there was worth six months' work of a revenue officer. Many of them stopped making whiskey. . . . They came off the side of the mountain to school. One of my students came out of a blockade distillery and his father made enough liquor to wash this house away. He'd haul likker to town as a little boy, like I did. He went to school with me and later went to preaching. I helped him out after he went to preaching. I'd help him get meetings to hold."

The old Dark Corner of pioneer days is gone. Today it is thickly settled and fine homes are perched on the mountainsides, alongside the road that crossed the mountain ridge from Hoback Mountain on across to Tryon, North Carolina.

As a footnote, you can't find Dark Corner on any map of South Carolina today.

On the coastal plain of southeastern North Carolina is an Indian settlement known for its whiskey-making. It is populated by Lumbee Indians, who are concentrated around Pembroke in Robeson County. Famed for their energetic battle against the Ku Klux Klan in the 1950s, the Lumbees, like the Melungeons, are also said to have descended from Sir Walter Raleigh's Lost Colony settlers, which in the case of the Lumbees is much more plausible because the Colony was not far away. The theory is that in the late 1500s the members of the Lost Colony went to live with the friendly Croatan Indians on an island the Indians occupied. The Sir Walter Raleigh settlement disappeared between 1587 and 1591. The Indians subsequently moved inland and settled on the Lumber River around Pembroke. In the 1700s, the Scottish Highlander settlers coming into North Carolina discovered the Indians, who thereby became the Lumbees and were already speaking English.

Many of the surnames among the 40,000 Lumbees now residing in Robeson County, in North Carolina, are the same as those of the Lost Colonists. The Indians own fertile tobacco farms, and one can travel many miles in the county without losing sight of Indian-owned farms. The Indians are also active in moonshining—mainly using very small, family-type stills. At one time, it was estimated there were more illicit stills in Robeson County than anywhere else in the country. As a judge of the area said: "Put a Lumbee and a swamp together and you've got a still."

The stills were so numerous, according to a former agent in the area, Clarence Paul (now the ATF's laboratory chief in Atlanta) that "we could go to the Lumber River and chop up ten to twelve stills on any afternoon. . . . They were lined up beside the road. I had never seen moonshining in western North Carolina carried out to that extent."

The ATF's Tommy Thompson said, "They had an intertwined system—a network of producers. They would pool up a load. Say a person wanted a truckload of whiskey. The Lumbees pooled their whiskey for him."

Further down the coastal plains, in South Carolina, bands of moonshiners lived along the river swamps. All of the rivers through the coastal plain were noted for their moonshine nests, and this was particularly true of the Great Pee Dee River in Marlboro County. It was in Marlboro County that I received my introduction to moonshining as a fine art. Except that it turned out, for me, to be a very brutal art.

It was in 1961 and, at the time, I was associate editor of the *Florence Morning News*, located in the heart of South Carolina's coastal plain tobacco belt. It was a hot summer day when I drove up to Marlboro County in the Pee Dee River basin and interviewed one of the area's leading farmers about his conservation practices. The heat and humidity hung oppressively.

Leaving the farm, I elected to take a shortcut through a little crossroad community called Blenheim. To reach Blenheim required my driving a mile or two down a dirt road to a paved "farm to market" highway, which in turn would take me to the town. Soon I crossed a narrow blacktop, but was not sure this was the road since there were no signs. From one of the fields, a black farmhand walked up and I swung my Renault 4CV around in a U turn and asked directions.

"Just take that road back there," he said, with friendly courtesy. "Could I ride with you a piece down that road?"

I invited him to get in.

Before I could start up, a late model Ford pulled up beside me with two people in it. The passenger, a burly, bronzed young white man—not over thirty years old, it appeared—grinned broadly, almost jokingly, and said, "Howdy."

I could smell liquor on his breath; sort of a rancid, foul-smelling odor, something I hadn't smelled before.

"Who are you?" he asked, still holding his big grin seemingly frozen in a half-joking demeanor.

"I'm just a passing through," I told him, sort of mimicking his joking vein.

I drove off and left him parked there in the road.

A quarter-mile down the road, after I had let the black hitchhiker out at a shack, the Ford roared up beside me as if to pass, then stayed

144

alongside for a while. Except for our two cars, the road was free of automobiles. The car pulled in front, slowed down, and let me pass. Then it came up and bumped me from the rear. The thought flitted through my mind that the people in the car were local Klansmen, who didn't like it a little bit that I had offered a ride to a Negro. After a while, the car dropped back. I determined to get its license plate number if it came into Blenheim.

A wide place in the road, with big trees all around, Blenheim was virtually deserted except for a group of boys whiling away the humid afternoon in front of a store. I pulled under the shade of a tree near the crossroad intersection and got out to wait. South Carolina automobiles carry license plates on the front as well as the back, so I pulled out my notebook to write down the number. I didn't have to wait long. Around the bend the Ford eased in at about twenty miles an hour. I quickly wrote down the license number and jumped back into my 4CV.

This time, the smile was gone from the face of the young man. He barreled out of the car before it stopped rolling.

"Who *are* you, anyway?" he demanded through the window of my car. I could see he meant business. As he towered over me, I could see that he was really tough and strong and blocky.

I froze in fear.

"I'm a newspaperman. I'm with the *Florence Morning News.*"

"Let me see your *credentials*," he demanded.

I never did carry a press card in Florence, never needed one really. I desperately wished at that point that I had. I did have a few gasoline credit cards, and I thrust a plastic Gulf card out the window. Obviously he couldn't read. He studied the card very intently and deliberately.

I was getting more panicky by the second and wanted desperately to get out of there. So I jerked the card back.

This infuriated him. He yanked open the door, grabbed me in a vise-like grip under my arms and dragged me out of the car. Then he slammed a huge fist into my breastbone and sent me sprawling on my back in beautiful downtown Blenheim. He stood there mumbling in anger. I jumped up and ran over to the youngsters on the corner.

"Who *is* he?" I asked them.

No one would answer. It was obvious they were on *his* side, and that they appeared to be wondering, as he was, who *I* was.

My adversary, still in a fit of anger, stalked back to his friend's car, and I got back into mine and pointed it in the direction of Florence. *Very slowly.* Because he was following me again. After a mile or so, he turned back toward Blenheim. I floor-boarded my accelerator.

Arriving back home, I pulled off my shirt and discovered blue marks under my arms where he had manhandled me. Plus purplish and blue spots on my chest.

Still, I had the license number, and I called the gentleman farmer in Marlboro County whom I had interviewed and asked him if he could find out anything. He called back the next morning.

"You know who beat you up? Robert Lee Blue. He is one of the biggest *moonshiners* in Marlboro County! The driver was the son of the mayor of Blenheim. I suggest you come up here and swear out a warrant."

Later that day, I returned to Bennettsville and the picture began to clear up. Federal probation officers informed me that Blue, already on probation for whiskey-making, had been arrested by Federal ATF agents the previous weekend and had been implicated in a multi-state moonshine ring. When Blue spotted me in his area, he jumped to the mistaken conclusion that I was a federal agent, responsible for his arrest. He also concluded that the black farm worker was the local informer. I learned that following my run-in with Blue the previous day, the moonshiner beat the Negro unmercifully, practically blinding him in one eye.

Federal agents advised me not to bring a case in local court, but to testify in federal court. They were ready to try to get Blue's probation revoked. Blue had also beaten up a Bennettsville policeman.

As the agents suggested, I did not press local charges. Then at the hearing on a request for probation revocation, held before Federal Judge C. C. Wyche, in the U. S. District Court in Charleston on July 12, 1961, I testified as to Blue's attack on me in Blenheim. Judge Wyche revoked Blue's probation and sentenced him to serve out the three remaining years of his original five-year probation in a federal penitentiary.

The incident illustrated to me the character and nature of the modern-day moonshining business. It also gave me a greater appreciation for the skill of the Alcohol, Tobacco, and Firearms undercover men—those fellows who risk life and limb by getting out amongst the distillers and the bootleggers to build a case against them. In this particular case, ATF investigator Raymond Harrison, posing as a bootlegger, had on May 8 of that year bought forty-eight gallons of moonshine whiskey from Robert Blue for $176 and Blue apparently never suspected that Harrison was an ATF undercover agent!

Interestingly enough, Marlboro County, up until South Carolina adopted a legal liquor system for all counties (with no local option), had the distinction of having had the longest unbroken dry record of any community in the United States. The Charleston *News & Courier* of July 27, 1905, noted that Marlboro at that time had been dry for 100 years, a situation "brought about by public sentiment rather than legal enactment."

It would be impossible to attempt to catalogue all of the interesting moonshine pockets in a brief survey. For instance, we did not detail the colorful Prohibition moonshining center of Golden Pond, Kentucky, which today is a great park land flanked by two beautiful lakes on the Tennessee and Cumberland Rivers. Similarily, we skipped over Franklin County, in southwest Virginia, and areas throughout eastern Kentucky, West Virginia, Alabama, Mississippi, Oklahoma, and the Arkansas Ozarks.

But, the areas we have covered provide a fair reflection of the shape of the illicit enterprise throughout the region—an occupation still a long way from being totally subdued, but one that is on the road to extinction.

11

"Tripping" Moonshine: The Hard Chargers from the Hills

> Haulin' whiskey, that wuz our living.
> The old ones made the likker and the
> young ones hauled it.
> —Retired corn whiskey tripper

THE best liquor car I ever had was a Kaiser-Frazer. You know how big and bundlesome they were. We took the front seat out, and the back seat. You could get about twenty-five cases in it—150 gallons—and you'd be settin' on whiskey when you wuz drivin'. You'd stack it up to the window and put a big old Army blanket over it.

"That Kaiser-Frazer was just like a big ole hull. One day I was going to Atlanta with a load and right where Happy Herman's is now, on Cheshire Bridge Road, there was a wreck and a policeman was directing traffic. All he had to do was look in my window.

"So I said, 'What am ah *goin'* to do now? I'm caught *for sure.'* There was this wreck and a long line of traffic easing along. I knew that when I got to that wreck, that policeman'd be right on me. So I just opened the door on that Kaiser-Frazer and *helt* to the handle. And what I was goin' to do was what we call bailin' out. He woddn't [wasn't] goin' to get me. I opened it . . . just cracked it real good and right when I got up to him, he happened to turn his head the other way and blew his whistle for me to go on. I said, 'I'll talk to you later, podner!' "

To see and hear him now, a neatly dressed, sophisticated-in-the-rough, greying-at-the-temples southern gentleman who has become a millionaire entrepreneur in the last decade, you would find it difficult to imagine that twenty-five years ago he had gotten his start as a moonshine tripper, a liquor hauler, the transporter of illegal white booze from out of the hills of north Georgia. But such were the temptations available to bold, young men after World War II, that for the daring and the knowledgeable, there were fortunes to be made in moonshine, particularly in the bankrolling, hauling, and bootlegging of it. And of all the people who have had a hand in the illicit whiskey enterprise—the master distillers, the still hands, the servicemen, the bootleggers, the financiers, and the trippers—it was the latter, the transporters, who took the greatest gambles, the constant risks of being nabbed by the federal or state or local law officers, and facing the likely possibility of being sent to a United States penitentiary in Chillicothe, Ohio, or Atlanta, Georgia, for at least a year and a day of reflection.

One of America's first trippers was John Hancock, a Scotch-Irish Bostonian who, in addition to brushing the boldest signature on the Declaration of Independence, smuggled Madeira wine into Boston and once locked up the British customs officer there. In England, for centuries before, evasion of the excise had been a national pastime. The country's seacoast was honeycombed with smugglers' nests up to the mid-1800s. Where there has been illicit whiskey-making, there has always been some kind of illicit distribution system. In the saga of corn whiskey in America's Appalachians, the "tripping" of the liquid contraband has left an indelible mark—a story of good ole boys from the hills and coves rising up Cinderella-like from ignorance and isolation and poverty and becoming dare-devil somebodies with great speed and power and great wads of greenbacks, challenging anyone who stepped in their path.

But the true tripping phenomenon came only with the trauma of National Prohibition. Before that, in the 1700s and the 1800s, getting illicit whiskey to the consumer was a rather simple exercise. Other than the delivery of barrels and kegs of homemade liquor in horse-drawn wagons, on horseback or by boat, most of the traffic was in-house: the consumers came to the stills. Before and after the turn of the century, "rat houses" had been part of the Appalachian frontier scenery—small log cabins seven or eight feet square with tiny openings next to the road. The buyer would pass his jug into the hole, along with his money. From the inner darkness would emerge the filled jug, with only the hand of the seller to be seen.

Hollow trees had a big role in moonshine marketing folklore. In Cherokee County, Alabama, thirsty citizens would deposit their money in such a tree, ring the bell, and saunter down the road, returning a few minutes later to pick up their package of liquor. In the North Carolina foothills a choice watering oasis in the twenties was an old apple tree where one could call up a jug of the choicest nectar of the hills by blowing on a trumpet that hung from a tree limb—one blast per quart. From out of the woods would emerge an old gray horse with the jugs in a sack draped across his back. Upon the placing of the payment in the sack, the horse would turn around and slowly amble back into the forest from whence he came.

Often the method of delivery was more ordinary. In West Virginia, a moonshine bootlegger tromped the hills on foot, delivering to his customers house to house, carrying his contraband in hot water bottles. In another area, a peddler who hauled jugs of corn whiskey in his saddlebags found a ready market among people going home from church. Many bootleggers established regular routes, like a milkman, and deposited in the mail boxes of their customers daily jugs of whiskey inside shoeboxes. And as we have seen, mules and horses were often pressed into service, two kegs balanced on their backs.

But Prohibition's Volstead Act in 1919 changed the easygoing corn whiskey distribution system. Corn whiskey went big-time— attracting fabulous prices from thirsty consumers everywhere, but particularly in the major cities, where the big gangs contracted for every drop of homemade whiskey they could lay their hands on. Medium-size cities across the South, such as Knoxville, Chattanooga, Greenville, Asheville, Atlanta, and Columbia, and even smaller cities, such as Rome and Athens (Georgia), blossomed into attractive moonshine markets, and haulers and trippers (sometimes referred to as runners) suddenly were in big demand, and yielded to the attraction of the big money. They quit their two-horse wagons and bought touring cars, those big, old boxy Cole-8s, Packards, Lincolns, Franklins, Chryslers, Cadillacs, Buicks, LaSalles—and the smaller and cheaper two-door Fords and Chevrolets. In the 1920s, haulers found they could make enough money on one run of moonshine to buy a new Model A Ford. Many would trade their old car in on a new one every few months. The saying of the time in the rural South was that if a man owned an automobile, he was bound to be involved in illicit liquor in some form or fashion.

Jesse James Bailey of Asheville, North Carolina, now in his eighties but still standing almost as ramrod tall as he did when he was sheriff of Madison and later Buncombe County in far western North Carolina, remembers clearly the touring-car trippers of the '20s who chugged through the mountains of "Bloody Madison" with loads of white lightning from Newport in Cocke County, Tennessee, bound for Asheville, over on the other side of the Appalachians.

"I was on Walnut Gap one night in 1921 with my deputies—on the highway between Marshall and Hot Springs—and you could see them coming for three miles, making those sharp turns around those mountain roads. Those lights kept swinging around . . . swinging around those curves. We had this old Ford cranker. We got it across the highway. I put my two deputies out there beside the road. The usual method of the trippers, they'd come around a curve and see the road blocked, and they'd jump out and high-tail it and leave the car and the liquor. They figured they could lose every third car and still come out with a profit.

"In this instance, I had a double barrel shotgun. I put my deputies back down the road hoping to catch the trippers . . . only it didn't work out that way. They came around that curve in their three-speed Overland. They put the gas on and run right up close to me. When they seen they couldn't get by, their next thought was to turn around, and when they did, I let both barrels go into the righthand rear tire. It blew right off. My men jumped in my car and by the time I could get it cranked up, they were four miles ahead of us. You know, I run those sons-a-guns all the way down to the Laurel River. Ran them twelve miles and them on a rim! I just kept on and on. We run around this curve. They were stuck in a mud hole. They jumped out into the woods. We got the car and sixty-six gallons of white liquor. But we never did catch the men."

The story of the trippers is partly the story of their cars.

A favorite car among the early trippers was the 1926 Model T Ford roadster which could hold ninety gallons of whiskey in one-gallon cans, or thirteen or fourteen cases of half-gallon fruit jars. A mountain mechanic—not a tripper—installed a system on his '26 Ford that caused the headlights to turn with the wheels, a handy device for anyone traveling fast on winding roads. A moonshine tripper came along and talked the mechanic, "Uncle John" Wellborn, into selling it to him, which he did, for a price.

The 1929 Chevrolet touring car was modified into a liquor "trip" car by the installation of horizontal, box-like traps underneath the floor on either side. The cars were also outfitted with a storage area in the back seat. A false back seat was built with a door in it, providing a big storage area. Once the trap area behind the seat was stacked with cans or jars of liquor, the door would be snapped shut, and the upholstery cover draped back over the false seat. This kind of car had a capacity of around 125 to 135 gallons, none of it visible.*

But roominess soon gave way to speed and performance. With the exception of a few hot rod buffs, about the only people interested in high performance cars in the '20s and early '30s were the liquor runners. From the first, Fords were far and away the trippers' favorites. Some of the early Hudsons and six-cylinder DeSotos were fast, but they were conspicious by their rarity, in contrast to the Fords, which were liberally sprinkled around a community. On the 1934 Fords, the moonshiners' mechanics in Atlanta machined off the

---

* Up to the turn of the century, five and ten-gallon oaken kegs and one, two, and five-gallon ceramic jugs (demijohns) were utilized to haul the whiskey out of the mountains in wagons. Some of the earliest automobile trippers brought the spirits out in barrels, also. Later, a five-gallon "jimmy jug" was used, particularly in the Appalachians. It was a round, metal water cooler type jug with a plywood-like exterior. Big and bulky, the jug often leaked when jostled in a car. Soon the trippers turned to the container that became synonymous with moonshine—the open-mouth, half-gallon Ball and Mason fruit jars used by farm women to "put up" vegetables and fruits. The filled jars would be packed twelve to a corrugated paper box, constituting a six-gallon "case."

But the really popular moonshine container, at least in the region around Atlanta during the Prohibition era, came to be the one-gallon rectangular tin cans with cork tops. These "jackets" were packed in onion bags or burlap "tow-sacks" at five cans to the bag—with holes slit in it for the cork of each can. Once securely tied, a bag of five cans remained as a unit through many round trips between the distiller and the bootlegger. To avoid delay caused by the siphoning into the cans, many trippers kept their moonshiners supplied with bags of cans. "Every time we went up to Dawsonville, we took them a load of recorked cans," an ex-tripper recalled. "They'd have our other cans filled and we didn't have to wait for the siphoning." Many trippers insisted that the cans be filled at an angle to eliminate the "gurgle," which would change the center of gravity on a curve.

One-gallon glass jugs—in some cases used Coca-Cola syrup jugs—were another favorite container. In some areas, five-gallon "GI cans" were used successfully. Today, one-gallon plastic milk jugs are the universal container. Trippers can stack thirty plastic jug cases, or 180 gallons, into a car—much more than they can carry with jars or cans.

cylinder heads to raise the compression, and with the '37 and '38 models, bored out the cylinders, put in oversize valves and ground the crankshafts to increase the stroke. These changes speeded the cars up considerably. Some mechanics installed the larger Mercury engines, retaining the Ford connecting rod.

Along the new U.S. Highway 41, from Atlanta to Marietta, known as the "four lane," Atlanta's young crowd gathered for Saturday night dances on the Chattahoochee River Bridge at the end of the construction. On the same spot, a few years later, the liquor runners proudly displayed their souped-up machines, growling and roaring with the first taste of real speed. They considered they had a worthy entry for the moonshine-tripping big league if their charges would cross the bridge at 100 miles per hour and, after a mile-long climb up the new road to Marietta, could top the crest at no less than 75 miles per hour.

In the early '40s, the trippers developed into rip-roaring daredevils who literally tore up the dusty, red clay back roads from the hills of north Georgia leading to Atlanta or Asheville, North Carolina, and Greenville, South Carolina.

One of the transporters who quickly established a reputation for seemingly reckless abandon was a tall, dark-haired "Rudolph Valentino of tripping," who let his hair drape down over his ears. On one series of runs on the forty-five miles between Dawsonville and Atlanta, he burned up a set of tires. Arriving in Dawsonville for his fourth load, he called his boss in Atlanta and told him he needed to buy a new set of rubber. He was ordered back dry (empty) and told to find another job. His mechanic from Atlanta recalled the tripper's driving style: "He was just sliding around the corners and curves. He never even bothered to pick up his damn feet. He never knew what a brake wuz. When he come to a curve, he'd jus thow on the gas, pitch the car sideways and sail it through—skate through. That's the way you drive a sprint car on a dirt track. Drive with the footfeed and the front-end. You pitch it sideways and get it to corner and if you're not turning far enough you get in a little bit deeper, it makes you turn a little further. The front wheels will be actually turned in the opposite direction to the way you want to go, just as on ice."

The trippers had a number of alternate routes into Atlanta's downtown area which they dubbed the "Toddy Trail." A great percentage of the liquor coming out of northeast Georgia—particularly

153

from the Dawsonville–Dahlonega area—came down State Highway 9, today's U.S. Route 19 (also Roswell Road) then via an exclusive residential area, to the stash houses. One common route into downtown Atlanta was off of 9 south onto Piedmont Road, until 1950 a narrow, twisting street. The "moonshine Valentino" would whip around its winding curves with wild abandon, his cargo of liquor bouncing around merrily. A country boy riding shotgun on one run became panicky on the Piedmont stretch and held onto the dash for dear life. The story went that he bent the dashboard with his grip, leaving his fingerprints embedded in it.

"Valentino" met his match when two federal agents jumped him in Dawson County, ran him for eight miles, and shot off his tires. A retired ATF agent recalled the scene: "It was around two or three in the morning. The ground was frozen. The driver ran off in the woods and left his car load of whiskey. Then he came back to our car crying, saying he wished to God one of our bullets had hit him in the back of the head. He was ashamed of being caught by revenuers and having to go back home and face his friends. He was just a kid. But he was the best country driver I've ever seen."

Ford two-doors and coupes became increasingly popular with the transporters. The '39 two-door, for instance, could handle 125 gallon-size tin "jackets" of liquor (weighing in at 1000 pounds plus the weight of the cans), which served to give the car added stability on curves but slowed it down on hills. The haulers "hulled out" their automobiles, removing the bracing between the rear seat and the trunk, thereby providing payload space all the way from the trunk door to the front seat. Many drivers also removed the shotgun seat, leaving only the one bucket seat for the driver. To compensate for the heavy loads in the rear, mechanics put in override springs. Their favorite modification was to take the rear springs off of Model T Fords, heat and curl the ends and mount them onto the axles of '40 Fords, a favorite of trippers. With this "cross spring," the loaded car would sink no more than an inch. The trippers also over-inflated their tires to handle the heavy loads. In later years, they used load levelers, "clip coils," and air-lift springs.

Cars with stiff springs would bounce a lot on rough spots when empty, and were easily spotted by lawmen. Two in particular, Cal Cates and Burton Carroll, Fulton County (Atlanta) policemen, who patrolled the main roads leading into the city, always kept their eyes open for such stiffly bouncing cars. The two policemen, recalled an ex-moonshine mechanic, "wuz rough customers, son. Their favorite hangout was the old Speedway Service Station on old Highway 41, north of Atlanta. Carroll had a Buick. I believe Cates drove a Pierce-Arrow and a Packard. If they got atter you, you had to sack it up and go, because they wuz flat goin' to run you. But now, they wuz *good fellers*, understand."

During the early highway encounters, when the police were without the benefit of two-way radios, the chases that ensued were real car-to-car and driver-to-driver battles, the winners being the ones having the best engines and exhibiting the smartest driving strategy.

"We could catch up with 'em a lot of times, but then the problem was stopping them," said Carroll. "We either had to bump them off the road, wreck them, or puncture their tires." His favorite tactic, used by many, was to bump a car from the rear at the proper point on a curve, causing it to spin out. State revenuers sometimes spot-welded a ninety-pound rail around the frame of one of their cars, to bump their liquor-tripping adversaries. One month in 1937, State agents claimed to have put fourteen new liquor cars out of commission. "You run into the side of a car with that thing and he'd know he'd been hit," an ex-agent recalled.

One night, Carroll spotted a tripper on Atlanta's Marietta Street near the Chattahoochee River Bridge. The tripper deliberately slowed down going into the curve because he figured Burton was preparing to bump him. Just as Burton speeded up to make the kill, the tripper threw on the gas, roared out of sight, and the policeman almost lost control of his own vehicle.

Every moonshine tripper worth his salt had an "opera coupe" '40 Ford, which had folding seats (and a bucket seat for the driver) and seemed to be made to order for hauling illicit booze. In fact, the '40 Ford coupe became the all-time favorite car for hauling liquor because of its speed and maneuverability and because, when carrying a load of 120 gallons of liquor, it would hug winding mountain roads like a bobcat, even more effectively than when empty.

One night, Carroll was barrelling down Atlanta's Northside Drive, chasing *two* '40 Ford coupes, each of them driven by well-known members of the liquor-tripping fraternity. Carroll barked into his radio, "Am headed in on Northside Drive at Collier Road. They're both in front of me." A minute or so later, topping the hill, he came back on to say, "Damn, I'm meetin' them going back!"

The drivers had executed the "bootleg turn," the big turnaround, throwing their cars sideways, skating, and spinning around in the road. Some drivers did it by throwing the gear into second, making a sharp turn and letting the car swing around by itself. Others put the car into a skid, pulling on the emergency brakes lightly, turning the steering wheel sharply to the left, and then accelerating madly—all requiring split-second timing to avoid turning over.

Carroll got into another hot chase with a moonshine car in downtown Atlanta. It was a rainy, slick night when he spotted the car and gave chase. "We went up and down the streets downtown. We were slipping and sliding, bumper to bumper, all over the place." At Henry Grady Square, the cars merged into a merry-go-round race at sixty miles per hour around the statue of Henry Grady, the "New South" orator and editor. After a few tire-squealing two-wheel turns, Carroll angrily slammed on his brakes, jumped out, and captured his thoroughly surprised adversary.

In many cases, though, the police and revenuers, frustrated because their cars were inadequate to keep up with the finely-honed, high-powered machines driven by the liquor boys, turned to other tactics, such as blocking and "spiking."

"They caught a lot of 'em by spiking 'em," an old-timer recalled. The agents would take two-by-six boards and drive fortypenny nails through them. They would then pick a spot between two banks and throw out the spikes when they saw a moonshine car coming. "They like to got Jim H. one time that way. But only one man on one side pitched out his plank. Thought it was all that was necessary. Jim saw it in time and, flip, throwed his car up on two wheels just like that, flew over the spikes and set it back down and kept going. Then's when they started putting down *two* spike boards."

Retired ATF investigator Duff Floyd of Jasper, Georgia—something of a legendary figure—remembers using a set of heavy iron spikes embedded in a metal base. When unfolded on hinges, the spikes stretched twelve feet across. The agents would space the spikes at the entrance to a bridge and would erect a U.S. Treasury Department stop sign back up the road a piece, where they tried to flag down suspected cars. "If they ignored the sign, we just let them go, because the spikes would get 'em."

Some agents in earlier years blocked liquor cars on covered bridges, but the trippers considered this unfair and unsportsmanlike, similar to shooting a rabbit in a box. Most of the blocking in the '30s

156

"Bloody Madison" was the nickname given to Madison County, on the far western fringes of North Carolina. This photo, made in 1921, shows Madison's "still busting" sheriff, Jesse James Bailey, in a pile of moonshine stills he and his deputies had destroyed over a six-month period. The holes in the copper stills were made by the officers' picks. Note the World War I leggings, popular among mountain men of that day.

The war against moonshiners in Muskogee County, Oklahoma, in the 1920s netted this result— stills of all varieties. The campaign against the illicit whiskey makers was led by Sheriff J. F. Ledbetter (fourth from left) who won the nickname of "still-buster." (Photo courtesy C. H. McKennon).

The community of Gum Log, located in a remote section of northeast Georgia along the South Carolina border, was known far and wide as a prolific producer of corn whiskey during the 1920s and 1930s. Lawmen would cut up to 12 stills a day in the area—all copper stills such as the one above, which has just been seized. The Sheriff of Franklin County, Georgia, Tom Watson Andrews, poses in front of furnace and still pot. Note the thump keg and pre-heater and flake stand on the right. Lined up in the clearing in the woods are barrels of mash.

Possibly the largest dry land seizure of illegal moonshine whiskey on record in America occurred at Ingle Hollow in Wilkes County, North Carolina, during the 1930s—even though some of the whiskey had been moved out prior to the big raid. In the photo, federal agents look over one end of the hollow covered with 7,700 gallons of whiskey in six-gallon cases and five-gallon cans. Note condenser worms on the left.

The "pour out" of confiscated white whiskey was an every-three-month ritual in front of the sheriff's office in Buncombe County (Asheville), North Carolina, just as it was at courthouses across the South. This photo was taken in 1929, and the man in the right foreground, helping empty the half-gallon open-mouth jars into the gutter, was Jessee James Bailey, who had left Madison County to become sheriff of Buncombe. Bailey's left hand was wrapped up due to a gunshot wound inflicted by a criminal, not a moonshiner.

Frank Rickman, son of the long-time sheriff of Rabun County, Georgia, Luther Rickman, sits top of one copper pot still lashed to the front bumper of his father's automobile following a still raid in 1930. Frank, a moonshiner "catch dog" on still raids, is holding another still in his hand, a two-gallon "drinking liquor" still in which the moonshiners re-distilled their superb drinking whiskey. The other huge copper pot still at the left had a capacity of over 200 gallons.

During Prohibition, illicit white whiskey was transported over long distances. This photo, made in 1929, shows a 1929 Cadillac coupe and its load of 186 gallons of moonshine, captured by officers near Asheville, North Carolina. The Cadillac had built-up springs, typical of trip cars even in that early era. Posing with the "catch," second from the left, is Jesse James Bailey.

Fred Goswick, *left,* of Dawsonville, Georgia, a one-time corn whiskey "tripper," checking the trunk of a reconditioned 1939 Ford coupe, one of the all-time favorite of liquor runners and early stock car race drivers, due to its maneuverability, speed and power. "The day I got caught," Goswick remembers, "I was on a narrow road and couldn't get by the car in front, and the patrolmen were bumping me from the rear." He cut into a farm yard and jumped out but was quickly caught by the patrolmen. "I'll never forget the old woman who came by and said, 'Well, *ain't he young!*' "

Lloyd Seay, a whiskey tripper and one of the greatest of the early stock car drivers in the South, won the National Stock Car Championship at Atlanta's dirt track Lakewood Speedway on September 1, 1941, but was killed by a cousin the following day near Dawsonville, Georgia, in a dispute over a load of sugar. His family erected the above tombstone in the Dawsonville Cemetery, showing Seay in his 1939 Ford coupe, bearing Number 7. The carving is in bas relief, with a photo of Seay attached to the window. See page 158–59.

"Clip coils" used to level a car loaded with liquor.

Homer Powell, former agent in charge of the Augusta office of the Bureau of Alcohol, Tobacco and Firearms, learned how to blend into the countryside when out in the woods keeping a moonshine distillery under surveillance. Here he demonstrates how effectively an agent can hide by merely crouching behind a bit of undergrowth. At one time during his Augusta tenure, Powell had the national record for "known seizures"—arresting moonshiners at a distillery site.

Homer Powell. "The fastest information the ATF agent has got to work on is something a woman tells him. She's probably angry. When she gets over it, she'll tell her moonshiner husband and you have to get them before they find out."

Duff Floyd, a federal agent for 35 years in north Georgia and now retired, uses his "flame thrower" to light up his ever-present pipe. Although he engaged moonshine trippers in hundreds of high speed chases, he never wrecked a government car.

David Ayers, who retired in 1972 after serving as alcohol tax unit supervisor for northeast Georgia, remembers blocking tripper cars as a deputy sheriff. "Back in the 30s and 40s, wouldn't nobody be out at night in a car but a doctor, a drunk, a liquor hauler, or us."

A steamer still being destroyed in north Georgia during the 1940s. Officer in front is cutting hoops and smashing apart huge mash barrels, with the white, foamy, fermenting mash pouring out. The upright boiler at left is surrounded by a brick wall to help conserve the heat. (Photo courtesy Duff Floyd).

Large steamer distillery is viewed by officers in the 1940s following the seizure in north Georgia in the Graydon Evans section. In the foreground are large mash vats. In the background are the upright boiler, and, to the right, a "stack barrel" distilling pot. The still "shack" was typical of those at the time: a crude pole shelter with a covering over the top. Duff Floyd is at the left. (Photo courtesy Duff Floyd).

William N. Griffin, right, now director of the Southeastern Region of the ATF, had just raided an illicit distillery in Cocke County, Tennessee, when this photo was made in 1950. Note that the fermenter barrels as well as the pot still were buried part-way in the ground. Today, says Griffin, moonshining in Cocke County has been reduced 80 per cent from the late 1950s. "We'd go blow up forty stills one day and go back the next and find thirty in the same sites."

Modern day moonshine distilleries can be found in homes, barns, large chicken houses, caverns underneath buildings. There have been mobile distilleries built onto trucks, which moved to a site where fermented mash was ready and, following distillation, moved on to another location. In Haralson County, Georgia, an illicit distiller was found in an abandoned Catholic Church founded in 1893, it so happens, by immigrant winemakers. In the photo, county sheriff's deputies and state and federal agents are pouring out 374 gallons of liquor. They also destroyed two 2,160-gallon fermenting vats and a large quantity of sugar.

and '40s took place on narrow roads, between two banks. Otherwise, the hauler would merely throw on the power, cross a shallow ditch and climb a bank to get around. In many cases, the trippers would plunge like tanks right through a wooden barricade or even an automobile blockade. If they found themselves being chased on a main thoroughfare, they would turn off onto dirt roads which they knew like the back of their hands. In the trip to Atlanta, many drivers in the '30s and early '40s didn't really hit a pavement until they got to the outskirts of the city.

The trippers greeted with joy the arrival in 1939 of real hot rod equipment—the Ford cast iron "Pike's Peak" head, the first really high compression cylinder and dual manifolds and dual carburetors which came from California. By then, cars had bigger pistons, so the mechanics bored the cylinders out even bigger and ground four-inch cranks. It all meant more power and speed.

But the new equipment led to more than faster tripping. One of Atlanta's premier mechanics, who got his race car training by tuning up and building engines for whiskey trip cars, started drilling out the intake manifolds—which made it possible to install two or three carburetors instead of one, increasing the air and fuel intake and increasing the automobile's power tremendously. (This practice of the early moonshine mechanics has been copied in recent years by racing mechanics.) On Armistice Day, 1939, an Atlanta-based trip car with its manifolds drilled, the first one ever, won the first car race held on Atlanta's famed clay dirt track, Lakewood Speedway—and it was won by a tripper. Lloyd Seay, a daring driver from Dawson County, known for his tremendous automobile handling on the trippers' "moonshine trace" from north Georgia into Atlanta, won the race driving a 1938 standard two-door Ford. (His left arm was propped up in the window through the 100-mile event, and many fans thought it was injured, but it was merely his driving style.) Seay was described by a revenue agent as "without a doubt the best automobile driver of that time. He was absolutely fearless, and an excellent driver on those dusty, dirt roads. I caught him eight times, and had to shoot his tires off every time."

Seay won another race at Lakewood in 1941, but was killed the following day near his home in Dawsonville in a dispute with a cousin over a load of sugar. On Seay's grave in the Dawsonville cemetery, a monument erected by kinfolks and friends featured a bas-relief carving of Seay's 1939 Ford coupe, with a photograph of Seay attached to the window opening on the carving.

The movie *Thunder Road*—with Robert Mitchum as a young moonshine tripper/race driver—captured the speed-filled drama of the tripper's life. The picture was complete with high-powered engines and the multitude of gadgets the trippers used to thwart pursuers, including smoke-bomb tanks that would lay down a screen of black smoke, caused by the burning of oily cloth saturated in moonshine, creosote, hot peppers, and crankcase oil.

Federal agents Bub Kay and Tom Bowen were chasing a liquor car down Highway 17 in Georgia's mountainous Habersham County when the trippers turned on their smoker 200 feet from a river at a sharp curve leading up to a bridge. Virtually blinded in the "blackout," the agents plunged down a twelve-foot embankment and into the river, but came out unhurt.

David Ayers of Cornelia, state revenue supervisor for north Georgia, chased a smoker car twenty-two miles from Lavonia on through Royston, Georgia. "It was about four o'clock in the morning when I jumped him. I always set way off so that if they checked the road they wouldn't see me, but I could see them. I saw this car coming down 17, and I eased into Lavonia between two buildings and dropped right behind him. Quick as my lights hit him, he turned on his smoker valve. He had burnt cylinder oil, cayenne pepper, iodine, and creosote in those tanks. It made an awful black smoke. Quick as that stuff hit you, you'd have to roll your door window down to see out. And you couldn't turn on your windshield wipers—that just made it worse. That old smoke, you wouldn't feel too much effect at first. But it would burn your eyes and your face, too. My partner who rode with me, Moyce Andrews, he had to hang out the window with his shotgun to try to shoot off their tires. His hole face almost peeled off from that stuff. Well, we run this liquor car right down the ridge from Lavonia to Canon to Royston. He turned off onto 29 then. He'd get plum out of my sight and he could have lost me. But he left his smoker on and I followed that smoke. His pressure and ingredients finally run out and we got close enough to plug his tires and we caught him."

Trippers threw jars and cans of whiskey, tacks, spikes, and even spare tires into the path of the revenuers. Ayers remembers it well. "I jumped Legs Law [a well-known liquor runner] at Tiger one time.

A man had called me and told me he was coming down. Legs was in a blue 1937 Ford with a powerful Vogt motor in it. I had a big motor in my car too. Had to, to meet the competition. I was driving a two-door '40 Ford. I had a big Mercury motor in it, built up by Hugh Babb in Atlanta. Cost me $1500. You'd have just as big a block as you could get in flat-heads. I had a Mercury motor and its cylinders bored, with everything else [hot rod equipment] that came out of California. I had three carburetors, mechanically operated. It was good for 130 miles per hour on the road. When Legs came along, Moyce, my partner, as standing out next to the road and whistled to me. I cranked up and picked up Moyce but it took me twelve miles to catch up with Legs . . . almost to Tallulah Falls. We crossed Tallulah Falls and he was throwing liquor out at us in half-gallon jars all along. Coming on the straightaway before we got to Panther Creek, this boy riding with him got out the spare tire which was laying up on the liquor. He got it out and rolled it out the door. It hit the pavement and took a big bounce and I drove right under it . . . missed it about that fer . . . just inches. The liquor jars cut my tires some, but I didn't get a flat. Legs turned onto Bear Gap road at Turnerville, and on that dirt road, the jars didn't do no good. He was running hot then, anyway. We got up close to him and shot his tires. We caught the boy with him and picked up Legs later."

Congress passed a law exacting additional penalties for cars with gadgets such as smokers, and with the passage of time, the gadgets and tacks and spikes and smokescreens became passé. But the trippers continued to run even more powerful machines, installing bigger engines with higher compression cylinder heads and with modifications (including Offenhauser manifolds, which meant more carburetors), and the trips became wilder.

"I get scared just settin' and thinkin' about it. I had more nerve than brains. Usta come down out of those mountains in that hopped-up Ford, drove around those curves on narrow roads all the way from up there at Tate. Them roads were narrow, about like one lane today. Just barely room for two cars to get by. I've throwed one of them hopped-up Fords 100 miles an hour around them curves a lot of times."

Today the ex-tripper, heavily bearded and fifty-two years old, lives a life of retirement near Kennesaw Mountain north of Atlanta and confines his drinking mostly to beer.

159

"That '39 Ford. We had it fixed up. Had $2,000 in it. Had a Red Vogt motor in it. Cost me $700. German V-8 Mercedes engine. My brother ran a body shop. I'd take my old '39 Ford in there and say,

" 'Paint this thing, will you?'

" 'What color you want?'

" 'I don't care, whatever color you want to paint it, just change the color.'

"He'd paint it and I'd make about two runs and the ATF, they'd know my car. One day in Dawsonville, a revenuer told me, 'You're wasting money paintin' that Ford. I can sit up there on the hills in Ball Ground and hear that engine thumpin'. Even if you muffle it, when you come up that hill with that load on, I can hear that engine thumpin'. Big Sam, I know you and I know your daddy, old Big George. I like your daddy. We're good friends. I'd hate to catch you but I'm going to. I'm going to stop you from hauling liquor one way or another.'

" 'You can't catch me, old man. I can drive this Ford faster backwards than you can forwards.' "

The gauntlet thrown, both Big Sam and the revenuer were primed for the Big Day. It came early one morning in the spring of 1945. Big Sam came roaring down Highway 5 out of the hills and the ATF agent, parked up on the big hill at the schoolhouse in Ball Ground, heard the thumping whine and tore off. He radioed ahead and two highway patrolmen and several county deputies barricaded the road at Woodstock. The tripper takes up the story:

"I looked out there and they had the road blocked on the hill at Woodstock and old ATF was pushin' me. He'd been pushing me from all the way up there at Ball Ground. I was playin' with him, more or less. I'd let him get up about two hundred yards of me and I'd pull away from him. I'uz goin' on into Atlanta with a load, about a hundred gallons.

"I looked out there, and there was state patrol with high-powered rifles. So I turned it into a dirt road—the Old Alabama Road—number 92 now. Just flat *slid* it in there. Old ATF come in behind me, tryin' to make that curve fast as I did and turned his '40 Ford bottomside up. I got through and opened that old Ford up. They shot at me a couple of times. Drove about four miles back over there, turned off the road through the woods. Old sawdust pile up there.

Drove around behind sawdust pile and got out and climbed up on top of the sawdust so I could watch the road. They come shootin' by . . . varroooommmm. I set up there and watched 'em go out of sight. Sirens died down. I set a few minutes and they didn't come back. I said, 'Heck, they're going all the way into Cartersville lookin' for me.' I turned around and come back, went right back the same way I come in. Went back in the Canton Highway, Highway 5. There was old ATF's '40 Ford, layin' there with the wheels up in the air and they wuz a puttin' him in the ambulance. I pulled up. Whole crowd of people there. I said,

" 'What happened here?'

" 'Revenue officer turned over here chasin' a whiskey car.'

" 'Hurt him?'

" 'No, didn't hurt him much, don't think. They're going to take him down for a checkup.'

" 'That's too bad. Shudda killed the SOB.'

"They looked at me real hard. I drove on downtown to Atlanta and unloaded the whiskey."

The grizzled ex-tripper popped open another can of beer.

"Started haulin' whiskey 1935. Just a kid, fifteen years old. First load I ever hauled, two sixty-gallon barrels full in the back of a Model A Ford truck. Hauled it to Kennesaw in open truck in broad open daylight.

"When I was haulin' for my people, all I did was drive. My grand-daddy did the distilling, and all the family helped out. They'd load it up near Cartercay in Dawson County and lock the trunk; I'd haul it to where they told me. I'd pick up the money and bring it back and give it to the kinfolks. They'd give me my money for hauling it. I got $1 a gallon—$100 a trip. I was makin' $500 a week.

"Usta have a milk run to Atlanta. Unloaded a load every morning down there. Down at Central Avenue. A hundred gallons. They'uz a wholesale bootlegger there. We'd just back up in the alley. Big old two-story house. Had a basement in there. We'd just back up in the alley and this colored guy, janitor, he had a key to the trunk. He had a key to every one of 'em that was haulin' there. Me and Legs Law and Roy Hall. We could drive around in front of the place, park and go inside and the lady that run the joint, she'd pay ye off. You didn't have to put your hands on the whiskey.

"I was in there one time unloadin' a load. The janitor had about half of it throwed off. I was settin' there with my motor idling and a police car turned in there. I yelled for the colored guy to slam that trunk lid down. He slammed it down and run inside and locked the door. Wasn't room on the street to pass 'em, so I gunned that Ford and shoved that thing in second gear and went up on the sidewalk bank and just barely got by. They had to back out and turn around. Time they got backed out, I was across the river bridge, I guess, down here on the Chattahoochee. Still had eighteen gallons of whiskey in there—three cases. I told all the trippers they wuz on to us down there. Somebody turned us in. They caught the lady.

"I wuz a good country road driver. Better than on paved road. They'd get to pushin' me too hard, I hit the dirt. Then I had 'em lost then. I had a car built up with double shocks on it and special springs.

"Well, I tell you, you live kinda rough life up there in the mountains anyway. If you made any money at all, you had to make whiskey or haul it, one or the other. You got a hard way to go if you make a livin' farmin' in that rocky country up in there. It's hard to get corn out of rocks. And makin' likker is hard work. Don't let nobody tell you it's easy. You rawhide them 100-pound sacks of sugar and them big buckets of mash and all that stuff, and cleanin' out stills and bottling that stuff up and carryin' it miles out of the hills on your back, it's tough work. You earn ever dime you make. Your haulers are the ones who made the gravy.

"I quit haulin' in '47. That's when I got nine holes shot in the back end of that car. That's the closest they ever come to catching me. If I hadn't had a brother that lives up there in Canton, they would've got me that time. I shot in his garage and pulled the door down."

The era of the moonshine hot rodders really boomed in the early '50s, not only in north Georgia, but in east Tennessee and western North Carolina, particularly around North Wilkesboro where Junior Johnson got his introduction into fast driving by tripping from his daddy's still in Ingle Hollow down to Statesville—a training track that took him roaring into the stock car racing big-time.

Liquor hot rodding developed primarily in a relatively narrow slice of the Southeast—the Blue Ridge/Cumberland hills of the three states. Bill Griffin, the six-foot-six, no nonsense, tough-talking ex-pro footballer who directs the ATF agents throughout the Southeast, was stationed in Greeneville, Tennessee, at the time, and ran head-on

162

into the rising tide of the Cocke County moonshine runners who were racing into Asheville and Knoxville in their 1939 and '40 Ford coupes outfitted with aluminum Edelbrock heads, triple carburetors, and high-speed Columbia rear ends. Cocky and confident, and bristling with braggadocio, they put in high springs in the rear which made their cars "stand on their heads" when not "leveled" with a load of whiskey. They threw away their mufflers and came out with twin straight exhausts. "Made a helluva noise," said Griffin. "You could hear those things for miles on a clear night . . . carooooom . . . pop . . . pop . . . pop. . . . Those kids practiced like mad. I've laid up there many a night on the side of the mountains watchin' 'em practice spin-outs and turns . . . evasive maneuvers and escape maneuvers."

Griffin confessed to having lost out a few times in blistering, high-speed chases.

"The moonshiners built some good, high performance cars . . . the moonshiners *and* the ATF agents. You didn't have status unless you had a hot rod. What they had was far superior to what we had. We were driving six-cylinder '47, '48 Fords. But we'd seize one of their hot rods and put it into service against them. We were about as crazy as the damned moonshiners. A bunch of kids having a good time.

"Last case I was involved in, I damned near got fired over it," Griffin recalled. "We had just received two 1949 Ford six-cylinder cars. So we decided to block this runner on this bridge that comes across Douglas Lake between Cocke County and Knoxville. Sure enough, the guy came along like it had been reported he would. In a hot rod Ford. He had a passenger with him. He must have been doing about seventy miles an hour down the road. We had a lookout on the other side of the lake who radioed that the boy was on the bridge. So our agents pulled out side by side on a two-lane bridge with headlights on and red lights flashing, thinking the guy would stop or try to run around on the bridge. Instead, he tried to go between them! There was about eighteen inches between the two cars. The amazing thing, he *almost* got through. But the impact knocked the two front wheels off his car and he rode up over the tops of our cars. He was cut up pretty badly and his passenger was butchered up too. We had one boy who got a broken leg. I remember asking the runner, when they pulled him out of the car, 'What'n hell did you think you were doing?' He said, 'I was goin' for that gap!'"

The two ATF cars were demolished. "I wrote letters for several months," Griffin remembered with a wincing grin, "about why we had two new automobiles blocking a load of liquor."

The ATF stopped blocking after that and turned to more strategic tactics. They put investigators at the spots where the liquor was being delivered, took down the delivery car's license number, and, after the car left, seized the liquor, and then later picked up the car. Using this system, there was no chase, nobody got hurt, the car was seized intact, and the ATF ended up with a car they could either put in service or let the General Services Administration sell, for the benefit of the taxpayers.

Along about this time, a tough federal judge in Knoxville, Robert Taylor, began dealing sternly with the hot rodders. He sentenced the runner who "went for the gap" to ten years in the penitentiary. Between Judge Taylor and the ATF men, who began plucking off the whiskey cars right and left, the era of the hot rod came to a screeching halt.

The trippers shifted to the "sneak car"—an old beat-up automobile that they thought they could sneak in unnoticed. These cars were also called "slip bys." "The best one I can remember," said ex-tripper Fred Goswick of Dawsonville, Georgia, "was a '36 Ford. Had one bucket seat. Who would have thought of a raggedy old '36 Ford having 250 gallons of whiskey in it? I would just creep in [to town] . . . just ease in and out." Goswick ran more than a thousand loads of whiskey into Atlanta during his tripping career—between the tender ages of fifteen and twenty—hauling an average load of more than 200 gallons per run. "I'd go into Atlanta nice and quiet and easy, like you was going to mass . . . waving and smiling at everybody. And when a policeman seemed to be staring at me too long, I'd start picking my nose, because nobody is going to keep staring at you if you start picking your nose."

Retired federal revenue agents recalled a high-speed chase of a Ford coupe loaded with liquor coming out of Tate, Georgia. Going from Tate into Nelson, a straightaway abruptly ended in a sharp curve. It was a dark night and agent Bill Webster wasn't familiar with the road. He followed the coupe into the start of the curve but, going too fast, lost control and spun out and plunged into a pile of scrap marble. It demolished the car. Webster was thrown out and remained unconscious in a hospital for two days while his partner, state agent Tom Y. Harris, left the accident without serious injury, although, according to retired agent Duff Floyd, "he looked like he had been sortin' wildcats. He had the most scratches and scabs and skin tore up on his face of anybody you could imagine who still wasn't hurt seriously."

While Webster lay unconscious in the hospital, a big bouquet of flowers arrived, accompanied by a card that said, simply, "The Coupe."

The revenuers found out later that the flowers had come from Roy Hall. Such was the code of mutual respect between the revenuers and the trippers. Though they were on opposite sides of the law, a strong bond of friendship held them together.

The exciting days of whiskey-tripping are drawing to a close. Atlanta, which for decades has had the dubious title of the moonshine-consuming capital of the world, is losing its taste for illicit booze, and the trip men are having to find other employment. In the 1940s, trippers hauled around 50,000 gallons of untaxed whiskey into Atlanta each week. Today, the volume has dropped to below 8,000 gallons a week. During Prohibition and after, lawmen on the average often captured fifty whiskey cars a month in Atlanta. In 1972, they seized only seven during the entire year, and those yielded only 229 gallons of spirits. By the end of the decade, it is safe to predict, the moonshine tripper will be only a memory.

It is likely that America will never again see an era of similar camaraderie between lawmen and their adversaries, between the hunters and the hunted. The era of the moonshine trippers.

12

Fighting the Revenuers

Sometimes they'd raid you early in the morning, sometimes late. Sometimes they'd lay up there and watch you work for a *long* time, figuring out the best way to catch you. Sometimes they'd be so close, just in behind a tree, a log or a bush. We wouldn't even know they was there. . . .

—Georgia moonshiner

I was lying in the short grass, wearing my dark green shirt, pants and cap, watching the stash, when a car drove up the road and stopped, almost in front of me. It really surprised me. I didn't expect it to stop there. We had found this one stash of about six cases off to one side, but the car stopped directly in front of me and the moonshiner. Instead of walking to the stash we had found, the driver went over to the other side, just a few dozen yards from where I was lying, to still another stash that we didn't know about . . ."

The ex-Alcohol, Tobacco, and Firearms agent was talking, recalling a stakeout along Tobacco Road—the same Tobacco Road that Erskine Caldwell wrote about in *God's Little Acre*. Off United States Highway I about six miles south of Augusta, between Fort Gordon and Bush Field, amidst mini-mountains of whitish-grey sand covered with clusters of stunted "blackjack" scrub oaks, the Tobacco Road moonshiners tended their 1,000-gallon galvanized "groundhogs" like mother hens—big round stills which are heated by roaring gasoline flames fed from pressurized tanks. You could hear the "jet engine" roar of the stills for a quarter of a mile.

One of the tough illicit distillers on Tobacco Road, a blocky 240-

pounder with twenty-two inch biceps and a twenty-inch neck, was a legend among his own people, a sort of Hoss Cartwright of Tobacco Road. A modern-day Paul Bunyan, he would hoist a 100-pound sack of sugar onto his shoulder with one hand, flip a second one up with his other hand, then walk with the two sacks on his back a mile to a still site.

In addition to his physical power, John Black, as we'll call him, was an expert whiskey-maker.

But back to the revenuer in the grass:

"I was lying there, didn't have *any* cover from the moonshiner's direction, lying there in about eight-inch tall grass. The only thing that kept me from being seen was my dark green clothes. So I stayed very still . . . didn't move a muscle. This man got out of the car, walked into the woods right by me and got a case of liquor, brought it back and put it in the trunk of the car. He had two black customers who stayed with the car. When he put the case in the trunk, I had enough evidence to seize the car, along with the owner standing there.

"The moonshiner came back for a second case. I didn't recognize him, but he looked big and tough."

When he walked by on his second trip, the revenue man jumped up and took off after him. Down through the scrub oaks they ran. The tall investigator, with a long, flying lunge, tackled the man, pushing his head in the sand. The investigator, straddling and sitting on the back of his adversary, became a bit uneasy when he noticed the moonshiner's bulging, hard muscles.

"What's your name?"

"Black."

"You must be John Black, 'cause I've already met your brother Charlie."

"Yes, I'm John."

"I'm Homer Powell. I'm a federal agent."

"I know who you are, Homer."

"Before I let you up, I've heard you're pretty bad to fight. You've given the deputies a hard time. Are you going to give me any trouble?"

"No, Homer. I've heard about you, too. If I gave you any trouble, you wouldn't hit me, you would shoot me."

"That's right." (Powell said later, "You have to build your own reputation." He never intended to shoot any of his moonshining adversaries, nor did he, but it was part of his psychological warfare to make them think he would, if necessary.)

"No, I'm not going to give you any trouble," Black said.

"Okay. Let's go break your liquor up."

With axes, they smashed the half-gallon jars stacked neatly in the corrugated boxes at the two stashes and even joked a bit. Powell laughingly informed John that the second stash was quite a revelation—a new find for the federal agents.

John asked permission to save one jar of the corn juice. "I just got caught; at least I ought to get one drink," he pleaded.

"No, we can't have that," Powell replied, with firmness.

It was about five in the afternoon. "John, it'll be dark pretty soon," Powell told Black. "There's no need in me taking you to jail. I know where you live. I know everything about you. You go on home. Have your bondsman be at my office at ten o'clock in the morning. But you be there at nine, because I've got to get your picture and fingerprints. We'll have a hearing at ten o'clock. The commissioner will be there and you can be released on bond."

Black showed up on schedule and at his subsequent trial, Federal Judge Frank Scarlett gave him what the judge usually gave first offenders of the liquor laws—a two-year probationary sentence.

A few months later, on a hot summer day, Powell was helping raid a still a bit further down Tobacco Road. The ATF officers usually devise a strategy before conducting a still raid. They decide in advance which officers are going to "flush" the still and which are going to "catch" on the other side. A still may be flushed from the front, the back, or the side, depending on the lay of the land. In this particular case, there was a wide open hill in front of the stillyard—a hill that sloped upward at about thirty degrees for 200 hundred yards, with only a few scrub oak on the side. Powell, the ATF investigator in charge, who was assisted by another federal agent plus state and county officers, elected to send in a flush team from the woods, and he and another agent hid over behind the hill, serving as "catch men."

As soon as the flush team made contact—that is, as soon as the moonshiners saw the agents—the sand hills reverberated with whoops and shouts and the grunts of the 'stillers digging up the dirt

168

with their feet, trying to get away from the officers. A big fellow with a stocky build threw down his shirt and came chugging out of the stillyard, charging madly up the hill. It was John Black!

As he dug a path up the hill, Black smilingly looked over his shoulder every few seconds, obviously pleased that he was getting away from the Feds. It took him only a matter of seconds to cover the 200 yards up the hill. Just over the crest, he pulled to a stop to get his breath, ducking behind a pine tree about ten feet from Powell, who was also behind a pine.

"Well, John, you want to run some more?" Powell said.

Black whirled around, wide-eyed in surprise.

"Damn, Homer, what are you doing here?"

"Just waiting for you. You ready to go on back down?"

"I'm out of breath now; let me rest a minute."

"Okay, John, no problem; you get your breath and come on back to the still when you're rested." Powell walked down to see how the other raiders had come out in their footraces.

Since Black's first arrest by Powell, the moonshiner had had several altercations with sheriff deputies, two of whom had visited the federal agent to find how he had managed to handle the mean moonshiner without a fight. They had been unable to speak to the man, so it seemed, without a fight breaking out.

At the still, Homer found that two of Black's associates had been caught, including his brother Charlie, whom Homer had also arrested previously.

A half hour later, after having destroyed the still, the agents with their prisoners started to go, but discovered that John was missing.

"Charlie, where is John?" Homer asked. The brother did not know what had happened to him.

"I caught John on top of the hill," the ATF investigator said, "and told him to come on back down here. I don't like it, the fact that I gave him a chance and he didn't come down here. Charlie, I'm going to let you go home. Get your bondsman and get John and be in my office at one o'clock this afternoon."

"Homer, I don't know if I can get John or not."

"You'd better. If you don't, I'm going to be sitting on your door-step night and day and you can't live with that."

At one o'clock, John and Charlie and their bondsman, an Augusta restaurateur, arrived at the ATF office in the Augusta Post Office.

169

The federal agent talked to John like he was a disobedient child.

"John, why did you do that?"

"I'm sorry, Homer. I apologize."

"Don't do me like that. I can't stand that. I do you a favor, I expect you to appreciate it."

"Well, I *do* appreciate it, Homer. I'm sorry. I didn't mean to run off. I just couldn't stay there. I know it was wrong and I apologize, 'cause you treated me all right."

When Black's trial came up, Judge Scarlett gave him a year and a day behind bars, the traditional sentence for second offenders. Such a one-day add-on sentence actually has the effect of adding about seventeen days to the actual time an offender must remain behind bars before he can be eligible for a good-time release.

Several months went by and investigator Powell didn't think much more about Black until he received an excited call one night from the Richmond County (Augusta) jail. The chief jailer was frantic. "You'd better come down here, Homer, you're in deep trouble."

Arriving at the jail, Homer learned that Black was back in Augusta, bigger than ever and meaner than ever. Raising hell at a beer joint, he had whipped four deputies the night before and had put two in the hospital with severe cuts and bruises. The other two men virtually had to break a billy club over his head to subdue him, and he had to be sewed up before he could be put behind bars. The deputies had gone to quiet him down on a complaint from neighbors. He had vowed he wasn't going to jail, and he proceeded to plow into the officers.

The jailer now reported that Black was making the claim, loud and clear, that he was going to make it his business to "get" every one who had anything to go with sending him off.

The jailer said, "You know, Homer, *you* were the one who made the case against him that sent him off to Tallahassee. He might be coming after you. I thought you ought to know about this; you ought to be on your guard. He's due for release tonight. They'll probably post his bond in an hour or so."

Powell felt the overwhelming urge to go face Black.

"I knew John Black was bigger and stronger than me and could probably tear me up with one hand," Powell said years later. "At the same time, I couldn't stand to go overnight without it being settled."

Investigator Powell lost no time after leaving work. He dropped off his partner at his home and drove on out to Black's house on Tobacco Road. Powell hadn't told his wife nor his partner of his intentions—that he was going out for a face-to-face confrontation with John Black, right in his own lair. He figured that if worse came to worst, they would all read about it in the next morning's *Augusta Chronicle*. He pulled up to the moonshiner's frame shack—many illicit distillers and bootleggers, although relatively well off financially, lived in poor circumstances (and still do) to keep up the façade of poverty—and Black's wife came to the door.

"Hello, Mrs. Black, I'm Homer Powell."

"I know you," she said, her lips tightly drawn and her eyes barely visible between narrow slits.

"Where's John?"

"What do you want him for?"

"Just want to talk to him. I'm not going to arrest him. I don't have anything against him. I just want to talk to him. I heard he was out."

"You're sure you're not going to arrest him?"

"No, ma'am."

"All right, he's over at the place drinking beer. You know where it is, in the pine grove."

Powell drove over into the pines, pulled his gun belt off and stuck it under the seat. Just as he stepped out of his car, the blocky form of John Black appeared in the front door of the little cinder block building, on his way to the outdoor privy.

"John!"

"Who is that?"

"Come here a minute."

"Who is it?" Black asked, holding his hand over his eyes to shade the glint from the light over the door.

"This is Homer."

"*Homer Powell!* Why, you old sonofagun!" He stuck out his beefy hand and gripped Powell's hand with a vise-like crunch.

"Glad to see you, Homer. How you getting along? Come in and have a beer."

"No, wait a minute, John. I heard you were back. But I've heard something else, too, and I got to settle that before we go in. I heard you had a little trouble last night."

"Yeah, those sonsabitches tried to whip my head again. They're always doing that."

"Yeah, but I heard that you threatened that you were going to get even with everybody that had anything to do with your being sent off last time, and you know that I was Number One. I was the one that made the case. The other officers were just working with me. They were helping me. Now, if you got anything you want to settle with me I want to know it right now."

"No," John said simply.

"My gun's in the car," Powell declared. "There's nobody here with me. It's just you and me and the hootey owls and I want to know about it."

"No," John repeated. "Homer, I don't have anything to settle with you. As far as I'm concerned, you're all right. You never did mistreat me. You didn't try to take advantage of your badge at all. You didn't try to hurt me. You just treated me like I was a man. You caught me right, you arrested me, and you put me in jail, but you did it like a gentleman, and I got nothing in the world against you. *Come on in and have a beer.*"

Powell recalled: "That was the sweetest sound I ever heard, because he looked then like he was four feet wide. I could tell he hadn't lost any of his strength. You know they tighten up their muscles working on that road equipment when they're sent off to prison, and he wasn't any better looking as far as my having a fight with him than before he left. He didn't look too gentle then."

"Okay, John, that's all settled, now, and you got nothing you want to square with me? Because you know if you get back in the 'business' I'm going to be out there trying to catch you again."

"Hell, I know it, Homer. Don't worry about that. *Tomorrow's another day.*"

They walked together to the tavern, which was rocking to the country music of a jukebox. When Powell stepped inside, his eyes bulged. He saw the biggest gathering of moonshiners and bootleggers he had ever seen except in the hallway at Federal Court in Augusta, when they were all in trouble. The room was packed. "Every booth and every table was full of moonshiners and bootleggers and I knew most of 'em and they knew me."

John Black reached down and pulled the plug on the jukebox. The room became as silent as a tomb. All eyes turned to the two—the

Tobacco Road moonshiner and the revenuer who had caught him and sent him to the pen.

"Now all you sonsabitches sit still," Black commanded. "I'm going to tell you right now, Homer Powell is here as a friend of mine. We're going to have a couple of beers together and if one of you says a word, I'm going to whip your ass right now. None of you better say anything that's going to get you in trouble with me, because Homer is here. He's a friend of mine. I just got out of the pen. He sent me off and he's celebrating me coming back, so the rest of you fellers probably didn't give him enough business while I was gone. Tomorrow he might catch me again, but tonight we're going to have a beer together. Now the rest of you go on about your business and everything will be all right."

So with that, they took stools at the counter and enjoyed themselves while the rest of the room squirmed. One moonshiner crawled behind and under the bar when he saw Powell come in the door and stayed there during the federal man's visit. Between guzzles of beer, the moonshiner and his captor joked about the times of near capture and escape.

As Powell got up to leave, Black invited him to have a third beer.

"No, John, I've got to get back to work. I can see I don't have anything to do here because they're all corralled, and no still is running around *here*. I've got to go somewhere else and find one running *tonight*."

As he reached the door, John yelled:

"Hey Homer! If I was to buy you some new clothes, would you wear 'em?"

Powell hesitated. "Well, I don't know, John. What did you have in mind?"

"If I was to buy you a red shirt and a red pair of pants and a bright red cap, would you wear 'em?"

The room exploded in laughter. Powell had a reputation for being "good in the woods" and had slipped up Indian style on a lot of moonshiners, including John Black, thanks to the help of his camouflaged clothes, which blended into the local countryside.

"I appreciate it, John," Powell replied. "You buy it and I'll wear it to court. What about that?"

With that, the federal investigator made his exit. He arrested John

Black one more time, a year later, and locked him up again without any trouble. They saw one another several times, and John would always speak to him, and the investigator was always friendly in return.

"He just went on like everybody on Tobacco Road," Powell declared. "They did what they were gonna do and what they *had* done for generations, which was make liquor and sell it. That was a way of life with 'em. If you got caught, it was bad. If you didn't get caught, it was good. They had a completely detached attitude toward the whole thing."

Powell's ATF counterpart in northeast Georgia at the time was the late Bub Kay. Of all the big law men in the Habersham-Rabun territory, Kay was one of the most popular and respected among the moonshiners.

A rotund, jolly yet firm officer, Kay had the reputation among the makers and the sellers of white whiskey of playing "fare and square," and of being a true humanitarian. Every Christmas eve, he would put on a Santa Claus uniform and play St. Nick to the kids of poor moonshiners in the hills and poor blacks in the area. Quite simply, he was greatly loved by all members of the corn likker fraternity, even when he arrested them, and even though they often mispronounced his name. For instance, a moonshiner I talked to in Habersham County called him *Mc*Kay.

"He was as good an officer as I ever seed in my life. I don't believe he would swear a thing in the world on you but what he knowed. I always liked Bub McKay. Some of the revenuers would swear to you in court, whether they knowed you or not. Ever who done the reportin', I guess, would just let 'em know the name just to get the money, and the officer 'ud swear they knowed 'em. I don't believe Bub McKay would. I always had that confi*dence* in him. People thought well of him. I shore did hate it when I heered him and his wife got killed in that car wreck. I hated that awful bad. He was an officer, but still he was an awful good feller. Last time he was here I told him I didn't have nothin' to drink and I said to him:

"Bub, it looks to me like since you've got plenty of it, you would bring me a drink of it ever once in a while."

"Next time I come back up here I'm going to bring you some."

"Well, I'll be lookin' for it, Bub."

174

"What if I wus to tell you it had to be government likker, that I couldn't bring you any white likker?"

"Well, if it's that old govern*mint* likker, I'd jest as soon you'd keep it."

Bub never did bring the liquor. Shortly after, he and his wife died in a highway accident.

Another younger revenuer who worked with Bub but who treated his subjects with a little less benevolence—and took his mission as a deadly serious affair—rapidly attracted the personal animosity of the moonshine brotherhood. But they respected him. He was James Stratigos, who built fame as the nemesis of Persimmon—Persimmon being the most noted moonshine region of Rabun County, in far northeast Georgia.

"When you were a stranger to a new territory, the moonshiners always tried you, two or three of the fast young bucks," Stratigos said. "They always tried to outrun you, or whip you, or bluff you. If they couldn't do any of them, then you had no trouble. Every time you went to a new territory, you had to run down a couple of the fast ones, whip a couple of the strong ones, and prove to a couple of the smart ones they couldn't bluff you. From then on, everything was peachy keen. I moved a half dozen times and every time I had to whip two or three tails before it was over. But I never lost a man after I got my hands on him.

"I loved to walk. I'd have Bub Kay drop me off in Persimmon before daylight. I would start on one mountain and I would know every ridge and every trail and every holler that they make liquor in. I'd walk 'til dinner and Bub'd pick me up and we'd go eat lunch and come back and I'd start on another ridge. I just hit those spots so often, they couldn't make money out of it. Those people in there were so thick it was awful hard to slip in amongst 'em and catch 'em. You had to be real lucky. They watched every road. Had guards on every road and guards in Clayton. You drive through town and they counted you; when you'd get to Persimmon at the first house you passed, they counted you; then at the second house. It was pretty damn hard in daylight to catch somebody. You had to come before day and then they had guards following you. This was in the late '40s and early '50s. They had hot rods. Hot rod Fords were *the* thing. If you didn't have a '40 Ford, you weren't a bona fide violator. You were just some kind of cheap imitation. They'd come through with a

175

big damn motor in it, motor fill the whole engine cage, do 150 in
second gear. You'd be plodding along with some old government
mule they'd given you and get out of town about three miles and . . .

". . . Zeeeeeeeeeeeeeeeeoooooooooooooooommmmmmmmmmmm-
mmm . . .

"Just a streak would pass you. You'd know, *the word was going to
Persimmon.*

"I figured out a way to break 'em. I figured if stills couldn't stay up
long enough to make a profit on 'em, didn't matter whether you
caught the moonshiners or not. We started on this project of breakin'
'em financially. About every two weeks, I'd cover every hollow in
Persimmon. That's quite a few hundred square miles. We went in
there one morning at 4 A.M. We went until we stopped for breakfast
at 8:30. In between, we found five different stills. We 'saved' two or
three of them and waited and caught the violators later. On two
where it was obvious they had seen us, we went on and cut 'em up
with axes. We didn't start using dynamite until late in the '50s. Now
we blow up everything. Nowadays, if you can spot a still from the
air, you *know* it's operable. In the '40s, if you spotted a still from an
airplane, you weren't really sure about it until you came to it on the
ground. On a cut up copper still, they could go back in and repair
them, unless you really tore it up. They'd beat that thing back in
shape by hand and solder up all those joints and put it back in
operation. But eventually, I caught practically every one of the
moonshiners in Persimmon, some of them more than once."

Although Stratigos left the post some years ago, the folks around
Persimmon still remember him.

"Stratigos," a retired moonshiner recalled, "he was the worse one
the federal law ever put in here. He'uz a mean'un. He'd wait all
night. Have three or four with him. You wouldn't get away from
Stratigos. When Stratigos got after you, you might as well call in
your dogs."

"In the '30s, I got away many a time. I could run then. Generally
somebody would let us know the law was around. Last time I got
away, it was in 1951, snow on the ground. The boys seen him [Stra-
tigos], and there was a big chestnut log right nearby. I crawled
backwards into that holler log. Was in there so tight that after they
left I was stuck. Had to get my knife out and rip off my sweat
jacket."

One of the funniest incidents in Stratigos' career came when he was out walking along a ridge in the Batesville section near the Soquee River in Habersham County, accompanied by a deputy sheriff. A noted liquor-making family lived in the area. It was in the fall and Stratigos saw a little wisp of smoke coming up out of a hollow. He asked the deputy to go wait at the far end of the hollow while Stratigos came in on a 'flush' from the hillside.

"I didn't know but what it might be a teen-age boy. They used them as still hands, because they figured they could outrun you."

Stratigos tiptoed down to where he was in plain sight of the still, about a hundred yards. It sat in a thicket in a wide open hollow. If the moonshiner had looked up, he could have seen the revenuer approaching. Stratigos broke into a gallop down the hill, crunching through the deep leaves like a threshing machine. As he pulled up to the still, there was a man bent over, poking a stick of wood under a little copper pot. Stratigos reached over and tapped him on the shoulder. It turned out he was a little fellow, about five-foot-four and weighing about ninety pounds. But eighty-one years old, and deaf!

"You're under arrest," Stratigos told him.

"Eh?" he said, as he straightened up.

"YOU'RE UNDER ARREST," Stratigos yelled.

"Don't believe I know you."

Stratigos identified himself and looked over the still, a little copper outfit with two barrels of mash.

"You goin' to tear it up?" the old man asked.

"Yeah, that's what we have to do, tear it up."

"You goin' to pour out the likker?"

"Yes, we have to. That's the law."

"Just leave it. I'll pour it out when I get back."

"That's all right. I appreciate it, but I'll just pour it out now."

The deputy sheriff had arrived by then and asked Stratigos if he planned to make a federal case.

"Hell, no," the revenuer replied. "That's *your* prisoner. You take him in."

Together they took him to the justice of the peace, where the old man later pleaded guilty and paid a fifty-dollar fine.

There were some highly skilled women moonshiners in Persimmon, too. They put on overalls and ran stills, and tripped the whiskey in cars to Asheville, North Carolina.

One night Stratigos and a crew of federal and state agents walked

177

into a Persimmon still area after being put out of a car a mile away. Just as they got there and started across a field, a truck pulled up and two people got out and started unloading barrels. It was "dark as the ace of spades—no moon, no nothin'," Stratigos remembered, and the moonshiners used flashlights to unload their cargo.

"We crossed the grass and I got above 'em and just started walking down in the dark. State Agent Roy Gordon was right behind me. We were meetin' them and although they had flashlights, they were pointin' them to the ground and had something on their shoulders. I took off and ran down the slope and picked up first one man with one arm and ran on down and picked up the second man by the arm. Then there was a BA-LOOM, BA-LOOM. Both of them were carrying barrels on their backs and I had run 'em out from under the barrels, which came tumbling to the ground."

In the meantime, Gordon went to the truck and caught Emma German (not her real name), who, it turned out, owned and operated the still. The two fellows carrying the barrels were her still hands.

Stratigos led his prisoners to the truck and one was jerking and twitching. The agent shined the light on him, and he turned white and stiff. Alarmed, Stratigos laid him out on the ground and placed a blanket over him, and a cushion under his head.

"He has those epilepsy fits," said Emma.

Down through the woods came another flashlight. Stratigos grabbed a flashlight and walked along, bent over like the other man. He got right up to the moonshiner, reached over and grabbed him by his overalls gallus with one hand and snatched his pipe out with the other, and told him: "You're under arrest. Come on."

But when Stratigos asked the man his name when they got back to the truck, all he could say was "ugggghhhh."

"I'm James Stratigos, a federal officer. Now don't get smart with me, fella. You're under arrest and you're supposed to identify yourself. Now I'm going to ask you again, what's your name?"

"Ugggghhhhh."

Emma spoke up: "Dammit, tell him your name. I've never heard of anybody get caught at a still and not tell their name."

They got him down where they could turn the car lights on him and he was white as a sheet—in shock. He stood there for fifteen minutes, going "ugggghhhhh."

178

There they were, having arrested a woman moonshiner and three still hands, two of whom were in a state of disability. But the woman was very cooperative and Stratigos learned she was one of Persimmon's most talented distillers. She subsequently brought her still hands in for a hearing and the foursome pleaded guilty.

"When I first knew Emma," Stratigos said, "she was in her late thirties and she was a very attractive woman. They say when she was younger, she was a beauty. She had some daughters who would take the beauty prize anywhere. Her husband had deserted her years before and she made liquor just like a man. Wore overalls and worked at the still, just like a man. She could carry a 100-pound sack of sugar on her shoulders just as good as a man, and an 80-pound keg of whiskey."

"When her husband left her, there was nothing else for her to do, unless she wanted to apply for welfare. She had been raised in a liquor-making family, so she went to work with a still pot and fermenters."

A former deputy sheriff remembered Emma as having made moonshine on the first groundhog still to come to Rabun County. "She just made this giant-size still—eight foot high and six feet in diameter. She just put the mash in there and worked it off. Didn't have a box or anything. She just capped it and stilled it right in the same container."

And she was *some* automobile driver.

"I've seen her take an old '34 model Ford and outrun all the damn men in this country," said an old-timer from Clayton. "She ain't no farce or no make-believe like this likker bunch they is now. She went to the shack, made it, hauled it, every damn thing."

David Ayers, retired state revenue agent, remembered the time in the late '40s when he and Bub Kay were riding along Popcorn Road in Persimmon. "All at once, we just run into a wave of that odor. I said, 'Wait a minute, Bub. There's a still right at us.'" Two shots rang out.

Ayers wet his finger and stuck it into the air to catch the way the wind was blowing. It cooled his finger to the left. Kay went toward a house and Ayers went into the woods to the left, and soon ran into two little girls, one of whom began crying.

"You'all just run back to the house," Ayers told the little girl who was crying, "and nobody is going to get hurt."

"Yes, Mr. David," the little girl said. She knew Ayers from previous raids.

When Ayers got in sight of the still, Emma was taking the cap off the copper pot. She laid it down, picked up a ten-gallon keg of liquor, tossed it on her shoulder, and started walking off with it.

"Emma," Ayers yelled out, "what in the devil are you doing? You need'n run."

Emma looked around.

"Hell, you know I ain't goin' to run, Dave. You know me."

So with her word, he then proceeded to run after and arrest the other moonshiner, a man.

But Emma was not always so willing to comply. Her exploits also were recalled by Frank Rickman, son of the late beloved sheriff of Rabun County, Luther Rickman. When he was growing up, Frank, who was a muscular, swift youngster, served as one of his daddy's moonshine "catch dogs" on still raids.

"Daddy could always catch the car Emma drove, but she'd get out and escape on foot. Did that two or three times. One time she came through the Blue Ridge gap and he'd got word that she had gone after a load. He went up there and waited. She was hauling a load of whiskey to Asheville. Daddy blocked her off at the Blue Ridge gap, and then ran one of the damndest foot races with her when she got out of the car and took off on foot down this holler. Every time she'd jump one of those logs and rail fences, her long black hair would just wave behind her like a flag. But he finally captured her."

When Ayers caught Emma making whiskey, he always pleaded with the probation people to go lenient with her. Said Ayers, "She had those kids she had to support and no husband. Had it sort of hard. She had a garden to feed her family and she was going to make something of herself even if she had to go in the likker business. And she raced cars on a closed track, the short ones."

Some years ago, however, after Ayers again caught Emma with a load of ninety gallons of liquor in her '49 coupe, the judge asked her to leave Rabun County. The following week, Emma packed up and left Persimmon and returns now only on visits. At her new home, she has turned to other pursuits.

13

Duff Floyd, Revenuer, and John Henry Hardin, Georgia's "Moonshine King"

> I thought a lots of Duff Floyd. He's a fine man. You tell him if you see him anymore that I would *love* to see him. You tell him I can yet outrun him.
> —North Georgia ex-moonshiner, Hubert Howell

THE Department of the Treasury doesn't call its Bureau of Alcohol, Tobacco, and Firearms men revenuers anymore. Actually, they never did. It was a handle given them by outsiders, particularly the tabloid newspaper writers. But now that the ATF is a bureau separate from the Internal Revenue Service (a separation that took effect in 1972), its people really aren't revenue men. Today the ATF is an enforcement arm of the Treasury Department, and its men are "special agents"—"T-men." For several decades now, ATF has been staffed with agents college-trained in law and accounting, with a high degree of integrity, intelligence, stamina, judgment, and professionalism. As such, they're a force to be reckoned with by illicit whiskeymakers. Along with their skill and savvy as super-sleuths against violators of the federal liquor laws, today's ATF agents also still retain the best of the skills of the old-time "revenuers"—their tough physiques, their shrewd and uncanny abilities as woodsmen, and their Indian-like intuition to "read the sign" (trails) and sniff out illicit stills. Which helps to explain in part the steady decline of moonshining as a way of life across the South.

This combination of old and new is epitomized by men like Duff Floyd, referred to earlier. Now seventy-three, Floyd for thirty-five years was one of the most productive "still busters" in north Georgia, a tall, rangy outsdoorsman who during his career literally worked around the clock in an evangelistic commitment to slowing down the flow of moonshine whiskey and forcing the producers to seek livelihood in some other field of endeavor.

Often described as having the skill of an Indian in the woods, Duff Floyd often would walk into illicit distilleries going full blast, before the operators ever suspected anything.

Floyd and his Number 1 sidekick, Wallace Wheeler, were out hunting a distillery in the Roy Oaks section in Cherokee County and came across a "workway"—the telltale path that leads to a stillyard and is just like a road map. The two men got in relatively close and could hear the clanging activity down in the cove. Floyd asked Wheeler to give him fifteen minutes to get around to the other side and then go on the workway, and the two men would meet in a pincer movement.

Floyd worked his way around to the back side. "There were two moonshiners, and I knew them both. Vernon High and Lester Plemmons [fictitious names]. Vernon was up on the pre-heater box, pouring the mash up and Lester was bringing it from the fermenters in two buckets, and handing it up to Vernon."

Floyd eased through the edge of the heavy thicket of rhododendron, "mountain laurel," growing in a heavy cluster right next to the stream and stillyard. When Lester walked off to the pre-heater stand with his buckets of mash, Floyd tiptoed into the stillyard, backed up against a big beech tree, slid to the ground, and locked his hands around his knees.

Lester came back to within twelve feet of the lawman and began dipping mash from the fermenters. He happened to look up, spotted Floyd, and broke into a grin. Floyd merely shook his head at him. The moonshiner drew a long breath and yelled out to his partner.

"Vernooooon!"

"What."

"Look around here and see if you know this feller, over here against this tree."

182

Vernon whirled around and froze in mid-air.

"Hell, no," Vernon said as his jaw dropped, "never saw him before in my life."

The two surrendered peacefully to their friend Duff, went to trial, and were sentenced to a term in the penitentiary.

Throughout his career of three and one-half decades, Duff Floyd never had to use his pistol in arresting moonshiners, and he took special pains to avoid making an enemy of any of them. At the same time, he seldom broke up a "live" still without arresting at least one of the operators. During some years in his career, he and his colleagues seized as many as thirty-five stills in a month, and averaged cutting more than one a day.

Duff's attractive wife, Marjorie—his faithful companion through the years—explained: "I'll tell you something. When he got after a moonshiner, the other man didn't have much of a chance. Duff doesn't have those long legs for nothin'."

"You couldn't get away from him hardly, no sir," declared his longtime friend and moonshine-hunting companion Darb Rusk, for many years a deputy sheriff in Cherokee County. "Duff would ruther raid a still than eat. He'd stop eatin' to raid one. And when he got to running a moonshiner down, he wouldn't run fast, to start off. He'd just trot him until he'd trotted him down."

"When he retired [in March, 1964]," Marjorie commented, "he could still outrun 'em, even the younger ones."

His fierce determination to get his quarry "come hell or high water" came to the surface on his very first still raid after he signed on as a Justice Department Prohibition agent on February 1, 1929, four years before the end of National Prohibition. His post of duty was at Athens, Georgia, east of Atlanta. The county sheriff called on Floyd to help locate a suspected still south of Loganville. Floyd and his associate, W. E. Derry, joined the sheriff and deputies on a walking sweep of the area. Soon they hit a trail that paralleled a creek.

"First thing we knew, we walked around some bushes and we were right on top of these guys on this shelf at a little old drum steamer. There they were, emptying 100-pound sacks of sugar into the fermenters. When they saw us, they made a dive and hit the creek."

Duff dived in after them, then followed them into the woods and brought down one of the men with a flying tackle.

During the episode, the other officers just stood and watched. Duff was flabbergasted. "What in the heck did you fellows come down here for, anyway? I thought you came to arrest the violators." After turning his captive over to the sheriff, Duff plunged back into the creek and retrieved his pistol. Thus began the revenue career of Duff Floyd.

Duff's longest tour of duty was at the post at Jasper, Georgia, in the Appalachian foothills north of Atlanta, where he now resides in retirement with his wife. During much of the time in Jasper, his territory included two of north Georgia's most prolific moonshining counties—Gilmer and Dawson, the latter of which, from time immemorial, had been known as Georgia's biggest illicit booze factory.

At the time, Dawson County was a hotbed of young hot rod liquor trippers. They would race around the Dawson County courthouse, a tiny two-story red brick building in the center of the town square. One night, a tripper bet that he could make the turn around the courthouse without even slowing down out of the straightaway coming down the road from Dahlonega, the moonshine trippers' main drag to Atlanta.

The car ripped the corner off the town's post office. The sheriff of Dawson, Charlie Crawford, was furious. He and his deputy dropped shells into their double-barrel shotguns and took positions at the old courthouse. Later in the night, the sheriff's own son came roaring around the square, and the sheriff shot off his rear tires, causing his car to careen into a ditch. The sheriff pulled the youth out of his car and clapped him in jail.

Duff, meanwhile, was out chasing liquor cars in the vicinity and was driving a new car.

"We were sittin' up there on the Dahlonega road," Duff recalled, "and this car we were looking for, loaded with liquor, came out into the main road, and headed south. When we reached the schoolhouse curve going into Dawsonville, he was out of sight. I roared up into the square. 'Look toward Atlanta!' I yelled to my partners. They didn't see him and I shouted, 'Gone toward Jasper!' and shoved that gear into second and made a dive to go past the square. Somebody was waving a flashlight but I didn't pay any attention; I was trying to follow that liquor car. I really poured on the gas. Just as I did, this old double-barrel shotgun went KA-BALOOOOOM ! ! ! KA-BALOOO-OOM ! ! ! and I could hear the buckshot singing. Two tires went down. I slammed the brakes on and the sheriff came running up, the smoke pouring out of the end of that shotgun."

The sheriff looked in and saw his old friend Duff. "I will just be damned, Duff!" he said.

"Charlie, what in the world?"

"Duff, I didn't know who you were. They been trying to take this place over and we declared war on 'em tonight."

The sheriff took Duff around to the jail and helped him put on new tires and even offered to pay for them. "I never saw a pore old feller as sorry about anything as he was," Duff remembered. "Other people got it out that he shot my tires down a purpose to keep us from catching liquor cars."

Marjorie Floyd remembered Duff's life as a revenuer was in one respect just like the life of a doctor—he was on call twenty-four hours a day. "Sometimes he would come in completely exhausted and go in and lie down and get a call and would have to go out again when he was just dragging.

"He really had no life of his own. He could not have kept it up if he hadn't have loved it.

"As for me, I ran a 'short-order joint' at home. If he had to leave at 2 A.M., I'd have to get up and feed him. There weren't any all-night restaurants around here then. I've gotten up many a night and fed him, sometimes the whole crew. We'd usually give them country ham and eggs.

"They'd be gone sometimes two or three days at a time and we didn't know how to get in touch with them. He seldom saw the children when he did come home. I had to keep them from waking him up. It wasn't a normal life at all. For several years Duff had his office at home, too. He did all his reports here. When he came in at night, he'd write reports on his typewriter until late at night. And Duff and Wallace Wheeler would come in after a day or two in the field, then they would get on the phone and talk for forty-five minutes or an hour. He really loved his work."

On several occasions, the ATF sought to promote Duff to a supervisory job, but he liked field work so much—particularly being in the outdoors—that he always rejected the offers.

But his active life also caused him some problems. In 1936, Duff's car struck a stump, and he suffered a broken neck vertebra and was on his back for six weeks. Later, he received a severe head cut when he crashed his private airplane. He lost an eye and also his sense of smell, due to a severed nerve at the bridge of his nose. His family got a big laugh out of a feature article that came out later in the *Chicago*

Sun which told about how Duff could "smell a still for a half mile."
One of the children chuckled, "I'm so glad Daddy can smell a still
because he can't smell anything else." The loss of his sense of smell
may have been the key factor explaining why he was overcome later
by dynamite fumes while blasting a distillery.

But Duff's strong constitution overcame all obstacles. His ability
as a pilot stood him in good stead when the ATF began using air-
planes to spot stills from the air. He flew as an observer with the
Coast Guard for a number of years, beginning in 1935 in Augusta,
where he earned his private pilot's license.

"I'd take pictures from the air. In the winter time when the foliage
was off the trees, it was just like looking at a map drawn on a
blackboard. We also had radio contact with our units on the ground.
Sometimes we'd have men on top of them in fifteen or twenty minutes. The moonshiners got to where they'd run off and leave their still
running when they saw one of our planes. They got to building
shelters over the stills. They'd put limbs over the shelter to camouflage their operations."

The bulk of Duff's career was devoted to seeking out distilleries
in the woods, destroying them, and arresting their operators. "I
wouldn't hesitate to ever go into the biggest distillery in my territory
at any time, day or night, without even a pocket knife. I never even
had to wrestle a prisoner down. Biggest part of the time, after I had
worked a territory for a while, I learned 'em and if I could get in
close enough and call them by their names, nine times out of ten they
wouldn't even run at all." Duff's tall, commanding yet kindly appearance—and his reputation for "playing fair and square," although tough and firm—usually disarmed his adversaries.

As Marjorie Floyd pointed out, "He didn't have any animosity or
belligerency and they didn't resent him; they realized he was just
doing his job. He treated them with courtesy and they didn't feel hard
toward him. I don't suppose he ever made an enemy out of a one of
them."

"I hope not," said Duff in all seriousness. "I don't know of it if I
did."

A lot of information on stills came into Duff's home—mainly from
other moonshiners. Many times they would come to the Floyd home
while Duff was away on a raid and Mrs. Floyd would dutifully record the information. "They came at *all* hours," she said. "Any time,

186

day or night. I've written down a lot of information, just what they told me. It never did occur to me to be frightened when they came."

Duff also received a lot of "purported information" by mail. "If you got an envelope that was a great thick thing and you opened it up and it had six or eight pages in it, you might as well not read it, because it was from some woman somewhere in a community, who was telling you about so-and-so making liquor and selling liquor. You already knew every one of them and knew what they were doing. The only thing you were interested in was '*where?*' And she didn't know *that*. But if you got an envelope and opened it up and maybe it had a three-cornered piece of paper in there—maybe a piece of brown manila paper sack, and it said, in a pencil scrawl, 'Look down the branch below so and so's barn'—that's all it'd be, just one sentence—you could count on that."

One day in the 1940s, someone came to Duff's little white frame house on Highway 5 in Jasper and told him there was a drunk looking for him on Main Street.

"I went up there and found him and he was *lousy* drunk. I told him he was fixing to wind up in the Jasper jail. He said, 'I've got a still I want you to raid. You know where the Sam Harmon Road is over in Dawson County?' He was so drunk he began to repeat himself. I had to work with him a long time. Finally he told me where to park the car, where to walk, how to get on the workway to the distillery. He told me there'd be two men in there at work the next morning and he wanted me to catch both of them. I told him we'd try, because that was our job, but that we couldn't guarantee anything.

"We got the crew together and went in over there about daylight. Pretty soon somebody came in there and started work. We could hear a man cough every now and then, but nobody ever spoke. We waited and waited for the other man to come in. Two hours passed. Finally, we decided to raid it. This man ran out and we grabbed him.

"Lo and behold, it was the fellow who had come over to Jasper and reported the distillery the day before!"

"Who told on me?" the captive snorted.

"I can't tell you," Duff declared.

"I'll give you fifty dollars if you'll tell me who informed on me," he said. The man honestly did not remember.

Duff laughed about it for years afterward, but never did tell the moonshiner that he had reported on himself! "I figured out later that he had had a dispute with his two partners, and that his idea was to report the still so his buddies would get caught. But he somehow got all mixed up." Apparently, his partners got wind of the intrigue—and stayed away from the still that day.

While Duff and Wallace Wheeler and other federal officers of the period put in as much as eighty hours a week, and treated their jobs with dead seriousness, there were occasions of great humor—episodes that gave Duff grist for his great ability as a spell-binding storyteller.

There was the time the United States district attorney in Rome, Georgia, asked Duff to go to Lookout Mountain, which juts into the northwest tip of Georgia just south of Chattanooga, and check out a moonshiner who had failed to show up for trial. The accused violator had sent in a doctor's certificate that he was sick, and the DA considered it a fake. Along about noon, Floyd got fellow agents Roscoe Kimsey and Jack Plampin to accompany him to the house of the accused, one Joe Smith.

"It was the latter part of May," recalled Duff, "and we were all dressed for court. I remember I had on a Palm Beach suit and white shoes and a Panama hat. I was just as white and loud as I could possibly be.

"We got up to Joe's house and nobody was home, although he was supposed to be sick. We got to walking around and found a road that ran off from the house, out through a field. About a hundred yards from the house, this road crossed a little branch. We walked out that road and when we got to the branch, we saw this trail going up the branch. Jack and I followed the trail. We left Roscoe and he walked up the field road. Up the trail a way, we heard a crew in this distillery, at work. There they were. I told Jack to give me about ten minutes to circle and get around through the woods and for him to come in and try to get one, and if they came out on the other side, I'd get one.

"I got around there and I took that hat off, and that Palm Beach coat, and put them out of the way, but I was still just as white as a bank of snow, you know.

"Jack came up on 'em and *they tore out*. One came up through there, and I got behind that gentleman. There is a lot of rough country around there. Rocks everywhere. I was just about on top of him and he ran to this place and there was a drop-off in a gulch of a place about as high as this ceiling. He sat down and he slid off of it and landed at the bottom. I knew I couldn't slide off that thing without just tearing my pants and ruining them. Just as he hit the bottom, I jumped. The rocks down there were from the size of your fist on up to as big as your head. I hit one on the side of my foot and I heard my ankle pop. And just as I hit, I grabbed him too. I was right on top of him. Oh, I've never had such pain. I couldn't stand up. He got ahold of me and held me and helped me back to the still.

"My prisoner had run out of his shoes, kicked them off so he could travel, and he asked if one of us could go back with him to find his shoes. I told him to 'go ahead and hunt your shoes.' Jack looked at me and said, 'You won't see him again.' I said, 'Yeah, we will; he's not going anywhere. He could've jerked loose and run from me anywhere coming back to the still, because I couldn't walk. He helped me get back.' Sure enough, in just a few minutes, here he came back. Had his shoes on. We brought him out. When we came out back to the road, there came Roscoe Kimsey ahold of a guy. Well, I couldn't walk. I had to hobble around. My ankle turned just as black as these socks. I had to get me a walking stick when I got back to Rome."

Duff Floyd's reputation for never using his pistol in an arrest came to an acid test when he was sent into Jackson County, Georgia, as part of a posse of officers trying to catch two young black moonshiners who had shot and killed a state revenuer raiding their still.

Duff was part of a crew on twenty-four-hour watch at the shack of the moonshiners' parents, an old Negro man and his wife. The woods in the vicinity were crawling with people packing shotguns and rifles —"volunteers" for the big manhunt.

"We were convinced that the young men were somewhere in the community. We hunted everywhere but couldn't find a trace of them. There were three of us who maintained the watch at night at the home—state revenue agents Jim Poole and Jim Bishop and myself. I talked to the old man, and I knew that those boys—one was about nineteen and the other, twenty-one—were trying to make contact with him. I learned the killing was more accidental than anything else. In the excitement of the raid, they had shot and killed the state agent. Then they fled into the woods and wilds. I talked to the old man and old woman every time we went up there. They were afraid their boys would be shot. All in the world those people in the woods

189

wanted was to get the sight of one of the boys. They would've shot them. That's the way a crowd will do. I could see the dangerous potential of the thing. So the last night we were up there, I told them, 'I know what your apprehensions are. I know you've been in touch with your sons. If you'll get them and turn them over to me, I'll guarantee you that they'll not be harmed, that they'll be carried straight to Atlanta and none of this crowd that's out in the woods will ever see 'em.' I could see it made an impression on the old man."

There was a weekend cottage about 300 yards back up on the same place and the owner had given the agents access to it. Duff told his companions, "We're not going to put a surveillance on the old man's house tonight. We're going up to the cottage and give them the opportunity to get together."

"Well, we went up to the cottage and we pulled out a deck of cards and played setback, the three of us, until we got sleepy and then we went to bed. Just after daylight the next morning, we drove down to the house. The old man walked out in the yard and motioned for us to stop."

The old man spoke: "Mr. Floyd, will you promise me those boys won't be harmed, that you'll get 'em out of here without this crowd killing them?"

"I told you that. Where are the young men?"

"They're out in the woods."

"All right, send out for them to come on up here."

The trio sat in the car while the old man sent a ten-year-old girl down a trail behind the house. In a few minutes, she came back, with the two young moonshiners following her. The agents didn't get out of the car.

"Have you fellows had anything to eat?" Duff asked.

"No, sir. We haven't had a thing in the world except blackberries."

The mother was in the yard and Floyd asked her if she had something to eat in the house.

"I've got a good breakfast on the table now," she said.

"All right," Duff said, "go on in, boys, and eat."

As they went in, Bishop asked Floyd if they shouldn't surround the house.

"No," Floyd replied, "What do you want to do that for? They volunteered to come up here, didn't they?"

So the three agents remained in the car. They could see the young men at the table, and they were eating furiously.

190

When they finished, they returned to the car. The mother brought out some long pones of bread that she had fixed for them, about ten inches long and three inches wide, wrapped in newspapers. The three agents got in the front seat and Floyd told the two young men to get down on the floorboard of the back seat. "Lie down one on top of another, where nobody can see you when we meet a car," he instructed them.

As Duff drove off, he asked them the shortest way, the back roads way, to reach the highway to Atlanta. "We hit the road they said to go and I drove like fury to Atlanta. We got 'em down there in jail, in a safe place. Then we contacted the headquarters in Commerce by phone and told them we had them safe in jail in Atlanta."

Duff felt compassion for many of the moonshiners he had to arrest, particularly the younger fry, since they had been "borned into moonshining" and had been given no opportunity to learn any other means for making a living. Duff often quotes an old moonshiner he arrested, who told about going "to town" in Ellijay (Georgia) where he would look at the people and look at those children with their arms full of books, with good shoes on and good clothes. "He said he wanted his children to have shoes and clothes and go to school and he didn't have any money. That's the reason he made liquor and sold it."

By and large, Duff found that outside of the liquor business most moonshiners in the Appalachian foothills of north Georgia were fairly dependable and honest people.

"But there was a certain percentage who were just downright rotten. They were in it when I was working, they are in it yet. They'll be in it until they die or until they're incarcerated somewhere. Because it's become a habit with 'em and you couldn't give 'em a legitimate job. They wouldn't have it."

Sometimes, Duff felt anger and disgust at such moonshiners. He ran up onto a still in Gilmer County, in the woods behind a schoolhouse, and found a moonshiner who had his two young sons, about eight and eleven, running the rig. The boys were dripping wet with mash. Duff watched for a few minutes. The old man was sitting around giving orders and the little boys were carrying mash from barrels to the still.

"I never have been so disgusted. It takes a lot of restraint to keep from completely losing your patience with a feller like that. I got those little boys off to myself and I told them, 'All right now, do

191

what your daddy tells you to do, as long as he tells you to do the right thing. But you boys ought to both be up there in school.' "

Every chance he got, Duff counseled young men to get out of moonshining and many of them did. "Lots of these young fellows had the will power to get out and get a little education, and get away from their old ways.

"I never missed an opportunity, when I got ahold of a youngster working in the still, to talk to him, just like I was his daddy. I'd tell him what was in store for him if he stayed in the business. I'd try to talk him out of it."

Of all the people ATF agent Duff Floyd met during his thirty-five-year career as a federal liquor lawman, the man who stood out over all the rest was a tall, quiet, stoop-shouldered old Cherokee County man known as the "moonshine king of Georgia." He was one of the state's biggest farmers, yet, aside from his illicit liquor transgressions, was a man of great nobility and integrity and honor.

Duff thought highly of the old man.

"He was a *very unusual character*, John Henry Hardin was. Anything in the world John Henry told you at any time, you could depend on it. He would not lie to you. His word was his bond. And if an escaped convict got down in his section, he was the first man to get out and let the officers know about it.

"John Henry was a big farmer, one of the biggest in that country. He grew a lot of corn on the Etowah River around Proctor's Bend back before the valley became Lake Allatoona. He grew lots of cotton further up from the river. The story went that before World War I, there came an unprecedented flood, and his fine corn crop soured and John Henry was downhearted. He knew he was going to suffer a big loss. One of his farmhands told him that he could save the corn by grinding it up and using it as mash to make whiskey. Maybe that's the way he got into it. I don't know for sure.

"At the time, he was a strong churchman and superintendent of Sunday School and a very reliable fellow.

"I first got to know John Henry in 1932, when I was transferred from Atlanta to Rome. He was a big farmer. Had several dozens of mules. Grew lots of cotton and corn. Had his own commissary store. He had people farming, and he had another group making whiskey in the woods and coves between the fields, with big steamer distilleries. Six, eight, and ten horsepower boilers from Chattanooga.

"One morning we raided a large distillery on his place, and while we were waiting for the other officers and still hands to come in with the truck and supplies. I noticed squirrels around everywhere. It was along in the early fall. I don't think I've seen as many squirrels anywhere. After John Henry's still hands came in—we had caught three or four of them and their trucks and an upright boiler—I said, 'I guess you fellers have plenty of squirrels to eat around here, don't you.' One of them told me, 'No sir, the man we work for here will not let us bring a shotgun or a .22 rifle or any other weapon around the distillery. He tells us we're violating the law in the first place and if you take a gun in there, it's not fit for anything except to get you in trouble—serious trouble.' *That was John Henry.*

"We'd go in there and we'd arrest a bunch of those fellers, maybe in the morning, and we'd come by John Henry's house or his commissary up there, and he'd be there. We'd tell John Henry that his boys had to go before the U.S. Commissioner to make a bond or go to jail and that we knew he didn't want them to go to jail. We'd say, 'How about bringing these fellers and meetin' us at Jasper at the commissioner's office, say about two o'clock.' He'd say, 'Yes, sir, they'll be right there.' At a quarter before two, I'd look out there and there would be John Henry with all those fellows in the car.

"A funny thing was John Henry would not tolerate a drunk on any job on his place. That was one of his rules. Wouldn't put up with a drunk at all. He'd let him go."

The sharpest recollections of John Henry came from a neighbor farmer, now seventy-four, who was a moonshining moonlighter and who at times made whiskey for Hardin on contract.

"He was a fine old man, John Henry was. He was a great singer. We could hear him singing from a long way as he came down the road in his little T-model. We could always hear him when he reached the 'Obie Patch,' a bend in the road. He had a '16 or '17 T-model Ford. He cut it down and made a little truck out of it. A home-made thing. It was the only truck up there. I mean, didn't *nobody* else have no cars or trucks either at that time. You could hear him singing for a mile on a clear morning. It was quiet and still up there and you could hear that little car 'a-chick-a-chick-a-chicking' and you could hear John Henry singing. He had a purty baritone voice, a *real* purty voice. He'd sing church songs, religious songs, 'cause he had been a great church singer. He had been a deacon of the Sixes Methodist Church at Little River. He was a Sunday school teacher, too. He was

193

a *great old man*. When he told you something, *it was that way*. I would have believed him above anybody else. And if he owed you a nickel, he'd pay you. I've known him in bad weather, it pouring rain, to get on a mule and ride it to somebody's house to pay 'em. He could have waited 'til morning, but he wanted that debt paid right then. He owed it and he wanted to clear it up. And it didn't make no difference what he had, you could borrer it, anything that you wanted that he had.

"I've worked fer him by the day on the farm—fifty cents a day, nickel an hour. You couldn't get no work nowhere else. Wuddn't a thing in the world. It was in the '30s—'31 and '32. Those were rough years on poor people that didn't have no money. If you worked for him on one of his stills, you got fifty cents an hour. That was lots of money! One time, we got seventy-two hours in at the still before we quit . . . thirty-six dollars worth. *I was rich*. That was in 1931. I worked off and on for Mr. Hardin from 1925 to '42.

"I also worked my own outfit on my own place and sold the whiskey to Mr. Hardin. Sold it to him for two dollars, and he sold it to the haulers for four dollars. The haulers, I understand, got eight dollars for it from the bootleggers in Rome and Atlanter.

"John Henry stored his whiskey in barrels. He didn't have to keep the whiskey overnight. There was *somebody* there fer it *all the time*. Lot of 'em took 100 gallons at a carload. Packed those cans in there.

"Sometimes John Henry would have twenty stills a workin' at one time, or more."

During my investigation of John Henry Hardin, I asked an old-timer who had lived in the settlement for about fifty years to accompany me on a tour of the old homestead and farmlands that were occupied by the moonshine king between 1918 and 1943, when he died. Much of the farmland—the bottomlands on the Etowah River —have been inundated by the waters of a giant U. S. Government dam downstream. The fingers of the Alatoona Lake extend into many of the valleys and coves which once held John Henry's stills and those of his subcontract moonshiners. The uplands area of the farm are now owned by big paper companies which have cleared away all the old houses and accompanying buildings that Hardin built and occupied: his huge commissary-store; his grist mill that stood behind it; his log cabin private residence; his huge frame home;

and, across the street from it, the big two-story barn which was famous both as a stash-house for storing liquor and as the pick-up point for liquor trippers who came nightly from Rome and Atlanta and Marietta to pick up loads for their thirsty customers.

John Henry had rented out the huge farmlands from the Georgia Power Company, which had bought up the property anticipating the construction of a hydroelectric dam. Later, when the U.S. Government built the dam, paper companies such as Georgia Kraft acquired the lands that didn't go for the reservoir, and they now operate them as tree farms. A section also has been designated as a deer preserve, and once a year, for three days, the state allows hunters to go in and hunt deer.

My guide on the tour was a former neighbor and confidant of John Henry's who, as a younger man, had operated a "fifteen-horse farm" nearby and had worked whiskey distilleries for the "king" on a wage and also as an independent subcontractor.

Coming off Highway 20 east of Cartersville, we turned onto a narrow dirt road that went through a heavily-wooded area and a mile or so further on forded Hawk Creek. We parked near a cove and got out and walked to a branch where the old man had once operated a still.

"Haven't been down in these woods in forty years. It hasn't been burned off in twenty-five years. You can't tell where a rattlesnake might hit here. I always kept 'em burned off when I rented this land. No snake problem then."

Soon we found a still site, the fieldstone remains of a firebox, a furnace. All around, rusty gallon cans were scattered, buried down in the leaves and ferns, each bearing the mark of an ax.

"You ought to take one of these back and give it to Duff. He's probably the one that put the ax to these cans. Probably in the '30s."

The woods smelled pungent and sweet.

"If you want to smell something good, you should come here after a rain. Yeah, when it comes a little shower of rain, right soon of a morning, it does smell good. This air is just as fresh as it was seven thousand years ago when man took his first breath of it."

Back in the car, we drove toward the old Hardin homestead. Soon we came onto one of the present-day landmarks in the area, a state deer-weighing station, a green lean-to.

"We're at the old Laughingal settlement. This was the Cartersville-

Canton Road, old Highway 20. But it was never paved through here. There's the Laughingal Cemetery. My folks saw Laughingal, a Cherokee princess, in 1835. Just before the Cherokee Indians were drove out. My folks had come over from England. Uncle Josh Kite was a great-uncle of mine and he was just a baby then. Laughingal give him a piece of Indian dumplings, they called it—cornmeal wrapped up in a blade of a corn stalk and cooked in boiling water. He had it and didn't know how to unwrap it, it was so tight. Laughingal said, "Shuck it! Shuck it! Shuck it!'"

Across from the Laughingal Cemetery we made a sharp turn to the south, onto the road leading to the old John Henry Hardin empire.

"Duff and the other officers rode these roads *all* the time. They knowed what John Henry was doing *all* the time. John Henry lived in an old log house that stood over there."

We got out of the car and walked through the vines and bushes. The only signs left of the log cabin were rocks from its foundation and a Chinquapin Rose tree, bearing beautiful pink-petaled roses.

Across and down the road apiece, plum bushes and pines grew up around chunks of the concrete foundations remaining from the old store. To the left, covered with pine needles, were pieces of the little office-building foundation. Out back was the grist mill where the only surviving mementos were a few rusty barrel hoops.

A quarter-mile down the road toward the river were the remains of the old farm home and barn. On both sides of the road, giant old dead oaks stood as gaunt, silver monuments, their trunk barks having been "grooved" with a saw, and put to death—just as the pioneers "girdled" their trees to make room for their corn crops. Only here, the objective had been to eliminate the hardwood competition for the fast-growing pines. A thicket of lush blackberry bushes covered the old house-seat.

"Yep, right here's where he fed his hands. It was a big kitchen and dining room. It was built almost entirely out of glass, a big frame house with windows all around the kitchen and dining room. Two truck loads of hands would come up here to eat every day during the summer. I imagine about seventy-five. They'd have to eat at different times. The house was the last building torn down by the paper company."

We drove further down the farm road, reaching a flat stream, Dry

196

Branch, that my Maverick forded easily. On the other side, we climbed a gentle hill by the old Dry Branch schoolhouse, where the hulking skeletons of old trees again stood like sentinels to the past. From the top of a ridge overlooking the Etowah River Valley, we saw the site of the house of John Henry's son.

"Can you see that mountain range that looks smoky? Well, that's on the other side of the lake. John Henry first lived over there, back to the left. I'd say two miles. That's at Little River. That's where he got washed away"—in the flood that presumably led to his whiskey-making activities.

After standing and gazing across the quiet scene, as if from another world, we retraced our path back by the old homestead and to the Laughingal Cemetery.

"My daddy helped dig a grave out there and he dug up the awfulest bunch of deer horns, I guess buried there by the Cherokees."

A deer galloped gracefully across the road, darting from the woods on one side, to the woods on another.

"Now here's our old farm where I lived with my parents. That was our apple orchard down there. There was two rows on each side of that little branch. That was a *long* way down through there and it made the apples, too—Winesaps and Ben Davids. I sold John Henry 100 bushels of apples in '27 and he made apple brandy. He made lots of peach brandy, too."

The old man, now old and a victim of heart attacks, looked with reverence at the site of his home, long since torn down and removed.

"Ever holler that we've seen, might near, I've made whiskey in. *Ever holler*, ever one was decorated with a still. Some of 'em had lots of stills. Me and another feller built a still shack over there one time in a ditch. The ditch was almost as wide as the road. We covered it over with timbers and put a boiler over there and put broom sedge on top, to a kammy-flage it from the flying revenuers, like Duff Floyd."

I will let Floyd have the last word about John Henry Hardin.

"He was the biggest operator we had to deal with in Georgia at that time, in the '30s. He made a lot of money at one time. Some said he was worth a half million dollars right after World War I, but he died a pauper. Suffered a lot of losses, served several penitentiary sentences.

"While I was working out of Rome, John Henry was implicated in two liquor conspiracy cases. Federal cases. He was found guilty on the first and pleaded guilty on the second. He was about seventy-two or seventy-three years old at that time. And he had already served at least two sentences before that. I believe he ended up in nineteen federal and state cases all together.

"After that second case, when he was in the U.S. Marshal's lockup behind the courtroom, I visited him and took him some flowers. We talked with one another through the bars. I told him, 'John Henry, you are the best gambler I've ever known. You have been in the whiskey business in a big way ever since I've been working up here. You've made no bones about it. But before you go off this time—we may not get to see you again—I wanted to tell you something. You've been very kind to us. Every man that worked down here against you appreciates your attitude. I just want you to know that we never came over here to your place to raid your stills one single time because we didn't like John Henry Hardin.' Well, you know, he reached through those bars and got me by the hands and he just stood there, and squeezed my hands and shook. The tears ran off his face and he never could say a word.

"Well, John Henry went ahead and he served that sentence and he came out and shortly after he came out, he was almost an invalid.

"I passed through there one day and saw him settin' on his porch in a wheelchair. I stopped and went to speak to him. He reached up and got me by the hand and pulled me down to a chair, and we talked for about twenty minutes. He like to never let me go."

John Henry Hardin, ex-moonshine king of Georgia, died in 1943 at the age of seventy-eight, and Duff Floyd knew that it marked a milestone in the passing of a way of life.

14

Moonshine Tales:
Pure Corn, Unadulterated

"Hey, George, your corn's lookin'
pretty yeller out there."
"Yeah, I planted the yaller kind."
"Say, George, I don't believe you're
going to make over a half a crop."
"That's right, I'm workin' on halves."
"George, how much do you think
you're going to make to the acre?"
"Oh, about a hundred gallons."
—Story told by
Ex-Moonshine Tripper

OF all the enterprises in the world that have been subjected to humor, the moonshine craft is perhaps the most overworked. Not only by the spectators on the outside looking in but by the practitioners themselves and by their arch enemies, the revenuers.

But without the good humor displayed on the part of most of the whiskey-makers (to help overcome the extreme tedium and hard labor involved), as well as on the part of the big and little law, it would be a far less fascinating occupation for both sides. Certainly, American folklore would be greatly diminished.

In this chapter, we are going to round up a potpourri of tall tales, stories, flat-out lies and some possibly true anecdotes that have accumulated over the years about the corn likker craft. We warn you, dear reader, that you should take everything you read in this chapter with a grain of salt (salt, by the way, will "kill" a batch of mash). But please read it in good spirits!

First a few stories about "big drinking." In the old days in the mountains, the daily hardships incident to mountain living were such that they could scarcely be borne by a man who was cold sober. He *had* to have a drink in order to keep going. And since the federal and state taxes caused "legal likker" (or government whiskey) to be priced out of most people's reach, corn whiskey quickly and magnificently filled the breach.

John O. Morrell, a retired TVA land surveyor and now a practicing attorney and land surveyor at Sevierville, Tennessee, recalled a story told him by a Mr. Swearingen (not his real name), a stable boss for a logging contractor during World War I. "Now the winter of 1917–18 was the roughest winter I have ever seen. The Tennessee River at Knoxville froze over twice, and many riverboats were severely damaged. According to Swearingen, he didn't draw a sober breath all winter.

> I kept a jug, or a fruit jar, under the bed, and when the alarm went off at 4 A.M. I would get up, take a big drink and go out to the stable and feed the horses, come back to the house and take another drink before breakfast, then back to the stable to see that the teamsters showed up, and had their teams properly groomed and harnessed. Back to the house to mark up any absences and take another snort. Then back to the stable to doctor sick or injured animals, mend gear, and clean stables. Another drink before dinner and rest a little while, maybe bring in some stove-wood for the missus, and back out to put down the hay before the teams started coming in from work . . . check the horses back in and see if any of them had been hurt. Another drink before supper and a final one before going to bed.

So, in any case, said Swearingen.

Hamper McBee, one-time Cumberland moonshiner, tells the story about the time he and his liquor-making buddies had their black pot still fired up good and hot, and had a pretty good stream of liquor running out. A friend came by and issued a challenge: "I can drink whiskey faster than it's coming out of there." Hamper took him up on the dare, pulled the tub out from under the worm to make room for the ambitious visitor, and told him: "Hell, get down there and drink it, then!"

"He lay down under that worm," Hamper recalled. "He swallered and swallered and directly he just trembled all over and just rolled out from under it. He didn't come to 'til the next day sometime. He must have drunk a pint and a half. We were running alkihol. It was *strong*. It's a wonder it didn't kill him."

That's exactly what happened to a South Carolina moonshiner near North Augusta, South Carolina in the 1960s. A chief distiller and a still hand got to arguing who could drink the most liquor. The chief pulled out a large tea glass and with a bottoms up gesture, drank it down without hesitation. It was first run whiskey—130 proof. He drank it all, and dropped dead. The doctor who examined him found he died of acute alcoholism.

There was the story told by Judge Felix E. Alley, a distinguished federal judge in western North Carolina, in his book, *Random Thoughts and the Musings of a Mountaineer*. It concerned an old-timer in Macon County, North Carolina, Dave Lewis:

He came every election at daybreak, full of 'corn' in liquid form, and remained full till the last vote was counted. All day long at short intervals he would yell: 'Hooray for those and others!' It was never learned just what he meant by this expression. Finally his 'corn' got the better of him. The late Dr. S. H. Lyle was his physician; but the more Dr. Lyle applied his remedies, the more 'corn' Uncle Dave consumed. One morning he came to the doctor's office in a very 'soaked' condition and Dr. Lyle said to him: 'Dave, I don't know what is to become of you. I have been doing my best for months to cure you of this awful drink habit, but you persist in drinking to excess every day. You have drunk liquor until your system has become saturated with it to the extent that when you strike a match there is great danger that it will set you on fire and you will be burned alive. You know liquor will burn like kerosene oil.' Uncle Dave jumped up in great excitement and exclaimed: 'Doctor, have you a Bible in your office?' Dr. Lyle replied: 'Yes, I have a Bible here, but I am not going to let you take an oath that you will never drink any more, for I am sure you would violate your oath.' Uncle Dave replied: 'I don't want to take no such oath as that. I want to take an oath that I will never strike another match as long as I live!'

One familiar story about the moonshine drinking habits of some moonshiners goes this way. A fellow toting a shotgun and a jar accosted a stranger, pointed the gun at him, thrust the jar in his hands and made him take a good swallow. It made searing hog tracks all the way down his throat. Then the gunman handed his weapon to the stranger and said: "Now you hold the gun on me while I take a drink!"

One of America's great corn whiskey folklorists is Colonel Leland Devore (U.S. Army, retired), a native West Virginian, now of Maryland. Colonel Devore says that when the thought of "old-timey" West Virginia moonshine flits across the shadowed memories of his mind, his throat involuntarily contracts, his stomach prepares for an invasion, "and I hear, as if from far away, the gagging whisper of a long-lost friend of younger days whose favorite saying was, 'vile stuff—I WISH I HAD A BARREL OF IT!'

"The corn whiskey producer rarely aged his moonshine," Colonel Devore explained, "since he wanted to get it off of his hands as quickly and as profitably as possible. Aging, therefore, became the job of the purchaser. . . . The way to obtain the amber color, and incidentally to tame the stuff to where something resembling human speech was possible within five minutes after taking a sip of it, was to place the raw moonshine in a charred oak keg, add a few tablespoons of granulated charcoal, and keep shaking it at intervals for a few weeks—if you could wait that long and the keg held together."

According to Devore, many ingenious ways were devised to agitate the keg, including attaching it to the rumble seat of one's coupe or placing it on a rope sling on a closet door. One distiller in West Virginia would tie a keg of new liquor between the rockers of his grandmother's rocking chair, "And the gentle sloshing motion imparted a smoothness to that moonshine that was seldom equalled." This particular moonshiner sold his grandmother's knitted socks and mufflers to keep her busy knitting and rocking. "She liked to listen to the radio, and turned up the station loud, so the low gurgling of the keg bothered her not at all."

In East Tennessee around Gatlinburg, old-timers used three-gallon pickle barrels, charred on the inside, to age their whiskey. They would tie one to a chain and drop it in the river to bob around, with the chain anchored to the bank. Three weeks of such bobbing produced fine, red, well-aged whiskey. Other old-timers used hardwood sawdust which they put in a "Bull Durham" tobacco pouch and put it down in a barrel of whiskey, much like instant tea!

While many moonshiners liked to nip on their own whiskey periodically while working at a still, it was an equally popular pastime to drink the "distiller's beer" from the mash boxes.

There was the distiller at Lost Cove, Tennessee, who discovered to his chagrin that he had run out of whiskey. He made a bee-line for a friend's still. There sat two big 500-gallon fermenters and the mash was good and sour and ready for a run the next day. He and his friend cut a cane to stick down through the cap of the mash and sip the beer.

Lester said, "Harvey, I believe this box has more kick in it than that one."

Harvey replied, "Ain't we gonna drink both of 'em?"

They hung around the mash boxes all that day and night, drinking, and finally went home the following evening, with Harvey strapped across a mule, which was being led by Lester.

This story comes from a man who insists he knew the people involved. During the 1920s, some Kentucky moonshiners were sitting around a still in a cave waiting for a batch to run. Discussion got around to the good things of life which soon came down to the peak of every discussion of perfection—moonshine, women, and tobacco. As the first step of a fuzzy plan to contain all of these glories into one, the men wove green tobacco from a nearby field and suspended it as a mat at the top of a pot, so the stream percolated through the tobacco. They drank deeply of their "corn-bac." All of them became violently sick, one turned blind and deaf for about two weeks. Several teetotalers resulted. So that ended "corn-bac." "Besides," as one wag retorted, "ain't hardly any hollow-laiged fiddlin' wimmin' 'round here to try it out on!"

While some corn whiskey can be awfully powerful, it is not beyond being subdued. Professor Bill Egerton of Atlanta remembers his days as a young man in North Carolina when he found a way to conquer corn and make a cocktail out of it at the same time. Egerton created a corn drink he called the "nose dive":

"You got a jigger of corn likker and put the jigger in a water glass. You put enough tomato juice in the water glass to come up to the rim of the jigger. Then you turned it up and the juice held the jigger to the glass and kept it from knocking your teeth out. You got the moonshine in the middle of the mouth and two streams of tomato juice coming from each side. That was the best way we found to keep the taste down . . ."

Whenever moonshiners get a little of their own distillate down their throat, they become bold and rambunctious and become a little careless toward the always alert, usually teetotaling revenuers.

There was the case of ATF agent Roscoe Kimsey who, working out of the Gainesville, Georgia, post, had been trying for a long time to catch a moonshiner at his still in Lumpkin County. Roscoe had cut up the man's still many times but the moonshiner always escaped. On this occasion, Roscoe and his crew arrived at the site about 6 A.M. and they found the operator at the distillery at work. They had made several runs and were about to wind up their activity for the day. The moonshiner knew Roscoe's ambition to catch him in the act and just for the fun of it—with a few drinks under the belt—walked out to the edge of the stillyard, pulled down a tree limb and put it to his ear like a telephone. He got hold of another limb and cranked it.

"Operator, give me Roscoe Kimsey at Gainesville. . . . Hello. That you, Roscoe? This is Jack Sims [a fictitious name]. If you want to catch me, you'd better come on. We're just about through here and we're going to be gone in a few minutes. You'd better hurry up if you're going to catch me."

From out of the woods Roscoe stepped with a wide grin, handcuffs in hand. "All right, Jack, here I am."

The use of corn whiskey has not been limited only to drinking. There are stories about how it was often used to fuel the lamps of mountain cabins. And in the early 1930s, North Carolina state officials considered substituting the corn distillate for gasoline. The chief proponent was Capus M. Waynick, then chairman of the North Carolina State Planning Board. Apparently, he had heard about the two fellows who ran out of gasoline up in the hills on a stormy night, and got a jug of corn from a mountain man and put it in the gas tank. According to columnist John Parris of Asheville, "There was a series of explosions, sort of like a mule trying to break out of a barn and then the motor began to hum. Well, they drove that car almost twenty-five miles on that gallon of corn."

Waynick called a press conference and told newsmen that the state was using more than ten million gallons of gasoline in its trucks and buses, and he figured corn liquor would be more economical and equally powerful and would be a good way to dispose of the state's corn surplus. Chemists then found that corn alcohol would, indeed, power gasoline engines, but cautioned about the resulting foul odor. Whatever the reason, the state never did get around to using the high-octane corn, and many mountaineers were happy, declaring it would have been a shame to waste good corn likker in such a fashion.

Henry Ford the first also had a great hankering to try out double-distilled mountain dew in his tin lizzies.

A story goes that Henry was staying as Asheville, North Carolina's famed Grove Park Inn when Eph Lowman, the "mountain dew monarch" dropped by one night to visit him. He found Ford in the reading room and introduced himself. Ford motioned him to pull up a seat, and asked him what sort of business he was in. Eph informed him confidentially that he was a moonshiner, that he had blocked for almost thirty years.

Ford declared, "Do you know, I would give anything to test a sample of mountain dew." Eph felt sure that Ford had said, "taste."

"I can edzact yer taste fer you," Lowman whispered. "I brung a sample in my coat." He pulled out an elongated bottle, almost full with the pale, but athletic, fluid. Ford took the sample, and to Lowman's surprise slipped it into his pocket. He said he would "test it" later. The moonshiner left in disgust.

Subsequently, Ford reportedly tried to find Lowman. As he boarded a train for Detroit, he was supposed to have declared, "I would surely have liked to have seen that moonshiner. There is enough kick in his concoction to put mule-power into every tin lizzie on the globe."

The *Atlanta Journal*'s Hugh Park told about the fans who came out of the University of Georgia's Sanford Stadium following a football game to find their car wouldn't start. Out of the crowd stepped a fan who pulled from his car a whiskey bottle which contained gas. "All it needs is a drink of Scotch," he said as he turned up the half pint, pouring its contents into the carburetor. The car started perfectly. "Native Georgians who gasped at this miracle had heard that moonshine whiskey would start a recalcitrant automobile," Park wrote, "but none had ever seen one that had to be pampered with imported Scotch."

A corn whiskey expert in Smyrna, Georgia, relayed this story, told to him by his father, who recalled hard-drinking, cussing Uncle John of Rockcastle County, Kentucky.

Uncle John was out plowing his fields in the '20s. He was wont to pause frequently for a nip from his jug of 'shine hidden at the edge of the field. One of a crew of passersby, seeing this, asked his friends to hide and watch him play a joke. He climbed and hid in a large tree near where Uncle John passed. Soon Uncle John went by, preoccupied with his mule team and keeping a straight furrow. The jokester called in a grave, ominous voice, 'John . . . John.' Uncle John stopped, answered, looked around, and seeing no one, continued plowing. Well, the pause at the jug took extra time that trip. At next passing, the jokester again called out. John answered with a yell and looked all around—even up the tree. The wag was well concealed in a bushy fork and escaped detection. Uncle John naturally blistered the air blue with evidence of his chagrin. As he plowed on, the wag sent after him: 'John . . . your blasphemy . . . has been heard . . . and considered . . .' At the next passing, Uncle John less confidently answered, 'Who are you?' The wag replied, 'It is I . . . the Lord . . . come to test you . . .' Forthwith, Uncle John fell to his knees as if struck. 'What would you have me do?' The wag answered, 'Go Ye into the World and Preach the Gospel.' Well, Uncle John unhitched the team and became an inspiring revival preacher, gaining great local fame for the numbers of converts he made. The fact that lightning later struck both the tree and the nearby plow—and an accident or hot sun broke the jug— but heightened Uncle John's fervor.

Just about as equally wild was the story about the "still" ghost of Cocke County, Tennessee, as told by the Tennessee Folklore Society. In the early days of Tennessee's moonshining industry (when there were "government stills" licensed by the Treasury Department), the young men of a community often would go to a nearby still on a "gut-letting Saturday night." At the end of the night's celebration, they would return in fine form, singing and carousing along the mountain trails, and telling tall tales, including ghost tales. All of this made them more or less ghost conscious. On many occasions, they would see a ghost reclining on a stump in a low place. At this point, those who could run, did.

A young circuit rider preacher who wanted to shake the boys loose from their alcoholic habit decided he would give them a little additional scare. He wrapped himself in sheets, prepared a ghostly head-dress, and waited in the woods where the boys had reported seeing the ghost. When the preacher heard the boys singing and stumbling down the trail from the still, he mounted a stump and waved his ghostly arms. According to the Folklore Society, "the boys stopped 'stock-still' in a body, so frightened they could not speak for a moment. Then one issued a blood-curdling yell and shouted, 'Lord have mercy, look! There's two of them tonight.' " This time they ran like white lightning. The preacher looked around. And there sat the other one. He yelled for the boys to wait. Visiting at the still went into a decline afterward—for a few weeks, at least.

Some connoisseurs of corn liquor get so carried away after a few swigs that their imaginations understandably run loose. Take the case of a Social Circle, Georgia, businessman, who told me this story:

I used to have a great uncle by the name of Otto. Uncle Otto used to go fishing quite often and would usually bring about ten to fifteen real big bass home. One day I went with him to the lake and watched him fish. It was a great mystery to everybody how he always caught the fish every time and how he always caught such big ones. My great uncle, like everybody years ago, would take a drink of homemade white whiskey. So, naturally, when we got to the boat, he put a jar in with us. When we got to the middle of the lake, he told me he was going to show me how to fish for the big ones. He put a minnow on the hook, opened the jar of white whiskey, dipped the minnow in the jar, and threw the minnow over into the water. In about three minutes and a half, his pole bowed and the fight began. He and I fought the fish for about thirty-one minutes and finally got him in the boat. It was a big one. I asked Uncle Otto why the fish liked the minnow dipped in the white lightning. Wiping his mouth after taking the jar down, he said: 'Son, that fish don't like the liquor, but the minnow does. After that minnow took him a big drink, it made him real mean. That minnow swims around and finds him the biggest fish he can and then that minnow bites that big fish and holds on for the ride.' Sure enough, I like to fell out of the boat when I looked at that big fish and saw that minnow still hanging onto its tail.

207

The medicinal qualities of corn whiskey have long been revered by the people in the Appalachians, where its efficacy has been handed down from generation to generation, and where it has been credited with saving many a life. An old-timer in Dawson County, Georgia, remembered that "My daddy kept whiskey as medicine. He had a sick spell and the doctor told him the first thing to do when he got up of a morning, before he ate breakfast, was to take a drink of that corn whiskey. Lot of people took corn whiskey instead of medicine. Put cherokee tree bark in it and made bitters out of it."

Many mountain people dissolved camphor in corn whiskey to create a type of smelling salts, while another medicine was made by soaking cucumbers and poke root in white spirits. The *Knoxville Register* in 1820 published this prescription to cure a toothache: "Tablespoon of any kind of spirits, tablespoon of vinegar, teaspoon of common salt, mix and put in mouth. It gives great relief."

Many people around the Appalachians to this day swear by a special type of cough syrup made of corn liquor, rock candy, and glycerine. Sometimes peppermint candy is used, as well as honey and lemon juice.

A one-time distiller from Sugar Valley, Georgia, told of a corn liquor potion that will break up bronchitis in a hurry. "You take white whiskey and pour it in a saucer," he said. "Add sugar, about a fourth of an inch deep, and set it afire. Then you drink it hot. It'll really knock out bronchitis."

The students at Rabun Gap-Nacoochee School, in interviewing residents in the Rabun County area of northeast Georgia for their magazine *Foxfire*, unearthed many "hand-me-down" remedies that depend greatly on corn whiskey. Here are a few of them:

> *Croup:* For a baby, pour a mixture of turpentine and white whiskey into a saucer and set fire to it. Hold the baby over it until he breathes it deeply.
> *Dysentery:* Burned whiskey.
> *Toothache:* Hold whiskey on the tooth.
> *Headache:* Mix camphor and white whiskey and rub it on the head.
> *Colds and flu:* Whiskey and honey and lamb's tongue and whiskey.
> *Snakebite:* Cut open a freshly killed chicken and place the guts

on the bite to draw poison. Drink whiskey and also apply it to the bite.

An East Tennessean struck by a rattler (so a newspaper story goes) managed to get to his jug of whiskey in his back yard and guzzle down a quart. He credited the action with saving his life, although his arm remained paralyzed the rest of his life. (According to the newspaper, the victim grabbed the rattler and choked him to death!)

All authentic moonshiners are great outdoorsmen and woodsmen and their companionship with the animals gives them an intuitiveness that stands them in good stead when they are being surrounded by approaching revenuers. The mountaineer moonshiner nearly always takes his dogs with him to his still-house to keep a sharp eye out for the law. But there have been better lookouts than dogs. Mules, for instance.

"A mule is the handiest thing you ever seen to have around a still," says Hamper McBee. "That rascal, all you have to do is just *watch him*. Damn dog, he'd go to sleep on you. But a mule now, he'll flick those old ears up there . . . he can hear anyone a mile off. He'll point those ears forward just like a pointer dog. One time I remember, we'd faared up and had done run one charge and a recharge. We had an old mule with us. We were going to pack that whiskey out with him. Dad Damn, he just pointed those ears up the mountain. So I lit out from the still and circled around the road and walked up there for about ten minutes, to see who it was. It was a couple of boys squirrel huntin'. But it was *over a mile* up there."

Hamper also tells about a monkey that moonshiners adopted and kept at their still on the Cumberland Plateau near Tracy City, Tennessee.

"The old monkey lived only for three or four years. I reckon he finally had the DTs and died. But he drank that white booze all the time. They got him onto it. He'd *stay* on a drunk. Became an alcoholic. When they'd take his whiskey away from him, he'd just squall and have a damn fit. When they tried to get him on the wagon, he'd outfox 'em. He'd get up there and stick his tail down in the bung of that barrel full of corn whiskey and get that liquor on his tail and just slurp it through his mouth. He'd dip that tail into the barrel two or three times, then he'd *climb them trees*! Whoopeeee!"

209

As to dogs, it's true that some have made good lookouts but others have flunked miserably. There was the time when revenuer Duff Floyd and a local sheriff ran up on a small still, being operated by an old man. The old man had three dogs lying around him. The biggest one got up and ran straight to Duff. The agent patted him on the head and the dog elected not to bark. The second dog ran to the tree occupied by the sheriff, who was able to shush him and keep him from barking. Then agent Wallace Wheeler came down to flush the still, and the old man started to take off running through a briar patch. The commotion woke up the third dog, which jumped up and bit his owner three times!

Near Russellville, Alabama, ATF agents got information on an illegal distillery and planned a raid. Agent "Pic" Pequinot tells the story:

"So we went into the raid. There was high rock cliff going up close to the still. I came in on the patch. The moonshiner had a red bone hound, a big old dog, and a little old feist. I was on my hands and knees, just as careful not to make any noise at all. I raised up a bit and that feist *smelled* me. Here he come—yip, yip, yip. Well, that old man heard and went right up the rock cliff. Nothin' I could do. But then the old red bone came out there, and I made friends with him. So I took him around to the cliff where the old man went up and I said, 'Go get him, son,' and the old red bone went around through the pines and me right behind him, his old tail wagging and we got down there and finally reached the old man. The dog looked up at the old man and just wagged his tail. The old man said: 'You God-damn sunofabitch. *I'm a gonna kill you.*' "

There was the story of a noted moonshiner in Rabun County, Georgia, Fishbait French (not his real name), which had nothing to do with liquor but says something about moonshining gall. Fishbait was caught with a dead squirrel out of season. The game warden made a charge against him, and when his case came to trial, Fishbait pleaded not guilty, and, moreover, elected to serve as his own lawyer. The judge asked him:

"Well, Mr. French, do you have anything to say in your own behalf?"

"Yes, your honor."

"Well, you were caught with a dead squirrel, weren't you?"

"Yes, your honor."

"What else do you have to say?"

"Well, I killed it in self-defense, your honor. You see, it jumped out of a tree on me and I had to kill it in self-defense. It was about to eat me up."

In Hall County, Georgia, there was an old-timer—a merchant mariner who worked on the Great Lakes during the summer and who came home to north Georgia in the winter and made whiskey. He was proud of his workmanship. He had a copper still, with copper tubing and a copper radiator condenser. He kept his mash covered so bugs wouldn't get in.

But it was too good to last. On a Christmas morning, the sheriff and his deputies swooped in and cut his outfit down. The editor of *The Daily Times* in Gainesville at the time, Sylvan Meyer, was invited by the sheriff to witness the event. When they arrived at the still-house out in the Morgan district, they found the deputies busy cutting up the outfit. The moonshiner took the Christmas day raid very philosophically, however, and expressed his personal pride in the quality stuff he had been turning out. The sheriff spoke up:

"Okay, now give me what you've got under the stumps."

The man reached under one stump and brought out a half-gallon jar which he handed the sheriff and which the sheriff presented to the editor for Christmas.

"How about the rest," the sheriff pressed.

The man went to still another stump and brought out another jar. The sheriff just stood there and the man went to still another stump and brought out a third jar. Finally in exasperation, the merchant mariner-moonshiner declared:

"Good God, sheriff, aren't you goin' to let me keep anything for Christmas?"

Junior Samples (the "Hee Haw" star) tells about the time the Revenue men surprised him at his still near Coal Mountain in Forsyth County, Georgia. "They come so close to catching me, they broke my overhaul galluses and got my hat, but they didn't get me." Junior hid in the woods. As he lay there on the ground, his Ingersoll watch in his overalls was ticking so loud, he dug a hole and buried it. Junior adds: "I hain't drank any moonshine in five years. All the moonshine I get, I give it to my best friends."

IV

THE END

*It ain't like it was
years and years ago.*
Hamper McBee

15

Metro Moonshine: Where the Illegal Booze Buck Stops

> It's a different bunch of people that makes whiskey now than what used to. This bunch now, most of 'em are people who naturally want to be outlaws. Years ago, it wuddn't that way in this country. Some of the best people we had made whiskey. Old mountain people who didn't have any other way to make a living, who really stood for the right things.
> —Northeast Georgia businessman

EARLY one crisp morning in February, 1971, the people living near the Dunwoody County Club, a posh residential community on Atlanta's far north side, were roused out of bed by a thundering blast which reverberated through the wooded suburb. As the startled residents rushed to their windows and into the street, flames were shooting into the air from an $83,000 two-story brick house. From out of the burning building staggered three dazed, befuddled men in their shorts.

The neighbors rushed out with blankets and towels, but the men ran off into the woods, in a state of shock, confusion, and hysteria. One of them smacked into a pine tree; another ended up in a nearby creek. Bruised and bleeding, they were run down by DeKalb County policemen and taken to a hospital where they were treated for cuts and bruises.

As the embers cooled and the firemen withdrew, the neighbors gathered around. There, in the charred, smoky remains of the basement, plain for all to see, stood a whopper of a whiskey distillery—

an oblong, pan-type, gas-fired, 1800-gallon-large still together with four 1800-gallon copper fermenting vats filled with about seven thousand gallons of bubbly mash, almost ready for a run.

The three men, it turned out, were still hands, imported from old-time moonshining territory around Dahlonega, in north Georgia. They were turned over to ATF agents and charged with possession of an unregistered distillery and subsequently were convicted and sentenced, along with the owner of the house.

A homeowner off of the ritzy Northside Drive in Atlanta—who has about fifteen heavily wooded acres surrounding his large home near the Chattahoochee River—received a proposition through an intermediary. He would be paid $5,000, plus $500 a month rent, for the use of his property as a still site. One of the stipulations was that the house be returned to its original condition *after it was raided*. "Oh, they counted on its being eventually raided," the homeowner declared, "but they figured they could make a killing on it before it could be spotted and seized." The homeowner rejected the proposal.

In the Atlanta suburban county of Cobb, sheriff's forces destroyed an illicit distillery in a massive underground cavern. Containing two underground tanks with a capacity of more than 5,000 gallons of mash, the distillery had been turning out 900 gallons of white whiskey a week. Apparently the air vents were the giveaway. Neighbors smelling the sickly sweet-sour odor of the mash called in the sheriff, who dynamited the complex.

This, then, is the new face of moonshining. In recent years, illicit "big liquor-making" has been withdrawing from the mountains and foothills, moving into metropolitan areas, around major markets such as Atlanta, Augusta, Athens, Charlotte, Chattanooga, and Birmingham. And the modern-day "moonshine mafia" (my term), instead of putting up their stills out in the woods—where they can be spotted from the air and via walkways and trails—more and more are placing their rigs in homes and barns where the ATF agents must have a search warrant before they can enter.

Even more significant is the increased size of the illicit distilleries. The small-time operators are giving way to huge operations, usually financed by well-heeled syndicates.

In some areas, moonshining has also become gangsterized. In Walton County, Georgia, a sixty-seven-year-old country merchant, James Daws, who was scheduled to testify in a moonshine conspiracy trial, disappeared from his 300-acre farm on November 22, 1970. His body was discovered the following February in a creek in neighboring Barrow County. His hands and feet had been bound with wire, his mouth gagged with two neckties, and his body weighted with concrete blocks. The case has never been solved, although three men involved in the moonshine conspiracy trial were found guilty in Columbia, South Carolina, in July, 1972, on charges of manufacturing and selling moonshine liquor, and were given long penitentiary sentences.

The distiller is no more than a cog in the modern-day "moonshine mafia." He is merely a hired hand, usually earning from twenty to thirty-five cents a gallon for his output—not bad money for a man who probably is uneducated and unskilled in anything else, particularly if he can turn out a few hundred gallons a day, which is not unusual.

But the real moonshiner on the modern-day scene is the man who is not there—the man behind the scenes, a financier, say, who lives in a high-priced home and, more than likely, drives a late-model prestige car and moves in affluent society.

As an example of the mafia-type operation which has taken control of today's moonshining business, take the case of a north Georgia illicit whiskey entrepreneur and his nephew—both convicted liquor law violators—who were convicted again on charges of directing an operation that manufactured and distributed approximately twenty-one thousand gallons of untaxed whiskey during a six-month period in 1967. The defendants operated distilleries in nine counties in Alabama, five counties in Mississippi, and one county in northwest Georgia. They obtained their sugar, the key ingredient, from New Orleans, and hauled it to their stills in tractor-trailer rigs. The whiskey they produced represented a federal tax fraud of almost a quarter-million dollars. During the same six-month period, the two men also purchased about fifty thousand gallons of moonshine whiskey from other producers in south Mississippi, which they then distributed to illicit whiskey brokers in middle Alabama. This part of the enterprise contributed an additional tax bilking of the federal treasury of more than half a million dollars. Thus one organization, in just over half a year, defrauded American taxpayers alone of almost three quarters of a million dollars.

The ATF investigator who coordinated the massive, fifty-man

multi-state undercover campaign that put the moonshine master-
minds behind bars, declared, "They had their own mafia-type army
. . . their captains, lieutenants, trippers, still hands, and raw materials
boys. They had someone for every job and there were a number of
lieutenants. Just like the mafia, the people on one level didn't talk to
people on other levels. They knew who it was many times, but they
had absolutely no dealings with them."

The ATF's dramatic success in bringing the moonshine kingpins
in this particular operation to justice represented a validation of the
Treasury Bureau's strategy in recent years of going after the "major violators" by concentrating the necessary manpower and expertise
to nail them down. The ATF is quick to point out that it has no forgotten about the little illicit liquor-makers, the independent operators,
but their leading priority now is the really big production.

In every state of the southeast, the ATF has drawn up secret lists
of the major violators—the suspected financiers and brains behind
the big moonshine networks. Many of these people are respected
leaders in their communities and churches: just like some moonshiners of previous eras, many camouflage their illegal operations with a
front of farming, or raising cattle or chickens. A number of the
kingpins have rationalized their operation to the extent of dividing
marketing territories among themselves. Unlike old-time moonshiners, it is not unusual for them to travel long distances for raw materials. Operators of an illicit distillery seized in Myrtle Beach, South
Carolina, for example, were hauling sugar from New Orleans and
sending their liquor to New York and Philadelphia.

We can get a good picture of the degree to which moonshining has
assumed the character of a big business from the comments of someone who was part of that business as a stiller, a bootlegger, a trip boy,
and a still hand. Unlike the old-timers we have heard from, Roy
James Smith, as we'll call him, was not "raised in the liquor business," and today speaks with shame of his latter-day activities in it.

As a young man Roy James left the mountains in which he grew
up, came to the Piedmont plateau around Gainesville (in Georgia)
and got a job as an automobile mechanic, mainly working in a little
country garage. Soon he found that his courage was wanted much
more than his "mechanicking."

"These guys kept hangin' around the shop. You know how they

hang around a garage. They kept asking me to go to work for 'em. They offered me good money and I just went to work for 'em. And the first thing you know, I was in it with both feet. Soon I was driving everything. I bought me a new '65 Chevrolet pickup and was haulin' malt out of Atlanta on that pickup. My tires blew out one time with a 3000-pound load. I hauled that malt for about two months and really, to start with, I didn't know what I was haulin'! It was in bags that looked like horse feed. They'd tell me to go to Atlanta to so-and-so and bring it to so-and-so and we'll give you fifty dollars to do it."

The way he discovered just what business he was involved in was when he went to Canton, Georgia, on a hauling assignment and found a room full of jars! "Then I knowed what I was in."

Before long, Roy James, who grew up in poverty, was rolling in money.

"I never had made no money before. I dus went wild. I started to spending. I thought I had it made. Anything that any of the other boys was scared to do or wouldn't do, I would. I run a still one night when all the other boys in the county run off from it. They wuz afraid they would get caught. When they wuz scared like that, they'd come get me.

"After I seen what I was in and realized just how big it was, I tried to get out, but the boys wouldn't let me. It was about as big as the mafia. Eventually I had to move and leave out from up in thar. Everybody knew that I would do anything that came along. They'd come and get me up in the night to get me to do something they was too scared to do. When I moved, I just left. I ain't seen none of 'um since."

Roy James was in the "still servicing" business about a year, furnishing giant stills in north Georgia with malt and sugar and jars (mostly plastic milk jugs), and hauling whiskey out, the riskiest step in the illegal liquor business.

This was his *modus operandi*: "Let's say you had a big still and you come to me and want a truckload of jars. We didn't fool with the little operators. We told them they could get their supplies at a drugstore. I dealt in truckload lots. When an operator contacted me, I'd tell them that I had a tractor trailer and the only way I'd deliver them a load would be for them to give me half the money then and the other half when I delivered it. I'd tell 'em that 'If I don't deliver, you just lost that money.' That's the way I did business with 'em. After all, I was taking all the risk."

Roy James explained how his bosses set up their big stills. "Okay, you've got a farm leased and got a still. The first load of sugar and malt and jars have arrived. You can unload it all in that chicken house [which are usually 30 feet wide and perhaps 200 feet long], next to the still. But from there on out, you don't unload nothin' there. Three or four miles away, in yonder direction, you've got to have another building for your raw materials. Mainly sugar. Twenty tons of sugar don't mean nothin' in a big still. Twenty tons . . . that's just a load. Three or four miles this way, you got to have another stash for your liquor.

"It takes five men to run a big still, two of them just makin' the liquor. I know some boys up in Dawson County ain't done nothin' but make liquor. They're just still hands. They make it for thirty cents a gallon apiece and jar it up and set it in a chicken house. That takes two men—working right at the still. While one sleeps, the other is runnin'. They won't even talk to you unless you're makin' 200 gallons a day or better. They don't even want to know you.

"Okay. You've got the two men in the chicken house at the still; you've got another man over yonder where the raw materials is. Over here where the liquor is stashed, the fourth. Then it takes one man keeping that place supplied. If the operation closes down because of a lack of raw materials, if he's a makin' $2,000 a day, it'll cost something like $6,000 before he can get it started up again. You'll have to keep a tractor on the road all the time—just about solid; you gotta keep that still supplied."

Roy James went on to describe setting up a big still in an unused chicken house, to which water is pumped in a three-inch pipe.

"You get a twelve-horse steam boiler. Set it up in the middle of this chicken house. You build a vat [a still pot] out of wood or metal, just so it won't leak. Then you build mash vats—say that would hold 1,000 gallons of beer. The first day, you 'sweeten down' three vats, the next day you sweeten down three vats and the third day you sweeten down three. You've got nine vats of beer working. The fourth day, the first three is ready to run. You pump the beer over into the steam boiler [distilling pot]. It starts off at 130 proof. You check your proof—your bead, and when it gets to 70 proof, you shut it down and you pump the slop back into the first vat. You'll have just about as much as you had when you started. You'll wind up with about 900 gallons of the original 1,000 gallons. You let them cool a while, then you sweeten them right back down [with sugar]. The next day, you get your next vats run off. You run every day. It's just like a shift change on an assembly line.

"As to marketing liquor from a big stillin' operation today, the big markets are your major cities like Atlanta. In particular, cities with a black ghetto.

"There's a wholesaler in Atlanta that'll buy your liquor from you. This fellow out of Atlanta will send after it to your stash-house on the outskirts of the city. He'll send after it about twice a week and pay you for it. He's got the bread man, the telephone man, and everybody working for him. They're the retail bootleggers. The man that buys the liquor from you may never see it, but he'll get it sold.

"Now, the big liquor wholesaler in Atlanta doesn't want to talk to a small-still man. There's not enough whiskey to mess with. And really, the small moonshiner can't afford to sell it to him. He has to get eight or nine dollars a gallon. The big wholesaler will get it for about four."

Clearly, what Roy James was describing is an operation close to being a full-fledged industry.

"I don't believe the public comprehends the extent of the moonshine business," declares the Criminal Court Prosecutor, Hinson McAuliffe, of Fulton County (Atlanta). "The problem of liquor violations is Number 1 among the rackets in Atlanta. The economic decay of our low-income areas can be traced in large measure to the buying and selling of moonshine. Unquestionably it is a serious problem and we honestly don't know, for instance, how the overall activity is related to gang warfare, killings, or the bribing of police officers."

Five to seven thousand gallons of white whiskey pour every week into Atlanta ghettos, reputedly the "moonshine-consuming capital of America." After being cut with water (causing many imbibers to call it "cool water"), it is resold to thirsty customers in residential shot houses throughout the city's ghetto neighborhoods. Atlanta boasts more than two thousand of these crack joints, "good-time houses," and "gold mines"—the modern, ghetto version of the Prohibition Era speakeasy. They are usually located in the kitchens of run-down homes, where drinks are sold for thirty-five to fifty cents, and in many cases sold on credit. "If a shot house operator has a regular customer," says retired Fulton County Deputy C. E. Pequignot, "she'll usually let him have credit all week—from his first drink early Monday morning until he gets his pay on Friday afternoon. He likely purchases a few drinks every night, and may take home a half-pint on Tuesday and Thursday nights, for a dollar and a half."

Let's take a look at the economics of this new moonshining, some of which Roy James described. These are Atlanta area figures:

It costs the illicit distiller between $1.50 and $2 to make a gallon of moonshine, which is then tripped into the city to the wholesale broker. The tripper makes about $1 a gallon, and the wholesaler pays around $5 a gallon. The profit for the illicit distiller is around $2 or $2.50. The wholesaler then sells the whiskey to the shot house retailer for about $7 a gallon, delivering it right to the door by a "set-off boy." The shot house operator, often a woman, peddles it by the drink, the half pint, and the pint, getting around $16 to $32 for a gallon. If an operator sells two cases on a weekend—twelve gallons —the profit ranges between $200 and $350—tax free.

The shot house operator usually buys a case at a time, six gallons, and hides most of it in the weeds behind her house. She keeps one jar—a gallon—in the house at a time. When officers raid, they usually find the gallon jug with about a half pint of liquor in it, and the operator pleads guilty to possession. "But there's five gallons over the fence that we can't charge her with. We know she's been selling a lot because we'd find eight empty jugs in the garbage can." says Pequignot.

The shot house operators of Atlanta make an estimated $700,000 a month, tax free. Thus they willingly pay off the fines averaging up to $300 for possession of untaxed whiskey—a misdemeanor in most cities.

Larry Woods, a talented reporter for *The Atlanta Journal*, (now Atlanta Mayor Maynard Jackson's communications director) did an illuminating series of articles in 1969 on ghetto bootlegging, introducing shot house operators "Bad Eye Barbara," "Dirty Lil," "Hardrock Robinson," "The Gospel Singers," and "Suzie Q," who, he found, had been selling moonshine by the drink in her kitchen on weekends for fifteen years. Despite the changes in methods of distillation, the retail end of moonshining has not varied much over the years. Suzie Q's place of operation was her three-room shack, which was crowded with rats, roaches, and dilapidated furniture, and slept fourteen persons.

"In many respects," Woods wrote, "her house is typical of her competitors. She got into the business because she 'got tired of selling it for someone else.' On a good weekend, she'll take in $350, and can easily sell twenty gallons of 'shine by charging 50 cents a shot (a three-ounce baby food jar is the standard drink), or selling half-pints for 75 cents in cash or $1 on credit." Suzie lets a customer run up a $10 tab. If he doesn't pay up, he loses his drinking privileges. After she pays her wholesaler, Suzie Q nets about $200 a week, not counting the $5 protection money she pays an Atlanta policeman, a practice she had continued for eight years. Suzie estimates there are around twenty good-time houses such as hers within a six-block radius, and all of the houses also pay $5 a week to the cops. The concentration of good-time houses is duplicated in Atlanta's other ghettos, and in many ghetto communities in cities over the country.

Suzie Q doesn't drink the moonshine she sells because "that stuff is too nasty looking." But she told the *Journal* reporter that she thought most of the weekend brawls and cuttings in the black neighborhoods stemmed from "too much 'shine and wine."

This brings us around to the really devastating indictment against today's moonshine: its poison content.

Much of the moonshine produced today contains metallic salts which, in sufficient quantity and over a long enough period of time, can blind, paralyze, sterilize, maim, and kill. Or, less terminally, can give you a serious case of gout.

Many of the big-city moonshine wholesalers, after cutting their whiskey with water to a low proof of 50 or 60 (which is only twenty-five to thirty per cent alcohol), add adulterants to give it a "kick." Bootleggers also have been known to add petroleum beading oil, Clorox, paint thinner, a solvent like Solox, rubbing alcohol, laundry bleach, canned heat, and turpentine. Agents have found that some bootleggers mix one gallon of Solox for every gallon of low-proof whiskey. Wood alcohol embalming fluid has been used, giving drinkers, to make the point jocularly, a do-it-yourself embalming start.

But the really long-term poisoning effect of moonshine whiskey on habitual drinkers comes in the build-up of lead salts in one's body. These metallic salts, which you can't see or taste, are contained in

223

whiskey that is made on stills having lead-solder seams at vital connections or that is condensed through old car radiators, many of which have lead-solder repairs.

Here is how Eddie D. Hughes, special agent with the ATF's Georgia office in Decatur, explains it:

"At a legal distillery which has strict sanitary controls, a purified yeast strain is used to convert the starches into sugars and the sugars into ethyl alcohol. At an illicit distillery, where everything is open and unsanitary, wild yeasts are picked up from the air. These yeasts, instead of forming pure ethyl alcohol, create acetic acid [vinegar] along with the ethyl.

"During the distilling process, the hot vapors of ethyl alcohol, water, and acetic acid pass from the still through the connecting conduits to the doubler [immediate filter] and then to the condenser. At each joint where there is solder, the acetic acid attacks the lead in the solder, dissolving the lead and forming lead acetate. The lead acetate is carried over with the alcohol and water into the finished product."

Roy James described the process this way:

"When steam hits those old galvanized pipes and that old oil drum —and what they do, they pour gas in and burn it out and you get that old rust and stuff, and on a 500-gallon still, they'll stack up two radiators as condensers, and on your late model cars, your radiators are half copper and half lead—when that steam hits those fittin's, they take along all sorts of lead and rust poisoning into the condenser."

ATF chemists say the accumulation in one's brain of 1/250,000 of a gram of lead salts—about one-third the size of a pin head—is enough to cause spasms, blindness, death, or permanent disability. Dr. McLeod Patterson, of Columbus, Georgia, who had conducted research for many years on the moonshine lead-salts problem, notes that the lead collects in the body over a period of time, then attacks the brain, the liver, and other vital organs.

Moonshine alcoholics are pictured by the ATF as walking corpses. Their lips bleed, their skin shreds, sores pop open on their bodies, and they spend their nights vomiting.

At the Atlanta ATF regional chemical laboratory, more than four thousand samples of moonshine are received each year. Clarence E. Paul, lab chief, reports that at least ninety per cent of these samples contain lead-salt poison or some other harmful ingredient. The tolerable limit for lead salts in liquor is considered to be 1,000 micrograms per day per person. In thirty samples analyzed in one month, twenty-six contained lead salts. Of these, more than fifty per cent were found to have more than the tolerable limit.

Ironically, the tests also show that most of the moonshine registers as low as 50 proof. People in the ghetto, who can least afford the expenditure, given their meager wages, will pay as much as $2.50 for a pint of the illicit, possibly poisonous, liquid when they can purchase the legal whiskey for about the same price, and get a better quality liquor as well as a safer drink.

A well-known slogan among moonshiners over north Georgia, a phrase I have heard repeated dozens of times, is: "This liquor is made to sell, not to drink." As a result, you find many illicit distillers, like shot house operator Suzie Q, who will not drink the product of their own stills.

Some of the redneck distillers, who know their product is destined for the black ghettos, seem to get a perverse pleasure in making their liquor as mean as possible. If it's an "espacially good" run, they'll share some of it with their friends. But most of it is what they call "nigger likker" which they ship off to Atlanta and to bootleggers of black ghettos in smaller cities.

The most notorious case of illegal alcohol poisoning in America since the "jake paralysis" days of Prohibition, occurred in Atlanta in 1951, when around forty blacks fell victim to a poisonous potion mixed up by a 340-pound diabetic bootlegger named John Richard (Fat) Hardy. Actually, Fat's mixture couldn't be classified as moonshine. It really was a mixture of wood alcohol. But he palmed it off as the real stuff. It was on a Friday that Hardy, anticipating a heavy drinking weekend throughout Atlanta's black communities, bought fifty-four gallons of methyl alcohol at a drug wholesaler, declaring it was for his service station. From this, Fat and two friends concocted seventy-seven gallons of supposedly white whiskey, which he sold for $4.50 a gallon to three retailers. It was midnight Sunday when the first victim, Elijah Foster, fell dead of alcohol poisoning after suffering excruciating pain. Soon the emergency ward at Atlanta's big Grady Hospital echoed with wailing and moaning stretcher cases— terribly sick people whose central nervous systems were deteriorating, who were going blind, and who were all in terror. Thirty-five

225

victims died during the week and many were left blind and paralyzed. Hardy was sentenced to life imprisonment (though he eventually was released, and died a few years later).

Someone who witnessed the agonizing scene at Grady Hospital wrote a mournful ballad about it:

> *Don't want no Fats Hardy*
> *Toddy at the Party—*
> *(Great Lord, no . . .)*
> *Don't bring no Fats Hardy*
> *Toddy to the party—*
> *(Please, Lord, no! no! no!)*
> *Don't serve no Fats Hardy*
> *Toddy at the party . . ."*

This, then, is the modern day reality of moonshining—a far cry from the principles of the hardy, fiercely independent Scotch-Irish yeomen who brought the distilling craft to these shores in the early 1700s. And a long way from the few surviving old-time mountain distillers —the independent copper pot craftsmen who refuse to bend their standards to the new morality.

Modern day condenser on many illicit whiskey distilleries is the automobile radiator. The one pictured here is from the Moonshine Museum and is hooked up to a groundhog still. This "flake stand," through which cold water would be running over the radiator if it were in operation, is a portion of a 220-gallon barrel. On some bigger stills, particularly pans, operators have joined a number of automobile radiators in tandem to increase the condensing capability.

Huge commercial boilers, fired by coke, following the capture of this distillery setup in North Carolina. Wilkesboro type distilling pots, huge stave barrels, are in the center, with the thumper at the right.

Double drum or "stack steamer" distillery setup in western North Carolina. The steam comes from the two drum boilers at the left. The distilling pot is the stave-type large barrel to the right, followed by the thump keg and flake stand. The mash barrels are lined up across the front. A type of camouflage covering can be seen stretched across the top of part of the yard.

Showing how modern day moonshiners fill plastic jugs with whiskey are sheriff's officers of Haralson County, Georgia. The distillery setup, found in 1969 in a big chicken house within the city limits of Tallapoosa, Georgia, had four pan-type distilling units, each with a capacity of 1,660 gallons. The officers poured out 4,500 gallons of mash as well as 567 gallons of whiskey, most of which was in the one-gallon jugs. Officials said the still's daily tax fraud amounted to about $3,000.

Pan-type still used by modern day moonshiners in Burke County, Georgia. The officers stand around two of six huge tanks that were part of the distillery setup. Note the "shotgun" tube condenser which was used to condense the vapors from the pans. A "bootleg bonnet" filter is hanging from the business end of the shotgun, and the galvanized tin bucket underneath caught the fresh whiskey. The pans, fired by butane gas, were used for fermenting as well as distilling.

Eighty-six-year-old John Henry Chumley of Dawson County, Georgia. His reminiscences tell the story of the craftsmen liquor makers in the chapter "From Pure Corn to (Almost Pure) Sugar."

"Short" Stanton, *left*, of Greene County, Tennessee, has a good laugh with retired Federal Revenue man, Colonel L. B. Britton, who caught him one time on a still raid. They are now good friends, a relationship that is not at all unique among former adversaries in the illicit whiskey enterprise. Said Stanton: "I never did make any mean likker. I forget now which one of these Revenue officers told it right here in federal court. Said they could eat right off the top of the furnace of my still, it was so clean."

Hubert Howell, moonshiner during the depression years, now a skilled grower of gladioli, chrysanthemums, dahlias, and petunias, as well as corn, tomatoes, okra, turban squash, and four-leaf clovers, at his valley farm near Lake Allatoona, Georgia. "Ever hear of a Revenue named Barnes? Oncet I run away from him and hit a great big bottom and went a long ways down. Atter awhile, I seen Barnes a-comin', just a lookin'. I run on down the creek and I got up on a little hill. Atter a while, here he come trackin' me. That time, I went up a great mountain there, more than two thirds up it, and set down there. I was aimin', if he come on down there, to show him some new country he had never seen before."

Semmie Free of Tiger, Georgia. "Yeah, I drunk a lot of corn likker in my time. Now you can't hardly get it. The people don't make corn. They don't make nothin' right no more. Now, good sugar likker's *good*, though, if it's made right. But all this old bastard beading stuff they make it out of these days, hell, it'd kill a dead snake. Make it on old tin, sheet arn, anything but what they ort to. It'd kill a dead snake."

16

Double and Twisted:
A Final Backward Look

There's a fascination to moonshining. It
gets under your hide wors'n fishin' does.
—East Tennessee mountaineer

I T was watermelon time in Georgia—"hot as a pistol" as they say in the South—the time when the green stalks of corn shoot up tall and the golden tassels wave in the hot, humid breezes. The time when the corn whiskey market goes into a tailspin, to recover only with the arrival of the cool nights of autumn.

Leaning against his pickup truck outside Atlanta, the old man in his frayed but clean and pressed blue denim bib overalls seemed out of place, his blue eyes blinking under the rays of the noonday sun, in a big city suburb. But not really. For a true son of the rural South, and the mountainous South at that, bib overalls are *the* uniform, almost as revered in the Appalachian foothills as Mao jackets in China. Old-time southern mountain men wear them proudly, and almost always sport a big Elgin or Ingersoll pocket watch which they keep on a three-inch pleated leather strap, tucked conveniently in their bib pockets. Without these badges of identification, you would have difficulty placing this seventy-four-year-old Georgian in his former haunts. Robust and hearty, with a ruddy, smiling Scotch-Irish face and fringes of reddish-white hair on the sides of his head, he laughs a lot, reconciled to his new life-style as a carpenter in an Atlanta suburb. He lives in a little, two-bedroom white frame home perched on an acre of rolling red clay farmland, and has a bank account with a $400 balance. But when he talks about his former life in the hills eighty miles to the north, you can almost feel him being tugged by the magnet of nostalgia back to the days when he owned a 200-acre spread in a lush valley, distilled and bootlegged corn liquor by the carload, raised some chickens and corn and hogs, hunted foxes and coons and wild hogs, hauled his game roosters to cock-fights in neighboring towns in a cut-down T-model roadster, drank his own white whiskey as if it was going out of style, courted a little on the side and, during the same era, took an occasional turn in the pulpit to preach a fire-and-brimstone sermon in a little country church.

He remembers well how he got started in the illicit industry during the dark days of Prohibition and Depression:

"Shoot, I got where I didn't ask nobody to help me make whiskey. Just go and make it myself. Go cook it in myself. I even learned how not to have a still to cook in the mash. I'd take three eight-gallon lard cans, I'd set me up some rocks to set them on, and fill them lard cans with water. Got that water to boiling. I'd just reach and get me two big forked sticks and dip 'em into the barrel and pour me in a bushel of meal . . . ooooohhhhh, it'd make a mash! Cook it in. Make two gallons of likker to the bushel. Sweet mash. I'd go back in and break that up. I'd cook it in tonight, you see . . . ooooohhhhh, I'd get to where no light wouldn't show nowheres, you see. I'd go back tomor-rer evenin' and break that up. If it was in the wintertime, I'd go back about twelve tomorrer and break it up when it's hot and keep it from coolin' my beer too cool. Take my malt and let it work about two days and go back and throw me in a little sugar. Let that work off. Then if I wanted to make more, pour a still full of mash.

"If it was in the wintertime, cold, and you wanted your beer to work, what we did, we just lined them mash barrels up here on top of the ground. We toted in limbs and built a fence around them barrels. I usta cut down a bank and let the bank be one side of my fence. We left about a foot between the fence and the barrels. You tramp them leaves down in there, pack it up halfway. It'd make your beer stay warm, even in the cold of winter.

"Now that malt. I made it all the time. Summertime, you just throw a sack of shelled corn in a branch. Throw it in there like today and take if out in the mornin' and throw it out in the bushes, and by the morning the sprouts had done come up. In three days, it's ready to take out and dry. I'd grind it on a sausage mill. Dry corn malt is better than green. Makes a better flavored whiskey. Don't work your beer as hard.

"To make likker—if I'uz to make likker today, I'd double and twist it, I think. I'd go back to that. I'd put fifty pounds of sugar to a fifty-gallon barrel and a bushel of meal and put about a gallon and a half of good dry corn malt, and you got whiskey that's fit to drink. It would do for medicine.

"I've seen whiskey come out of the worm 160, 170 proof. Look like water, be so high. You could shake it and it's just flash off, just like that [as he popped his fingers]. They'd say, 'That likker's dead.' I'd just reach and take a pint bottle and get it half full. It's so high when it first starts runnin', it'll take a good third of a pint of water to temper half of it down. It'd be close to 175, 180 proof. But I've drunk it. Oh, yes. I'd take and drink and it'd go down—GOD AL-MIGHTY, SEE SEVEN STARS, just heat ye. Just like rubbin' you with some kind of hot linament. Don't take but a little of it to heat ye. I left my drinkin' likker at 120. I've drunk lots of it 130. Drunk it straight. No such thing as tempering. . . .

"Yeah, I was in that business for thirty-three years and we really had a time.

"One time, we had a 300-gallon copper still, boiled 300 gallons of cold beer, a barrel and a half of beer. We had two hundred and twenty gallon mash barrels then. We had our still back out in the woods behind the barn. You'd go through a chicken house, go out through the little back door and cross the branch. We had a Army truck there to haul our sugar and supplies.

"The revenue came down and saw some sugar in that chicken house and they went up there and they got the truck and cut the still down. They went in there without a search warrant, and when the trial come up in Gainesville [Georgia], the judge throwed it out. But we lost I don't know how much on that operation. We was running about fifteen gallons of likker to the sack of sugar and we had twenty-eight sacks of sugar on it. Three of us. It'd cost a man $500 to build a still like them things now. Copper, everything copper.

"Later on, we decided we'd make some ground hog likker, and we had two big ground hogs. We paid so much a gallon for this feller to run it—about fifteen cents a gallon and so much to get it in and out. The federal come in and cut the hogs and got a stash of whiskey in the chicken house and took up the fellers.

"Then we got into that steamer business. Boys, you could *make* whiskey on 'um, but you could get caught.

"We had one steamer to blow up. *Blowed up.* Boys was a runnin' it. They had just passed by it and walked over and set down and was a eatin'. A little old five-horse upright boiler. It 'uz on a bluff. That thang blowed up. Tall trees there and it cut the tops out of 'em. The fire box, we never did see it. It went down and out of sight in the ground. Beat anything I ever seen in my life. A man found the boiler up in his field at the Chattahoochee River a good quarter of a mile away. That sonofagun throwed dirt 'til it burned blisters on 'em, that dirt did, and set the woods on fire.

"The winding up of it, they moved a still up to my farm over there and I didn't have anything in it. I was a gettin' $100 a week jest to watch it.

"This feller out of Murphy, North Carolina, he was so dumb. He was smart in business, but he was dumb in likker. He brought a federal man in with him that he thought was a bootlegger. But he was really an undercover man. You don't take anybody where that likker is being loaded, or where that likker is being made. You make your likker over here. But you'll have your stash five or ten miles away. You don't tell another likker man what you're doin'.

"Yeah, I was in it thirty-three years. During that time, I farmed, coon-hunted, and all that stuff. Sometimes just run a little whiskey. If you got any good likker to drink, most of the time you had to make it yourself.

"I had a little old roadster cut down. Hauled lots of likker in it. I foxhunted in that, hauled my dogs. Hauled my likker and hauled my game chickens. Used to fight chickens, condition them. Last fightin' I done was at Hiawassee. We fought nine, won seven, drawed one, and lost one. All of us were drunk.

"But I've quit all that stuff. I've lost my farm. Used to, I could strut around and pop my suspenders. I'uz worth $200,000.

"But I've been humbled. Now I'm livin' for the Lord.

"I was converted on the twentieth day of October, 1961, and I laid my likker down. I come across the Blue Ridge and I have never drunk another drop of likker since, nor made any."

He jabbed his right index and middle fingers in the palm of his reddish and splotched weatherbeaten hand, in the gesture of a preacher quoting from the Bible:

"God just struck me down there in the house. I just fell there in the floor. I was tryin' to raise a row with my wife. She'd been in the hospital. She moved to the kitchen and I went in there and set down on the arm of the chair. Next thing I knowed I was layin' thar in the floor a beggin' for mercy. It wasn't long 'til I got the answer. Me and my wife got in the car and went down there to call the preacher. I had talked awful ugly to the preacher the Sunday before. I called the preacher and he come up there and he didn't know why. He got there as quick as he could, at about nine o'clock that night. We talked awhile and I told him I had a job for him to do. We walked down the trail and I hunted up the whiskey. I was down to three gallons. It was my drinkin' likker. We went down the road and got these half-gallon jars out from that holler stump, brought it up to the house and he poured it out in the yard . . . *poured it out.*"

He looked longingly at the distant sky and was silent.

Within another decade, the gentle art of illicit whiskey-making will be only a "heard-of thing," recounted in the folklore and the stories of such old-timers as our carpenter friend who remembers the corny smell of the mash tubs in the springtime, mingled with the scent of sassafras and dogwood blossoms and the ever-constant odor of the leafy, pungent woods-earth of the Appalachian outdoors. . . .

But wherever good whiskey is appreciated the memory of the pure corn copper pot craftsmen will live on.

Bibliography

Adams, Leon D., *The Commonsense Book of Drinking*, New York: McKay, 1960.

Alley, Felix, E., *Random Thoughts and the Musings of a Mountaineer*, Salisbury, N.C.: Rowan Printing Company, 1941.

Arnow, Harriette Simpson, *Flowering of the Cumberland*, New York: Macmillan, 1963.

Asbury, Herbert, *The Great Illusion*, New York: Doubleday, 1950.

Atkinson, George W., *After the Moonshiners*, Wheeling, W. Va.: Free and Campbell, 1881.

Baldwin, Leland D., *Whiskey Rebels*, Univ. of Pittsburgh Press, 1967.

Bolton, Charles K., *The Scotch Irish Pioneers in Ulster and America*, Boston, 1910. (Reprinted 1967 by Genealogical Publishing Company, Baltimore.)

Brown, John Hull, *Early American Beverages*, New York: Bonanza Books, 1966.

Callahan, North, *Smoky Mountain Country*, Boston: Duell, Sloan and Pearce, Little Brown, 1952.

Campbell, J. C., *The Southern Highlander and His Homeland*, New York: Russell Sage Foundation, 1920.

Carr, Jess, *The Second Oldest Profession*, Englewood Cliffs, N.J.: Prentice-Hall, 1972.

Carson, Gerald, *Social History of Bourbon*, Dodd, Mead, 1963.

Caudill, Rebecca, *My Appalachians*, New York: Holt, Rinehart and Winston, 1966.

A Compleat Body of Distilling, London: 1731.

Coulter, E. Merton, *Georgia: A Short History*, Chapel Hill: University of North Carolina Press, 1933.

Crowgey, Henry G. *The Formative Years of Kentucky's Whiskey Industry*, Ann Arbor: University Microfilms, 1969.

Crutcher, J. B., *Spurrier with the Wildcats and Moonshiners*, Nashville, Tenn.: University Press, 1892. (Facsimile reprinted 1968 by University Microfilms, Ann Arbor, Mich.)

Daniels, Jonathan, *Tar Heels: A Portrait of North Carolina*, New York: Dodd Publ. Co., 1941.

Dunaway, Weyland F., *The Scotch-Irish of Colonial Pennsylvania*, Chapel Hill: University of North Carolina Press, 1944.

Dykeman, Wilma, *The French Broad*, New York: Rinehart, 1955.

Dykeman, Wilma, and James Stokely, *The Border States*, New York: Time-Life Books, 1968.

Earle, Alice Morse, *Home Life in Colonial Days*, New York: The Macmillan Co., 1898.

Emerson, Edward R., *Beverages Past and Present*, New York: Putnam, 1908.

Eubanks, John Evans, *Ben Tillman's Baby*, Augusta, Georgia: published by author, 1950.

Fisher, Ronald M., *The Appalachian Trail*, Washington: National Geographic Society, 1972.

Ford, Henry Jones, *The Scotch-Irish in America*, Princeton: Princeton University Press, 1915.

Frome, Michael, *Strangers in High Places*, New York: Doubleday, 1966.

Furnas, J. C., *The Late Demon Rum*, New York: Putnam, 1965.

Garrett, Franklin W., *Atlanta and Its Environs*, Athens: University of Georgia Press, 1954.

Glasgow, Maude, *The Scotch-Irish in Northern Ireland and in the American Colonies*, New York: Putnam, 1936.

Hall, Harrison, *The Distiller*, Philadelphia: published by the author, 1818.

Hanna, Charles A., *The Scotch-Irish*, Vol. I and II, New York: Putnam, 1904.

Hannan, Alberta Pierson, *Look Back with Love. A Recollection of the Blue Ridge*, New York: Vanguard Press, 1969.

Hawke, David Freeman, *Benjamin Rush, Revolutionary Gadfly*, Indianapolis: Bobbs-Merrill, 1971.

Kephart, Horace, *Our Southern Highlanders*, New York: The Macmillan Co., 1913, 1922, 1949.

Kellner, Esther, *Moonshine*, New York: Bobbs-Merrill, 1971.

Kincaid, Charles, *The Wilderness Road*, New York: Bobbs-Merrill, 1947.

Kroll, Henry Harrison, *Bluegrass, Belles and Bourbon*, Cranbury, N. J.: A.S. Barnes & Co., 1967.

Lee, Henry, *How Dry We Were*, Englewood Cliffs, New Jersey: Prentice-Hall, 1963.

Leyburn, James O., *The Scotch-Irish. A Social History*, Chapel Hill: University of North Carolina Press, 1962.

Mason, Robert L., *The Lure of the Great Smokies*, Boston: Houghton Mifflin, 1927.

McDowell, R. J., *The Whiskys of Scotland*, New York: Abelard, 1970.

Merz, Charles, *The Dry Decade*, New York: Doubleday, 1930.

Morland, J. Kenneth, ed., *The Not So Solid South*, Athens, Georgia: University of Georgia Press, 1971.

Morley, Margaret Warner, *The Carolina Mountains*, Boston: Houghton Mifflin, 1913.

Morrison, Samuel Eliot, *The Oxford History of American People*, New York: Oxford University Press, 1965.

Needham, Walter, and Barrows Mussey, *A Book of Country Things*, Brattleboro, Vermont: Stephen Greene Press, 1965.

Nixon, H. C., *Lower Piedmont Country*, New York: Duell, Sloan and Pearce, 1946.

Oertel, J. F., *Moonshine*, Macon, Georgia: J. W. Burke Co., 1926.

Parris, John, *Mountain Bred*, Asheville, N.C.: Citizen-Times Publishing Co., 1967.

Parris, John, *My Mountains, My People*, Asheville, N.C.: Citizen-Times Publishing Co., 1957.

Pearce, John Ed, *Nothing Better in the Market*, Louisville, Ky.: Brown-Forman Distillers Corp., 1970.

Peeke, Hewson W., *Americana Ebrietatis*, New York, 1917. (Reprint. New York: Hatcher Art Books, 1970.)

Pennsylvania Cavalcade, Philadelphia: University of Pennsylvania Press, 1942.

Powell, Levi W., *Who Are These Mountain People*, New York: Exposition Press, 1966.

Raine, James Watt, *Land of Saddle-bags*, Richmond, Va.: Presbyterian Committee of Publication, 1924.

Randolph, Vance, *The Ozarks*, New York: Vanguard Press, 1931.

Rawson, Marion Nicholl, *Handwrought Ancestors*, New York: Dutton, 1936.

Rawson, Marion Nicholl, *Little Old Mills*, New York: Dutton, 1935.

Reynolds, T. W., *Born in the Mountains*. Privately published, 1964.

Rice, Otis K., *The Allegheny Frontier*, Lexington,: University Press of Kentucky, 1970.

Robb, Marshall, *Scotch Whisky*, New York: Dutton, 1951.

Roberts, Leonard W., *Up Cutshin and Down Greasy*, Lexington: University of Kentucky Press, 1959.

Robinson, Henry Morton, *Water of Life*, New York: Simon and Schuster, 1960.

Roueché, Berton, *The Neutral Spirit*, Boston: Little, Brown, 1960.

Rouse, Parke, Jr., *The Great Wagon Road*, New York: McGraw-Hill, 1973.

Rouse, Parke, Jr., *Planters and Pioneers. Life in Colonial Virginia*, New York: Hastings House, 1968.

Sann, Paul, *The Lawless Decade*, New York: Crown, 1957.

Scomp, H. A., *King Alcohol in the Realm of King Cotton*, Chicago: The Blakely Printing Co., 1888.

Shepherd, C. W., *Wine, Spirits and Liqueurs*, London: Ward, Lock and Co., Ltd., 1958.

Sheppard, Muriel Early, *Cabins in the Laurel*, Chapel Hill: University of North Carolina Press, 1935.

Sillett, Stephen William, *Illicit Scotch*, Aberdeenshire, Scotland: Beaver Books, 1965.

Simms, William Gilmore, *The History of South Carolina*, Redfield, N.Y.: 1860.

Sinclair, Andrew, *Prohibition: The Era of Excess*, Boston: Little, Brown, 1962.

Smith, Rev. George Gillman, *The Story of Georgia and the Georgia People*, published by author, 1900.

Stapleton, Isaac, *Moonshiners in Arkansas*, Independence, Mo.: W. F. Lackey, 1948.

Stedman, Ebenezer H., *Bluegrass Craftsman*. Edited by Frances Dugan and Jacqueline Bull. Lexington: University of Kentucky Press, 1959.

Steed, Hal, *Georgia, Unfinished State*, New York: Knopf, 1942.

Stewart, George R., *American Ways of Life*, New York: Country Life Press, 1954.

This Fabulous Century, Vol. III, by the editors of Time-Life Books, New York: Time-Life Books, 1969.

Thomas, Jean, *Ballad Makin' in the Mountains of Kentucky*, New York: Henry Holt and Co., 1939.

Thomas, Jean, *Big Sandy*, New York: Henry Holt and Co., 1940.

Thomas, Jean, *Blue Ridge Country*, New York: Duell, Sloan and Pearce, 1942.

Tunis, Edwin, *Colonial Living*, Cleveland: World Publishing Co., 1957.

Walden, Howard T., *Native Inheritance: The Story of Corn*, New York: Harper and Row, 1966.

Watkins, Floyd, and Charles Hubert Watkins, *Yesterday in the Hills*, Chicago: Quadrangle Books, 1963.

Waugh, Alex, *Wine and Spirits*, New York: Time-Life Books, 1968.

Way, Frederick, *The Allegheny*, New York: Farrar and Rinehart, 1942.

Weiss, Harry B., *The History of Applejack or Apple Brandy in New Jersey*, Trenton: New Jersey Agricultural Society, 1954.

Whitener, Daniel Jay, *Prohibition in North Carolina*, Chapel Hill: University of North Carolina Press, 1945.

Wigginton, Eliot, *Foxfire*, New York: Anchor Books, Doubleday, 1972.

Willkie, H. F., *Beverage Spirits in America*, New York: Newcomen Society, 1947.

Wilson, Ross, *Scotch Made Easy*, London: Hutchinson, 1959.

Wilson, Samuel T., *The Southern Mountaineers*, New York: Board of Missions of the Presbyterian Church USA, 1914.

Wiltse, Henry M., *The Moonshiners*, Chattanooga, Tenn.: Times Printing Co., 1895.

Wolfe, Tom, *Kandy Kolored Tangerine Flake Streamline Baby*, New York: Farrar, Straus and Giroux, 1963.

Woodward, William E., *The Way Our People Lived*, New York: Liveright Publishing Co., 1944.

Index

238